# Understanding the Role of Indonesian Millennials in Shaping the Nation's Future

The **National Research and Innovation Agency** (Badan Riset dan Inovasi Nasional, BRIN) is a cabinet-level government agency functioning directly under the President of the Republic of Indonesia that conducts integrated research, development, assessment, and application, as well as invention and innovations, and the implementation of nuclear energy and space policies. BRIN is also responsible for the regulation of science, technology, and national innovation, and is Indonesia's implementing agency for research and innovation.

**BRIN Publishing** is an established scientific publisher in Indonesia under The National Research and Innovation Agency (BRIN). BRIN Publishing holds a high responsibility to enlighten society's intelligence and awareness through the provision of qualified publications available to the public at large. Our main work revolves around planning, acquiring, designing, and distributing scientific knowledge to the public. BRIN Publishing has collaborated with various researchers and academicians as well as global publishers to publish high-quality publications that have passed thorough quality control mechanisms and editorial processes, including peer review.

The **ISEAS – Yusof Ishak Institute** (formerly Institute of Southeast Asian Studies) is an autonomous organization established in 1968. It is a regional centre dedicated to the study of socio-political, security, and economic trends and developments in Southeast Asia and its wider geostrategic and economic environment. The Institute's research programmes are grouped under Regional Economic Studies (RES), Regional Strategic and Political Studies (RSPS), and Regional Social and Cultural Studies (RSCS). The Institute is also home to the ASEAN Studies Centre (ASC), the Singapore APEC Study Centre and the Temasek History Research Centre (THRC).

**ISEAS Publishing**, an established academic press, has issued more than 2,000 books and journals. It is the largest scholarly publisher of research about Southeast Asia from within the region. ISEAS Publishing works with many other academic and trade publishers and distributors to disseminate important research and analyses from and about Southeast Asia to the rest of the world.

# Understanding the Role of Indonesian Millennials in Shaping the Nation's Future

EDITED BY

JU-LAN THUNG

MARIA MONICA WIHARDJA

First published in Singapore in 2024 by
ISEAS Publishing
30 Heng Mui Keng Terrace
Singapore 119614
*E-mail*: publish@iseas.edu.sg
*Website*: http://bookshop.iseas.edu.sg

and

National Research and Innovation Agency
(Badan Riset dan Inovasi Nasional, BRIN)
Gedung B.J. Habibie
Jl. M.H. Thamrin No. 8
Jakarta Pusat 10340
Indonesia
E-mail: penerbit@brin.go.id
Website: penerbit.brin.go.id



This publication is made possible with the support of Konrad-Adenauer-Stiftung.

**ISEAS Library Cataloguing-in-Publication Data**

Name(s): Thung, Ju-Lan, editor. | Wihardja, Maria Monica, editor.
Title: Understanding the role of Indonesian millennials in shaping the nation's future / edited by Ju-Lan Thung and Maria Monica Wihardja.
Description: Singapore : ISEAS-Yusof Ishak Institute, 2024. | Includes bibliographical references and index.
Identifiers: ISBN 9789815104608 (soft cover) | ISBN 9789815104615 (ebook PDF) | ISBN 9789815104684 (epub)
Subjects: LCSH: Generation Y—Indonesia.
Classification: LCC HQ799.8 I5U55

Cover design by Lee Meng Hui
Index compiled by Raffaie Nahar
Typeset by Superskill Graphics Pte Ltd
Printed in Singapore by Mainland Press Pte Ltd

# CONTENTS

# LIST OF FIGURES

# LIST OF TABLES

*Tables*

# LIST OF ANNEXES AND APPENDIXES

# THE CONTRIBUTORS

***The Editors***

**Ju-Lan Thung** is a senior researcher at the Research Center for Society and Culture, the National Research and Innovation Agency (BRIN), Indonesia. She graduated from the PhD programme in Sociology at La Trobe University, Melbourne, Australia in 1998. She has written several articles on Chinese Indonesians, ethnicity and various social issues, such as (1) "Agama dan Identitas Orang Tionghoa di Indonesia (Religion and Identity of Chinese Indonesians)", in *Revolusi Tak Kunjung Selesai: Potret Indonesia Masa Kini* (Kepustakaan Populer Gramedia and IRASEC, 2017); (2) "Confucius Institute at University Al Azhar, Jakarta: The Unseen Power of China", *Wacana* 18, no. 1 (2017); (3) "Memahami Etnisitas di Perkotaan: Politik Inter-Ruang di Kota Multikultural (Understanding Urban Ethnicity: Inter-space Politics in Multicultural City", *Jurnal Masyarakat dan Budaya* 19, no. 3 (2017); (4) "Chinese Indonesians and China-Indonesia Relations: A Juxtaposition of Identity and Politics", *Jurnal Masyarakat Indonesia* 43, no. 2 (2017): 197–206; (5) *Iptek dan Masyarakat: Problematik Agrikultura di Indonesia* [Science, Technology and Society: Agricultural Problematics in Indonesia] (LIPI Press, 2019); (6) "Politics of Difference: Ethnicity and Social Class Within the Indonesian Middle Class in Digital Era", *Jurnal Antropologi Indonesia* 41, no. 1 (2020): 41–51, http://journal.ui.ac.id/jai; (7) "Managing Multiculturalism in 21st Century Indonesia amid Ethnic and Religious Diversity", in *Indonesia at the Crossroads: Transformation and Challenges*, edited by Okamoto Maasaki and Jafar Suryomenggolo (Gajah Mada University Press, Kyoto University Press, Trans Pacific Press, 2022); and (8) *When East Asia Meets Southeast Asia: Presence and Connectedness in Transformation Revisited*, co-edited with Yumi Kitamura and Alan H. Yang (Singapore: World Scientific, 2023), pp. 29–55. Email: thung_julan@yahoo.com; thun001@brin.go.id

**Maria Monica Wihardja** is Visiting Fellow at the ISEAS – Yusof Ishak Institute, Singapore and a former World Bank Economist in the World Bank's Poverty and Equity Global Practice. She was the recipient of the Nikkei Asian Scholar 2023. In 2017, she was seconded to the Executive Office of the President of the Republic of Indonesia as a senior advisor to the Deputy Chief Staff in charge of strategic economic issues, where she oversaw the food policy reforms and stunting prevention agenda. From 2012 to 2014, she represented Indonesia at the Think20 meetings at the Los Cabos, Saint Petersburg and Brisbane G20 Summits. Her main research topics are food security and agricultural reforms, jobs, the digital economy, and regional and global architecture. She has a PhD in Regional Science from Cornell University, an MPhil in Economics from Cambridge University, and a BA in Applied Mathematics-Economics from Brown University. Email: maria_wihardja@iseas.edu.sg

*Chapter Authors (in alphabetical order)*

**Ahmad Budi Setiawan** is a senior researcher at the Institute of Governance, Economy and Community Welfare, the National Research and Innovation Agency (BRIN), Indonesia. He obtained a bachelor's degree in information technology from the Institute Technology Indonesia and a master's degree in information technology from Universitas Indonesia. He also holds Information Security Management System Lead Auditor and Associate Professional Engineer certificates. Email: ahma109@brin.go.id

**Ahmad Helmy Fuady** is a senior researcher at the Research Center for Area Studies, the National Research and Innovation Agency (BRIN), Indonesia. He was trained in economics and development at Gadjah Mada University, Yogyakarta and the Australian National University, Canberra, from where he obtained his bachelor's and master's degrees, respectively. In 2012 he obtained his doctorate from the University of Amsterdam, with a dissertation comparing development in sub-Saharan Africa and Southeast Asia, entitled "Elites and Economic Policies in Indonesia and Nigeria, 1966–1998". He has worked on a wide range of development issues, such as poverty alleviation, local development, regionalism, and industrialization issues at global, national and local levels. Email: ahmad.helmy.fuady@brin.go.id

**Andrian Wikayanto** is a contemporary art researcher at the National Research and Innovation Agency (BRIN), Indonesia, with expertise in

Indonesian animation studies, and new media studies such as augmented reality and virtual reality. On the sidelines of his research activities, he also makes documentary films, short animations, and illustrations on online comic media platforms since 2005. He is currently pursuing doctoral studies (PhD) in the field of animation. Email: andr038@brin.go.id

**An Nisa Astuti** is a researcher at the Collective for Action and Mobilization Studies (Koalisi). Her research interests centre around issues related to contentious politics and social movements. Email: annisatriastuti2810@gmail.com.

**Ari Cahyo Nugroho** received his bachelor's degree in communication (journalism) from the Jakarta Institute of Social and Political Sciences (IISIP) in 2003. He later earned his master's degree in communication with a focus on business media from Mercubuana University in 2022. From 2001, he worked as a journalist for various national newspapers. In 2007, he became a civil servant (PNS) for the Ministry of Communication and Information in the Republic of Indonesia, where he currently works as a Researcher, Editor, and Structural Officer for Human Resources. Email: aric001@brin.go.id

**Arief Hartanto** is a researcher at the Center for Research on Society and Culture at the National Research and Innovation Agency (BRIN), Indonesia. His favourite research topics are illustration in the context of practical art, history and visual communication. In addition, he is interested in exploring research on illustration including issues of culture, identity and industry. Email: arie030@brin.go.id

**Caecilia Suprapti Dwi Takariani** has been a researcher at the National Research and Innovation Agency (BRIN), Indonesia since 2022. Previously she joined the Ministry of Communication and Information of the Republic of Indonesia in 1989. She graduated with a bachelor's degree in law from the Faculty of Law, Diponegoro University, Semarang and a postgraduate of Communication Science, Padjadjaran University, Bandung. Her research focus is on communication and media, and has researched on communication, media, digital literacy and competence. Email: caec002@brin.go.id.

**Carolus Bregas Pranoto** is a researcher at the Collective for Action and Mobilization Studies (Koalisi). His research interest revolves around political ecology, forestry and concessions, and state-making. Email: cbregaspranoto@gmail.com.

**Chabib Duta Hapsoro** is a PhD candidate at the Department of Malay Studies, at the National University of Singapore. He received his MA from the Faculty of Art and Design, Bandung Institute of Technology (2014). He was the in-house curator of Selasar Sunaryo Art Space, Bandung (2010–20). Chabib's research interest usually deals with the social production and dissemination of art in Indonesia, deliberating the role of ideologies, elites, dominant class, markets, and governments. Chabib published a book entitled *Alam Terkembang Hilang Berganti* (Comma Books, 2020), comprising his writings on art. He also co-edited a book series, *Pusaka Seni Rupa II: Seni Patung Indonesia Modern* (Directorate General of Culture, Ministry of Education and Culture, Indonesia, 2020). His writings have been published by *Tempo* magazine, *Art Asia Pacific, and Wacana Journal of Humanities of Indonesia,* among others. Email: chabib.d.hapsoro@u.nus.edu

**Diana Sari** has been a researcher at the National Research and Innovation Agency (BRIN) since 2022. She joined the Ministry of Communication and Information of the Republic of Indonesia in 2009. Her focus of research is on science, technology and innovation policies. Several studies were conducted and focused on ICT policies, digital literacy and competence, smart cities, e-government, the preparation of the long-term ICT roadmap book up to 2045 at the Ministry of Communications and Informatics, the compilation of ICT indicator books, and research on regional aspirations. Email: dian083@brin.go.id

**Dida Dirgahayu** is currently an associate researcher at the Center for Research on Society and Culture of the Social Sciences and Humanities (IPSH) of the National Innovation Research Agency (BRIN), Indonesia. He has been a researcher since 2000 with expertise in journalism, communications and media. In addition to writing scientific papers, he is active in contributing to newspapers and the mass media and is a member of the Indonesian Journalists Association (PWI) West Java. Some of his latest scientific papers include "Literary Journalism in Mass Media",

"Journalists' Perceptions of Investigative Journalism Activities", "Literary Journalism in Local Mass Media", "Between Mainstream Media and Citizen Journalism", "Existence of Sundanese Language Press", "Contribution of Local Television Media, Between Journalistic Ethics and Press Freedom", "The Hyperreality of Social Media", "Contribution of Cimahi Technopark to SMEs", "Contribution of Mass Media in Election Activities", "News of Violence and Terrorism on Television Mass Media", "Literacy of Persons with Disabilities", and "Communication Lead of the Archipelago Capital Development (IKN)". Email: dida001@brin.go.id

**Endi Aulia Garadian** is a lecturer in State Islamic University Syarif Hidayatullah (UIN) of Jakarta. At the faculty, he teaches Indonesian Historiography and Colonial History in Indonesia. He obtained his MA at the University of Indonesia, majoring in Colonial History. He also serves as a researcher at the Center for the Study of Islam and Society (PPIM) UIN Jakarta. Endi's research topics focus on socio-economic change in Muslim society and Muslim activism in the digital world. His works on those issues, among others, are "Religious Trend in Contemporary Indonesia: Conservatism Domination on Social Media" (2020) and "Javanese Noble and the Misuse of Mosque Cash, 1890–1942" (2020), "Beragama di Dunia Maya: Media Sosial dan Pandangan Keagamaan di Indonesia" (Practising Religion in the Virtual World: Social Media and Religious Views in Indonesia) (2020). Email: endi.garadian@uinjkt.ac.id

**Feisal Nadhirrahman** is Head of Business Operation at tanamduit. tamanduit is an investment application that provides a variety of online investment options, ranging from mutual funds, retail government securities (SBN) and others. Email: feisal.nadhirrahman@gmail.com.

**Fuji Riang Prastowo** is an Assistant Professor in Sociology at Universitas Gadjah Mada in Indonesia. He delves deeper into some expertise in Ethnicity (Postcoloniality, Identity, Diaspora, Social Inclusion), Religious Studies (Abhidhamma Buddhist Psychology, Spirituality, Folk Religions), and Mental Health (Meditation, Education, Youth Wellbeing, Social Counseling). Apart from being a lecturer, he primarily works as a practitioner in some international advocacy projects in social inclusion and hidden populations. In social services, by the Theravada name of Saccavacako, he is a preacher of Buddhism and a teacher of interfaith meditation at several monasteries in Yogyakarta. See https://acadstaff.ugm.ac.id/ for his detailed academic portfolio. Email: fujiriangprastowo@ugm.ac.id.

**Genardi Atmadiredja** was born in Bandung in 1987. He completed a master's degree in fine arts at Bandung Institute of Technology (ITB) in 2017. He currently works as a junior expert researcher at the National Research and Innovation Agency, Indonesia, in the field of expertise in visual arts. Some of his scientific works that have been published include "Awarding in Major Exhibitions of Indonesian Painting and the Jakarta Biennale 1974–1989" in *Mudra Journal*, "Periodization of Artist Societies in Indonesia from 1930 to 2000s" in *Patrawidya Journal*, "Transformation of Fine Art Presentation Media in News Media Coverage" in the 2nd International Conference on ARTESH 2020, Bandung Institute of Technology, Indonesia, 2020, and "Management of State-Owned Fine Art Works in Indonesia: Conservation of Fine Art in Indonesia" in the International Conference on Aesthetics and Art Science, 2020. Among his research topics of interest are art history and art criticism. Email: gena001@brin.go.id

**Harun Arrasyid** is a graduate student in the Master's programme of Islamic History and Culture (MSKI) at the State Islamic University Syarif Hidayatullah (UIN) of Jakarta. He completed his bachelor's degree in the Department of Islamic History and Civilization and wrote on Islamic Populism. Currently, he serves as a volunteer to manage databases and a website at the Master Program of Islamic History and Culture (MSKI). His research interest is the politics of Populism and its influence on the Muslim community both in the past and the present. His previous contributions to this study include "Populism, Identity Politics, and the 2019 Election" (2019) and "The Dynamics of Indonesian Politics 1955–1959: Dialectics between Populism and the Politics of Islamic Identity" (2019). Email: harunarrasyid21@mhs.uinjkt.ac.id

**Ibrahim Kholilul Rohman** is a senior research associate at the Indonesia Financial Group (IFG) Progress and a lecturer at the School of Strategic and Global Studies, Universitas Indonesia. Email: ibrahim.kholilul@ifg.id

**Kevin Bagas Ksatria** is an Associate Consultant at Bain & Company. Email: kevinbagasksatria@gmail.com

**Kurniawati Hastuti Dewi** is a senior researcher at the Research Center for Politics, the National Research and Innovation Agency (BRIN), Indonesia. She obtained a bachelor's degree in politics from Diponegoro University (2000), a master's degree in Asian Studies from the Australian National University (2007), and a doctoral degree from Kyoto University (2012). Her doctoral dissertation at Kyoto University was published as a book entitled *Indonesian Women and Local Politics: Islam, Gender and Networks in Post-Suharto Indonesia* (NUS Press and Kyoto University Press, 2015). She has worked on a wide range of gender and political issues, women and politics, and women's leadership at global, national and local levels. She has been actively building networks with international feminists and scholars and was appointed as Secretary-General of the Asian Association of Women's Studies (AAWS) 2020–22. Email: kurniawati.hastuti.dewi@brin.go.id

**Meirina Ayumi Malamassam** is a researcher at the Research Centre for Population, National Research and Innovation Agency (BRIN), Indonesia, with primary research interests in population mobility and regional development. She is currently completing her PhD candidacy in the School of Demography, the Australian National University. Email: meir001@brin.go.id

**Muhammad Fajar** is Research Fellow at the Institute for Advanced Research at Atma Jaya Catholic University (IFAR-Atma Jaya). His research interests revolve around social movements, state formation, and youth politics. He obtained his doctorate in the field of comparative politics from Northwestern University. His dissertation unpacks the impact of Indonesian student movements during the regime transition period (1998–99). Email: muhammad.fajar@atmajaya.ac.id

**Raka Rizky Fadilla** is a Research Analyst at the World Bank and a Research Assistant at LPEM FEB UI. Email: rakarizkyfadilla@gmail.com

**Riri Kusumarani** completed her PhD at the Korea Advanced Institute of Science and Technology in 2019 majoring in Business and Technology Management. She has diverse research interests, mainly in digital behaviour, social media, information systems, crowdfunding, and game studies. She has presented at various conferences and contributed to book chapters. Riri is currently working as a researcher at the National Research and Innovation Agency (BRIN), Indonesia. Email: riri001@brin.go.id

**Sentiela Ocktaviana** graduated from the Master of Development Practice Program at the University of Queensland, Australia. She is a researcher at the Research Center of Society and Culture, the National Research and Innovation Agency (PMB-BRIN). She researches gender and development, women's issues, and human rights. For the last three years, she has been interested in studying new media, pop culture and masculinity. Email: sent002@brin.go.id

**Yuly Astuti** is a researcher at the Research Center for Population, National Research and Innovation Agency (BRIN), Indonesia. Her focus area of research is health-related social problems. Her recent research works are mostly focused on maternal and child health. She is currently pursuing a PhD program at Mahidol University, Thailand. Email: yuly.astuti@brin.go.id

# Introduction

## Understanding the Role of Indonesian Millennials in Shaping a Nation's Future

Ju-Lan Thung and Maria Monica Wihardja

Millennials or Generation Y—those born between 1981 and 1996—represent the population cohort who are moving into the prime of their careers and lives. It is this generation that is being groomed to take up leadership roles in various sectors of society. How millennials mature and develop, the values they hold and the capabilities they acquire will be crucial determinants of the outlook for a nation going forward. Millennials may not be digital natives, but they have grown up amid what is known as the Fourth Industrial Revolution—the current era where virtually every industry is being transformed by the exponential pace of technological change and digitalization. Unprecedented technological changes and what is known as hyper-globalization have caused disruptions to cultural and societal norms. The values and work ethics of millennials are shaped by their exposure to digital social media (Smith and Nichols 2015; Tulgan 2016). These characteristics—their exposure to technology and their world views, among others—place a huge gap between millennials and previous generations. As Hoffman (2017) and Tulgan (2016) have noted, millennials are the most misunderstood among the generations, particularly by their parents' and grandparents' generations, the Generation X and baby boomers.

In Indonesia, those from the millennial generation are slated to take up positions as leaders in various important spheres of society—from the political, economic and business spheres to the education, arts and culture sectors. Experiencing the prime of their lives amid the Fourth Industrial Revolution and the COVID-19 pandemic, millennials have acutely experienced disruptions to their family and working lives as well as ways of doing business.

Indonesia's demographic changes call for understanding the intergenerational gap that is at the core of the so-called millennial disruptions. The gap is a complex one—it exists not only between different generations but also between the millennials living in rural areas and those living in urban areas, as well as between rich and poor millennials. Several phenomena might indicate where to look in order to understand what has changed and how such change has disrupted our lives. Firstly, technology has created closer relationships between those separated by distance while making strangers of those living in close proximity to one another. Consequently, family and people-to-people relations have changed to the extent that the well-known solidarity of the Indonesian people, *gotong-royong*, has been completely redefined by the millennials. Millennials use different tools to empower and help each other. Secondly, materialism has taken hold of our lives to the extent that competition for acquiring material possessions, particularly IT gadgets, has become intense, even among youths in rural areas. The Internet and mobile phones are no longer luxuries but necessities. Thirdly, the Internet has created not only an instantaneous flow of information but also an overload of information (or "infodemic") that people are unable to digest properly, let alone evaluate for accuracy and truthfulness. Consequently, hoaxes and disinformation have begun to circulate extensively over the past five years, indicating the detrimental influences of digital technology on our lives.

Moreover, the impact of hyper-globalization and increasingly cosmopolitan lifestyles have shaped the worldviews of, and sense of identity among, Indonesian millennials, affecting their interpretation of religion, art and heritage, and their engagement with global issues and challenges, such as climate change and gender equality. The rise of globalization and the growing pervasiveness of online religious communities have influenced traditional religious values and social cohesion. As new religious ideologies emerge, the observance of religious rituals in some cases has begun to differ across communities professing the same faith. Differences in ideology and religious practice have resulted in growing polarization between conservatives and progressives, the increasing exploitation of religion for political ends, and the increasing difficulty of promoting moderation in religion. Such changes may also affect the religious views and activities of Indonesian millennials.

Indonesian millennials have generally grown up in the post-Soeharto period of socio-political change known as *Reformasi* and have been at the forefront of Indonesia's democratic transition. "Millennial generation" became a trending issue during and after the Jakarta gubernatorial election of 2012, when millennials campaigned through social media for Joko Widodo ("Jokowi"), now Indonesia's president, and his running mate, Basuki Tjahaja Purnama ("Ahok"), who eventually won the election. The millennials' social media campaign was discussed as a new trend in Indonesian politics, particularly after many of them supported Jokowi in his bid to become president in 2014. Their important role gained greater prominence soon afterwards with the establishment of Partai Solidaritas Indonesia (PSI, or Indonesian Solidarity Party) as the millennials' political vehicle. However, millennials started to become a national phenomenon when Jokowi attempted to appeal to unicorn start-up companies, many of which were founded by millennials, to win his second presidential election in 2019, where young generations made up a significant share of the eligible voters. Jokowi even introduced seven millennials aged 23–36, some of whom were start-up founders, as his special staffers when he started his second term in November 2019. This generation, in the mid-twenties to early forties, is now in a position to contend for the country's political leadership. How they think about politics and governance will be pivotal in Indonesia's political development in the future.

In industry and the business sector, Indonesian millennials have been forging alternative paths and innovations in the digital economy. Millennial business leaders have catalysed Indonesia's buzzing start-up scene. In the last few years before COVID-19 struck, we saw the rapid development of online businesses such as Gojek, Bukalapak, Tokopedia and eFishery. How these start-ups develop, grow and lead in these areas will influence Indonesia's economic dynamism in the coming years.

In the field of art and culture, we see that Indonesia's millennials, who have been raised in a globalized culture, have brought disruption not just in the art production process and in how art is enjoyed itself, but also in the art market, where the use of cryptocurrencies has revolutionized the transaction and ownership process. Even though this artistic revolution can be seen as a new interpretation of various art forms that adapt to the conditions of each era, three dimensions of art, namely art objects, art creators and art audiences continue to be involved in the process of acculturation, inculturation and cultural transformation through a continuous process of dialogue and synthesis across generations. The continuation of dialogue between the traditional and the contemporary has led Indonesia's millennials to a greater propensity to search for their local identity, which in turn brings them closer to Indonesia's traditional heritage and culture. We might find the involvement of this generation in various activities that empower local culture such as the creation of Indonesian anime. Clearly, art and science are close to young people's hearts and minds, a trend that was reflected in 14,000 innovations by youths (branded as "Insan BRILIan MUDA") submitted to the Millennial Innovation Summit 2020, an event organized by a government body (CNBC Indonesia 2020).

**********

Few studies have been conducted to understand the role of millennials in Indonesia's social, economic and political landscape today. The first book on Indonesia's millennials was written by Dr Muhammad Faisal, the founder of Youth Laboratory Indonesia. The book, titled *Generasi Phi: Memahami Milenial Pengubah Indonesia* (The Phi Generation: Understanding Millennials, the Transformers of Indonesia), was published in 2017. According to the writer, the book was intended as "a public narration to stimulate changes". It was followed by the 2018 book *Mempersiapkan Generasi Milenial ala Psikolog: Kiat-kiat Pendidikan Anak bagi Orang Tua and Guru* (Preparing the Millennial Generation in a Psychological Way: Child Education Tips for Parents and Teachers), written by a team of lecturers from the Psychology Faculty of Atmajaya University in Jakarta, and another book in the same year titled *Statistik Gender Tematik: Profil Generasi Milenial Indonesia* (Thematic Gender Statistics: Profile of Indonesia's Millennial Generation) and published by the Ministry of Women Empowerment and Child Protection in cooperation with Badan Pusat Statistik (BPS) or the Central Agency on Statistics. A 2019 book by Tsamara Amany et al. of PSI that was intended to explain millennials' political expression is *Ekspresi Politik Milenial: Dari Anak-Anak Muda untuk Indonesia* (Millennials' Political Expression: From Young People for Indonesia).

**********

This book is the outcome of a webinar we conducted on 15–16 August 2022 titled "Millennial Disruptions: Understanding the Role of Indonesian Millennials in Shaping a Rapidly Changing World". It was jointly organized by the ISEAS – Yusof Ishak Institute and the Research Center for Society and Culture, Indonesian National Research and Innovation Agency (BRIN). The webinar covered six broad themes: (1) Defining and debating millennials: Demography, worldview and consciousness; (2) How Indonesia's millennials are changing politics in Indonesia; (3) How Indonesia's millennials are changing the economy and business in Indonesia; (4) Millennials in culture and heritage; (5) Millennials' art and artists; and (6) Millennials' religious engagement. Twenty-five speakers addressed these themes and generated lively discussions. A total of 329 participants attended the two-day event.

Through a careful selection process, we picked nine of the papers presented at the webinar for inclusion in this book. One of the chapters covers the demographic theme, two cover the political theme, two touch on the economic aspect, two cover the religious aspect and two cover the theme of art. The selection was intended to provide a broad picture of the role of millennials in a changing Indonesia. But each chapter also draws attention to the generational differences between millennials and previous generations.

Does technological development really change the behaviour of millennials? Or is the growing adoption of technology just one reflection of the kind of socio-political, demographic and other changes that occur from one generation to another? We pose these two questions as areas worth pondering over not just when reading this book but also as a continuation of it.

**Meirina Ayumi Malamassam** and **Yuly Astuti** in Chapter 1 examine the generational differences in the occurrence and timing of life course events that mark the transition to adulthood, including first marital union, entry into the labour force and migration. They seek to find out the extent to which the demographic behaviours of young Indonesian adults can be explained by generational differences. They find that the remarkable variation in educational attainment across the generations has a significant impact on demographic behaviours over time. Moreover, the expansion of labour market opportunities, including digital jobs, and the improvement of regional connectivity in recent years may have influenced generational differences in life course events.

**Kurniawati H. Dewi** and **Ahmad Helmy Fuady** discuss in Chapter 2 the growing political participation of Indonesian millennials, particularly their participation in the 2020 direct local election (*pilkada langsung*). They provide detailed explanations of the winning strategies of millennials who have been assuming political office at the local level as district heads or vice heads. However, the writers' main concern is the fact that these millennial leaders represent a continuation of dynastic politics.

For their part, **Muhammad Fajar, An Nisa Astuti** and **C. Bregas Pranoto** explore in Chapter 3 the institutional foundations of youth organizations and highlight some of their progressive characteristics. The authors conclude, on the basis of an online survey and in-depth interviews, that even though millennials as youth activists have been drivers of a progressive agenda, they lack a broad social base. The authors argue that youth organizations require a stronger organizational foundation (better work distribution, wider geographical networks, as well as long-term education programmes) in order to bring about any societal change.

In Chapter 4, **Ibrahim Kholilul Rohman, Raka Rizky Fadilla, Kevin Bagas Ksatria** and **Feisal Nadhirrahman** study how financial literacy affects risk behaviours towards investment in various financial products across generations. They address the question of whether Indonesia's younger generations are financially illiterate or so literate that they become more risk-tolerant in managing their portfolios. The authors find that, compared with Generation X, i.e., those born between 1965 and 1980, Gen Y as well as Gen Z (those born between 1997 and 2010) have higher financial awareness of most financial products, including the high-risk asset types such as cryptocurrency and non-fungible tokens. However, higher financial awareness of certain financial products does not mean they own more of these financial products compared with Gen X. For example, even though those from Gen Y know more about cryptocurrencies and NFTs than the Gen X do, they prefer to spend their money on lower-risk financial products, such as mutual funds, bonds and gold but not insurance products. This finding also shows a significantly weaker relationship between awareness and the level of ownership of financial products for Gen Z, compared with Gen X. It indicates that Gen Z youths, despite being generally more knowledgeable of various financial products, do not necessarily own more of these products.

The digital divide exists not only in terms of device ownership and access but also in terms of digital competency. Besides owning financial products, some millennials are able to use their digital competence to exploit the challenges and opportunities presented by the digital economy and establish micro, small- and medium-sized enterprises (MSMEs). Focusing on West Bandung District, **Diana Sari** and **Caecilia Suprapti Dwi Takariani** in Chapter 5 compare the digital competence of business actors among the millennial generation to that of business actors from other generations. Their findings show that there is a significant relationship between digital competence and the education of millennial MSME actors although some elements of digital competence such as ethics and responsibility are not directly correlated with education. Additionally, the study found that Gen X individuals with higher education exhibit significantly higher levels of collaboration competency.

Two separate chapters examining the religiosity of Indonesian millennials show the interesting differences between this generation and their predecessors in responding to religious authorities and in their spiritual journey to embrace the adulthood process of "social becoming". Examining the views of millennials on the cryptocurrency economy and their responses to the *fatwas* issued by the Islamic authorities that declared cryptocurrencies to be haram, **Endi Aulia Garadian** and **Harun Arrasyid** formulated five typologies, ranging from Sharia compliance and reinterpreting *fiqh* (the body of juristic interpretations of Islamic law) to spiritual opportunism and spiritual relativism. Through their classification, the authors found that most millennials view the *fatwas* as religious opinions, not as legally binding exhortations. Their views are carried in Chapter 6.

**Fuji Riang Prastowo**'s chapter, on the other hand, locates the religious identity of digital natives within several concepts in youth studies, particularly relating to the transitional phase to adulthood, when digital natives are vulnerable to identity crises revolving around religion. He found that Buddhism has become the favourite choice of many Indonesian millennials who claim to be agnostics and atheists while studying meditation, yoga, veganism and other characteristics of the Buddhist lifestyle. The reason for their partiality towards Buddhism is that its doctrines are organically based on secular culture and rationality, particularly the so-called *Ehipassiko* principle of critical thinking, and inclusive of all types of youth identity, including sexual identity. Moreover, there are no absolute conversion rules in Buddhism, that is, conversion to Buddhism does not entail renouncing one's original religion, so anyone can learn Buddhism without having to leave the religion taught by their parents. As such, Fuji Riang Prastowo concludes in Chapter 7 that while experiencing spiritual disruption, some millennials negotiate their identity by converting to Buddhism or reconstructing a hybrid identity in a process of self-discovery.

In Chapter 8, **Chabib Duta Hapsoro** addresses participatory art among millennials, which differs from that of previous generations. He argues that while taking cues from an existing tradition that has emerged organically in Indonesia, millennials develop their own form of participatory art practices. The dominant discourse fails to provide a sufficient perspective on millennial artists, who are only seen as dealing with recent opportunities in virtual and commercialized art distribution under the blockchain system. Millennial artists who practise participatory art no longer fit into one rigid ideological categorization, particularly since they encounter more complicated challenges today: the neoliberal economy and education regime, a commercialized and depoliticized art sphere, and regional feudalism, among others.

In the past decade, the art industry has been one of many sectors influenced heavily by the presence of platforms for non-fungible tokens (NFTs)—that is, unique digital objects validated and protected by a digital encryption technology known as blockchain, which guarantees the authenticity of digital transactions. Many, including Indonesian millennial artists, have quickly responded to the NFT phenomenon with a view to utilizing the technology as a medium for publishing their artworks. In Chapter 9, **Genardi Atmadiredja** and his colleagues from Indonesia's National Research and Innovation Agency discuss how millennial artists respond to NFT technology and the impact of NFTs on their art creation process. Their findings show both opportunities and challenges for Indonesian millennial artists in the NFT world. The opportunities include direct access to the NFT digital art market; flexible time; wider freedom of expression; the potential for networking and collaborating between fellow artists and collectors; and an inclusive space for women. The challenges include lack of regulation; instability of cryptocurrency rates; the threat of cybercrime; and the susceptibility of digital artworks to being lost in cyberspace or being copied without authorization.

## References

CNBC Indonesia. 2020. "BRI Ajak Insan BRILiaN Muda Berinovasi di MIS 2020", 26 April 2020. https://www.cnbcindonesia.com/market/20200426234310-17-154564/bri-ajak-insan-brilian-muda-berinovasi-di-mis-2020

Hoffman, Fred. 2017. "Working with the Most Misunderstood Generations: Millennials". *American Fitness* 35, no. 3 (Summer).

Smith, Travis J., and Tommy Nichols. 2015. "Understanding the Millennial Generation". *Journal of Business Diversity* 15, no. 1. https://www.researchgate.net/publication/324922926_Understanding_the_Millennial_Generation

Tulgan, Bruce. 2016. *Not Everyone Gets a Trophy: How to Manage the Millennials.* New Jersey: John Wiley & Sons.

# 1

# Generational Differences in Life Course Trajectories of Indonesians in Their Mid-twenties
## Comparing Millennials and Older Cohorts

Meirina Ayumi Malamassam and Yuly Astuti

**ABSTRACT**

*Life course events related to the transition to adulthood have been a critical part of social transformation within society. One's birth cohort or generation is argued to be one of the important determinants in explaining attitudes, beliefs and behaviours towards life course events. Therefore, to have a thorough understanding of the demographic behaviour of a society, it is important to examine generational differences in life course trajectories. Taking advantage of longitudinal information from the RAND Corporation's Indonesian Family Life Survey (IFLS), this study examines generational differences in the occurrence and timing of marital unions, labour market entry, and first adult migration of Indonesians. By using descriptive and regression analysis, this study compares whether the life course transitions experienced by Indonesians in their mid-twenties have changed between the current young adult generation, the millennials, and older cohorts, i.e., Generation X and baby boomers. The study found distinctive characteristics in the transition to adulthood for each generation. Moreover, remarkable variations in educational attainment across the generations have had critical effects on the demographic behaviour patterns of young Indonesians. The findings of this study can provide insights into societal changes in Indonesia and act as a basis for designing social policies to anticipate potential future trends.*

## INTRODUCTION

Life course transitions are an integral part of an individual's life cycle. People face various options at critical stages in their life trajectories. Their choices might be shaped by distinctive attitudes, beliefs and behaviours and create societal changes over time. Major life course events, such as getting married, entering the labour market and moving out from the parental home constitute critical phases of transition to adulthood and play important roles as markers for social transition and intergenerational change in a society (Berngruber and Bethmann 2022).

An individual's birth cohort or generation may act as an important determinant of the shifts in the patterns of transition to adulthood. Birth cohorts reflect structural changes over time in a country, including changes in the governmental system and economic development (Vidal and Lutz 2018). Therefore, *cohort effect* explains how each generation has different behaviours due to variations in the temporal situations they experience. However, birth cohorts may not be sufficient to explain changes in people's behaviours over time. Variations in people's attitudes and behaviours can also be influenced by period and life course effects (Duffy 2021). The *period effect* demonstrates how attitudes and behaviours of societies change consistently across generations in response to a major event that affects everyone, such as a pandemic or economic crisis. The *life course effect* shows how people's preferences and attitudes change as they encounter major life events, such as leaving the parental home, getting married, or entering the workforce. Every shift in societal values and attitudes over time can result from one or a combination of these three effects.

Viewing variations in demographic-related events through the lens of generational differences enables a more nuanced understanding of individuals' life trajectories, demographic transitions, and the embedded time and place contexts (Bailey 2009). Demographic events—such as getting married, entering the workforce, or moving out from the parental home—are highly associated with the generational dynamics of a society (Berngruber and Bethmann 2022). For example, the occurrence and timing of marital unions and childbearing vary across generations (Van Winkle 2018). In contrast, variations in employment trajectories across cohorts are found to be relatively negligible (Van Winkle and Fasang 2017). Moreover, it has been argued that the prominent reason why some postpone entering the workforce, setting up a family and delaying migration till a later age is their prolonged duration in education. This is particularly the case among the younger generations (Mulder 1993). Consequently, there is a greater tendency towards late and protracted transition to adulthood among younger cohorts, whereas the older cohorts mainly experienced transition events at earlier ages (Billari and Liefbroer 2010).

Although there have been extensive studies of generational behaviours in the Indonesian context, research focusing on cohort behaviours related to demographic events is still scarce. As a highly populous developing country that has experienced rapid economic growth and social transformation in the past few decades, Indonesia provides a unique context for studying demographic behaviours. Therefore, this study aims to fill the gap in knowledge by examining generational differences, particularly regarding the occurrence and timing of life events that mark the transition to adulthood, i.e., marital union, entry into the labour force and migration. This chapter addresses the following research question: To what extent can the demographic behaviours of young Indonesian adults be explained by generational differences? The generational analysis in this study contributes to the existing research by providing a more nuanced understanding of demographic behaviours across generations and the contextual factors that shape individuals' and societies' values and attitudes in the Indonesian context.

## LITERATURE REVIEW

### Life Course Transitions Across Generations

Life course is defined as an "age graded sequence of socially defined roles and events enacted over historical time and place" (Elder, Johnson, and Crosnoe 2003). In other words, life course illustrates the transitions experienced by specific population groups and shows the general patterns of particular institutional norms (Aybek 2011). The changing influence of structural constraints and opportunities and individuals' preferences and characteristics over time are critical in explaining variations of life course trajectories (Mulder 1993). Additionally, multiple factors potentially increase or diminish individuals' propensity to experience particular life events, and all these factors are not necessarily isolated from each other (Schittenhelm 2011).

Life events related to the transition to adulthood, in particular, are considered critical markers in individuals' life trajectories (Berngruber and Bethmann 2022). The standard life trajectories in young adulthood usually start with completion or termination of schooling, followed by labour market entry, moving out of the parental home or to a new region, and family formation (Shanahan 2000). The timing of the initial experience of these follow-up life events acts as a strong basis for understanding the normative social conditions and cultural context of a society. Moreover, shifts in the age patterns of these events can illustrate fundamental contextual changes in a country's social, political, cultural and economic spheres (Berngruber and Bethmann 2022).

Age at marriage has been a critical determinant of population dynamics in a country (Qibthiyyah and Utomo 2016). Many countries have experienced fertility declines during the last few decades. This decline is mainly due to the use of modern contraception as part of family planning programmes since the late 1960s (Qibthiyyah and Utomo 2016; Warwick 1986). In addition, the expansion of education and labour market opportunities has influenced delays in marriage and childbearing, resulting in lower fertility rates (Qibthiyyah and Utomo 2016). Unsurprisingly, in the more developed countries with low fertility rates, family-related transitions, marital unions and childbearing are generally experienced later (Hofäcker and Chaloupková 2014). Rising individualism, a value characterized by the habit of living alone and the practice of prioritizing individual needs, is believed to affect the postponement of marital union among younger cohorts (Mulder 1993). However, while social values related to family norms have been observed to be changing gradually over time, it is suggested that the ideal norms for the occurrence and timing of marriage are still followed by all generations, particularly in less developed countries (Hofäcker and Chaloupková 2014). Therefore, Van Winkle (2018) suggested that differences in family trajectories are more likely to be influenced by spatial variation than by generational distinctions.

A different trend can be observed in employment trajectories. These trajectories involve individuals' entry into the labour market and their efforts to gain adequate employment and pursue successful working careers (Kogan et al. 2011). Prior studies found that changes in employment trajectories across birth cohorts are relatively insignificant (Biemann, Fasang, and Grunow 2011; Van Winkle and Fasang 2017; Virtanen et al. 2011). Further, the presence of a large number of baby boomers in the population amid the lack of extensive job opportunities during their adulthood created a situation of excess labour supply (Saragih, Widodo, and Prasetyo 2016). This puts the baby boomer cohort in tight labour market competition and results in high unemployment among them. Meanwhile, younger generations such as Generation X and millennials, have experienced rapid development of labour market structures alongside technological advancement, which has provided extensive working opportunities (Frian and Mulyani 2018; Gunawan et al. 2020). In many developing countries, rising informal economic activities in recent years have also acted as a critical determinant in the younger generations' entry into the labour force at earlier ages (Ginsburg et al. 2016; Jones et al. 2016). It can be said that the employment trajectories of each generation are shaped within the country-specific labour opportunity structures.

Life course events related to housing transitions are commonly marked by leaving the parental home or moving to a new region. This situation can be influenced by one or a combination of several events in the transition to adulthood. Family formation, labour market participation and schooling influence one's aspirations and evaluations regarding preferred living environments. This situation may result in the initiation of migration. During young adulthood, in particular, the onset of family and employment trajectories might act as a critical push factor to move out from one's place of origin (Plane, Henrie, and Perry 2005). Mulder (1993) explained that, for older generations, marriage-related motives had been the main feature in migration during their young adulthood. However, this consideration is less significant for younger cohorts. Their postponement of marital union to a later age is argued to be the main reason for this phenomenon. For the younger generation, increasing education participation rates have a higher significance in their migration trajectories. In recent years, pursuing tertiary education has become a prominent motive for migration in the initial years of adulthood. However, the extended years that they spend in education have decreased the level of migration during the later years of their adulthood due to their subsequent entry into the workforce.

Family, employment and migration trajectories are critical factors in explaining individuals' life course. Moreover, variations in educational attainment across cohorts generate distinctive opportunities in different trajectories throughout their life course. This situation results in variations in the occurrence and timing of individuals' major life events (Mulder 1993; Uhlenberg 1996). However, the generational differences could be negligible if all generations hold the same cultural values and social norms and are exposed to similar patterns of external events that influence and shape their life course (Hobcraft, Menken, and Preston 1985; Ting et al. 2018).

## Life Course Events in the Indonesian Context

As one of the most populous countries in the world, Indonesia has experienced rapid growth in population size, from 119.2 million in 1971 to 270.2 million in 2020 (Statistics Indonesia 2021a, 2021b). The 2020 census found that the population is dominated by Generation Z (28 per cent) and millennials (26 per cent), followed by Generation X (22 per cent), baby boomers (11 per cent), post-Generation Z (11 per cent), and pre-boomers (2 per cent) (Statistics Indonesia 2021b). The rapid growth in population over the years has been accompanied by economic growth and social development that have shaped a country-specific opportunity structure.

As in other countries, Indonesia's demographic dynamics over the years have been marked by the expansion of educational opportunities owing to several developments. Before the 1970s, school-age children or the baby boomer generation faced inequalities in educational provision (Bjork 2005; Thomas 1969). During the 1970s and early 1980s, the Indonesian government started its effort to bring equal access to education by establishing primary schools in every village (Rosser 2018). In the mid-1980s the government legislated compulsory education for six years and then extended it to nine years in the mid-1990s (Suharti 2013). A large-scale, intensive national effort to improve access to education has increased the educational attainment of Indonesians from an average of 1.1 years of schooling in 1950 to about 8.7 years of schooling in 2015 (Barro and Lee 2013).

That the younger generations have benefited from the development of the education system can be observed from their increasing enrolment rates, compared with the older generations. In addition, Suharti (2013) revealed that about 66 per cent of the Gen X cohort completed primary school, but only 44 per cent continued to junior secondary school. The millennial cohort showed remarkable progress in terms of graduating from primary school (81 per cent) and continuing to junior secondary school (66 per cent). The significant improvement in Indonesians' educational outcomes can be seen in the increasing proportion of the population aged 15 years and above who have completed junior secondary school i.e., from only 20 per cent in 1980 to 56 per cent in 2015 (Muhidin 2018).

A country's education system is expected to affect demographic behaviours across generations. For example, increased human capital development might impact supply and demand in the labour force. In Indonesia, the changing nature of the labour force, alongside the country's evolving economy in recent decades, implies a growing need for workers with middle-level technical skills (Suryadarma and Jones 2013). Jones et al. (2016) found that the rapid growth of the informal sector in Indonesia's big cities and metropolitan areas has also resulted in high labour absorption of low-educated workers. For instance, an inordinately high share of Gen X with lower educational backgrounds and from rural areas worked in the informal sector as self-employed workers or agricultural workers as of 2014 (Kudrna, Le, and Piggott 2021). While the minimum age for employment, according to Indonesian law, is 15 years of age (ILO 2014), the informal sector is rarely bound by this regulation. Therefore, it is not uncommon to find that most Indonesian labourers have started their employment trajectories at relatively younger ages (Suryadarma and Jones 2013). Rather than the cohort effect, the employment trajectory has been greatly affected by major macro-level events, such as the global financial crisis of 1998. During this period, many people, particularly baby boomers and Gen X, were unemployed (Permata, Yanfitri, and Prasmuko 2019).

The preferred arrangements of life course events among Indonesians seem to be completing schooling first, getting a job and then getting married (Sundaram 2005). Moreover, the minimum age for marriage was regulated by Indonesia's Marriage Act in 1974, which ruled that the minimum age for marriage is 16 years for females and 19 years for males.[1] Statistics Indonesia (2017) found that one in five Indonesian women aged 20–24 was married by 18 years of age. However, there was a shift in the age of marriage across cohorts. About 37 per cent of female baby boomers were married between the ages of 15 and 19, while fewer than 10 per cent of millennials were married during this age period (Nobles and Buttenheim 2008). Also, the average age at marriage was 19 and 21–22 for female baby boomers and millennials, respectively (Adioetomo, Posselt, and Utomo 2014; Sundaram 2005). The pattern among the male population showed delayed marriage, but there was also an increase in the average age at marriage from 24 years for baby boomers to 26 years for Gen X (Adioetomo, Posselt, and Utomo 2014). Another study, by Jones (2004), found that almost one-sixth of Gen X women aged 30–34 and living in Jakarta had delayed marriage and were still single. The postponement of marriage by the younger generations is argued to be influenced by wider access to higher education and longer time spent in school (Sundaram 2005; Utomo and Sutopo 2020).

Migration in Indonesia is mainly motivated by family- and economic-related reasons (Muhidin 2018). Family-related reasons include getting married or following family members, while the spatial movement for working and looking for work is categorized as economic-related reasons. However, among the young population, there has been an increasing trend in recent years of migration to pursue higher studies (Muhidin 2018). Migration is considered an essential element that is closely linked to some stages during the life course transition (Pardede and Muhidin 2006). Migration in Indonesia is highly concentrated in the early twenties (Bell and Muhidin 2009). It is also suggested that nearly half of young Indonesians have experienced spatial movements before age 30 (Muhidin 2018). Data from the Intercensal Survey in 2015 showed that the share of individuals who have migrated at least once is relatively similar across cohorts. Among Gen X, nearly a third have migrated at least once while the corresponding figures for baby boomers and millennials are approximately 27 per cent and 29 per cent, respectively.

Previous empirical studies of transition to adulthood events in Indonesia and other countries have emphasized the importance of contextual settings in explaining the occurrence and timing of life course events. Educational trajectories, especially, have been highlighted as the prominent factors in explaining various patterns of transition to adulthood across birth cohorts. Figure 1.1 illustrates the conceptual framework of this study. Socio-economic and cultural settings as well as economic development are noted as important considerations when examining generation differentials in education trajectories. This study argues that differences in educational attainment across generations shape variations in transition to adulthood events, i.e., first marriage, entry into

**FIGURE 1.1**
**The Study Framework**

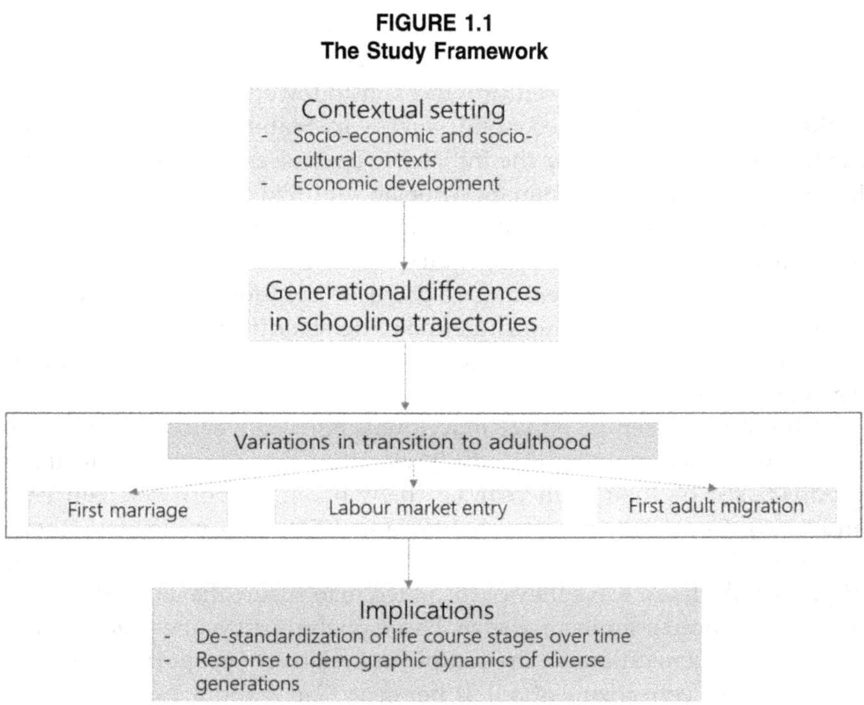


the labour force and first migration. Therefore, a deeper examination of generational differences serves as a critical foundation for obtaining a more nuanced understanding of demographic dynamics among young adult Indonesians.

## DATA AND METHOD

This study examines the occurrence and timing of major life events during young adulthood across generations in Indonesia. It uses data from all five waves of the Indonesian Family Life Survey (IFLS), a multi-topic longitudinal survey conducted by the RAND Corporation, USA, and several Indonesian universities that includes various demographic information (Frankenberg and Karoly 1995; Frankenberg and Thomas 2000; Strauss et al. 2004, 2009; Strauss, Witoelar, and Sikoki 2016). The survey collected retrospective information on major life transitions such as education, marital status, employment, and migration in each wave. In its initial run in 1993, IFLS interviewed 7,224 households with more than 22,000 individuals in thirteen provinces. It followed the sampling frame of the 1993 national socio-economic survey by Statistics Indonesia, hence the household selection for the initial wave represents 80 per cent of the Indonesian population (Strauss, Witoelar, and Sikoki 2016). Subsequent IFLS waves were conducted in 1997, 2000, 2007 and 2014/2015.[2] Due to its limited geographical coverage, analysis of IFLS data sets should not be seen as depicting a representative profile of the Indonesian population. However, IFLS provides a more nuanced understanding of the demographic behaviours of the population since it offers richer information than other nationwide surveys.

This study observed 30,422 individuals born between 1945 and 1989. For generational analysis, this study classifies these samples into three groups based on their birth year, i.e., baby boomers (born between 1945 and 1965), Gen X (born between 1966 and 1979), and millennials (born between 1980 and 1989). The samples are restricted to individuals aged 25 years at the latest wave they participated in to ensure that all participants have experienced a similar age span. Based on the birth year categorization, the shares of generations in the sample are relatively proportionate, with baby boomers comprising about 31 per cent, Gen X about 38 per cent and millennials approximately 31 per cent.

Plane et al. (2005) argued that various critical life course events occurred within young adulthood, such as leaving the parental home, family formation and childbearing, and entering the labour market. The present study specifically focuses on the occurrence of major life events by the age of 25 that can be marked as a mid-point of young adulthood. Moreover, previous studies have shown that marriage, entry into the labour force, and migration in the Indonesian context generally peaked around late adolescence and the early twenties (Muhidin 2018; Suryadarma and Jones 2013).

This study conceptualizes the occurrence and timing of major life course events by looking at the participants' year of first marriage, labour market entry, and initial youth migration. Annex 1.1 lists the questions from the IFLS modules that were used for this study. The first step of the analysis examines the propensity of each generation to experience major life course events by the age of 25. By employing logistic regression models, this study explores factors related to the occurrence of marriage, employment, and migration across generations. The explanatory variables included in the models are sex, highest educational attainment, hometown type, and ethnicity. Next, the Kaplan-Meier survival estimator is applied to estimate the yearly hazard of the occurrence of the observed life events across generations.

## RESULTS AND DISCUSSION

Figure 1.2 presents the share of the population in each generation that has experienced major life course events: first marriage, labour market entry, and first migration. It is shown that the majority of individuals in each generation have married and started to work by the age of 25. However, the share of married individuals is lower for younger cohorts. While nearly three-fourths of baby boomers were married by the age of 25, only 58 per cent of Gen X and about two-thirds of millennials had entered a marital union by that age.

Further, the level of labour market participation in the mid-twenties is notably higher for the youngest cohort. Millennials show a significantly high level of labour market entry at a younger age, with about 87 per cent

**FIGURE 1.2**
**The Proportion of Individuals Who Experienced Major Life Events by the Age of 25**

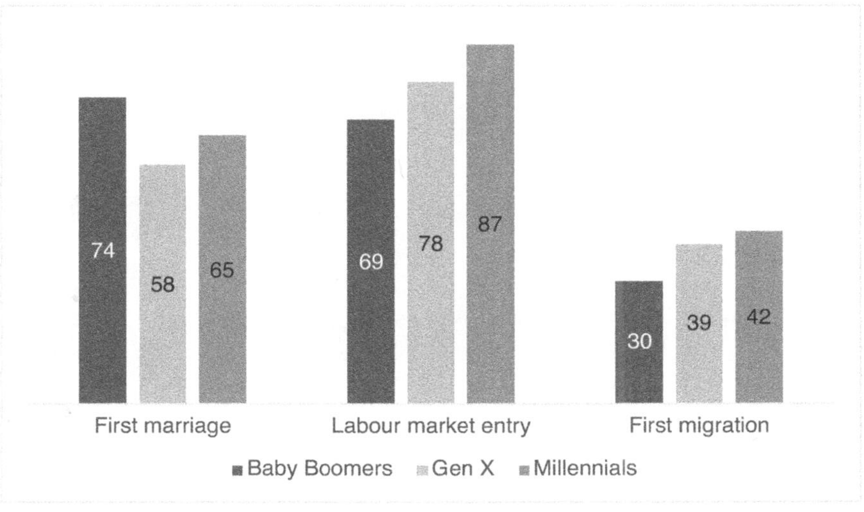

starting their employment trajectories by age 25. The rise of digital-based jobs in recent years has been crucial in the absorption of many young workers into the labour market in Indonesia (World Bank 2021).

Moreover, about 42 per cent of millennials had moved out from their hometowns before turning 25, a remarkable increase from the migration rate for baby boomers. The improvement of regional connectivity through ease of transportation might explain the increased share of migration among the younger generation. However, this situation could also imply a stronger influence of migration determinants in recent years, such as wider gaps in employment and education opportunities between regions (Malamassam 2022).

Increasingly, Indonesia's established school systems and improved educational attainment could critically affect individuals' trajectories. Figure 1.3 shows the changes in educational outcomes across generations in Indonesia. Millennials are better educated than the older generations. Remarkably, the proportion of those with primary level education or below decreased by about 50 per cent between the baby boomer generation and Gen X. Only about a fifth of the millennials did not proceed with their schooling beyond primary level. Additionally, the share of tertiary-

**FIGURE 1.3**
**The Distribution of Highest Educational Attainment by Generations**

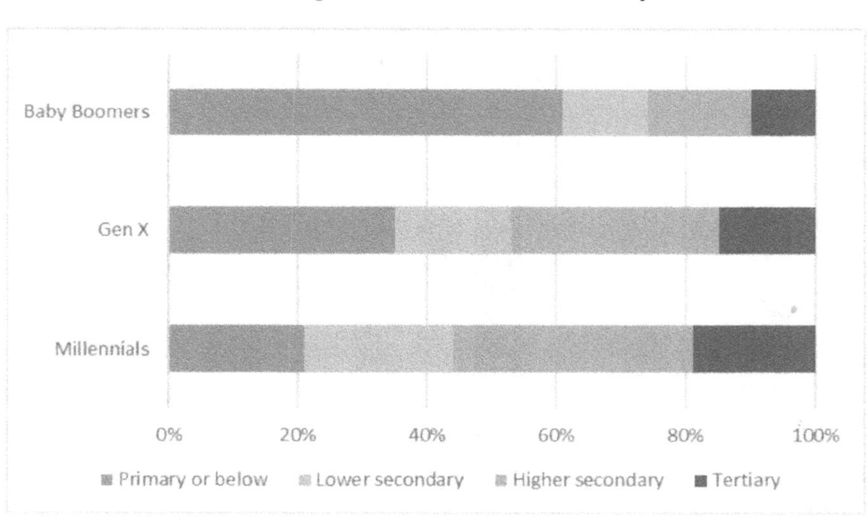

**TABLE 1.1**
**Pearson Chi-Square Test for Association between Marital Status, Labour Market Entry, and Migration Status at the Age of 25 by Generations**

| | *Baby Boomers* | | *Gen X* | | *Millennials* | |
|---|---|---|---|---|---|---|
| | *Labour market entry* | *First migration* | *Labour market entry* | *First migration* | *Labour market entry* | *First migration* |
| First marriage | 39.03** | 10.04** | 32.71** | 4.71* | 0.92 | 1.31 |
| Labour market entry | | 55.85** | | 57.00** | | 45.48** |

*Notes:* * and ** indicate significance at the 95 per cent and 99 per cent levels, respectively.

educated individuals in the millennial generation was nearly twice that of baby boomers.

Transition to adulthood events might not necessarily be isolated from one other (Schittenhelm 2011). One's exposure to a particular life event can lead to exposure to transitions in other life trajectories. Table 1.1 illustrates that, in general, the occurrences of first marriage by age 25 are significantly interlinked to labour market entry and first migration. However, the millennial cohort shows a slightly different pattern since the association between the first marriage and the other two events is statistically insignificant. This situation could imply that the earlier transitions to the labour market and migration by millennials decrease their propensity to get married at younger ages. Also, the weak association suggests an older age at first marriage for the younger generation compared with their older counterparts.

The choice of demographic behaviour across cohorts might indicate that contextual changes and social norms shift over time within society. Therefore, it is important to look at the variations in the factors that determine major life events between generations. Figure 1.4 shows the estimations of first marriage occurrence for the three generations. In every generation, females are consistently shown to have a higher likelihood of being married by the age of 25. It is also shown that there is no significant difference in the occurrence of marriage between those who grew up in capital cities and non-capital cities for the youngest cohort. Moreover, the effects of education on delayed marital age are persistent across cohorts. The tertiary-educated group has the lowest likelihood of being married at

**FIGURE 1.4**
**Logistic Regression Estimates of First Marriage by the Age of 25**

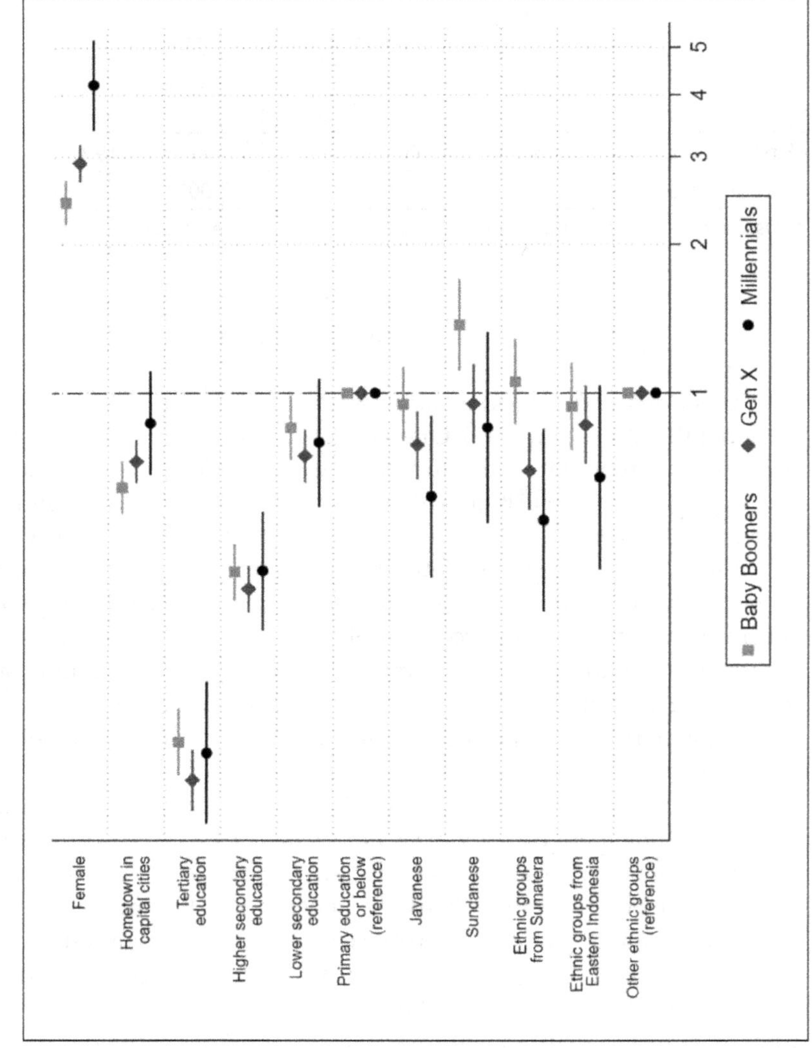

earlier ages compared with their less-educated counterparts. Interestingly, the effects of cultural background are significantly lower for the younger generations. This finding may illustrate that cultural norms have less influence on family trajectories for the millennial generation.

The predicted probabilities for labour market entry by the age of 25 among baby boomers, Gen X and millennials can be observed in Figure 1.5. Tertiary-educated individuals are consistently shown to have a lower propensity to be employed by the age of 25 across all generations. Prolonged schooling trajectories have caused delayed entry into the labour force for highly educated individuals. Moreover, tertiary-educated individuals from Gen X show the lowest likelihood of being employed at younger ages. This finding might indicate the period effect on the variations in the labour participation rate. A large proportion of Gen X in their early twenties experienced the global financial crisis in 1998. During this period, the labour market was greatly affected and the unemployment rate was extremely high (Permata, Yanfitri, and Prasmuko 2019). Further, it is interesting to note that millennials show a different pattern of labour market entry by educational attainment. It is estimated that educational attainment has no significant impact on labour market entry by millennials. The rapid economic growth in recent years has led to more opportunities in the informal sector, especially in the low-productivity services sectors, partly powered by digital technologies, but embedded with precarious and unsecured employment conditions. This type of work is generally not tied to working age regulations; consequently, low-educated workers can be employed at very young ages. The development of the informal sector, alongside the expansion of formal economic activities, has been a major feature of economic growth in Indonesia's metropolitan areas (Jones et al. 2016). This situation might have worked as a critical catalyst for the millennials' high rate of labour participation at younger ages regardless of their educational background.

Figure 1.6 shows the likelihood of migration by individuals in each generation by the age of 25. There is no significant difference between millennial men and women in their youth migration behaviour. This pattern differs from the two older generations, where females are less likely to migrate than males. This difference could conceivably be shaped by variations in the situations they experience during their lifetimes. Millennial females are more likely to have access to opportunities elsewhere due to shifting gender-specific social norms in recent years, which can be seen

**FIGURE 1.5**
**Logistic Regression Estimates of Labour Market Entry by the Age of 25**

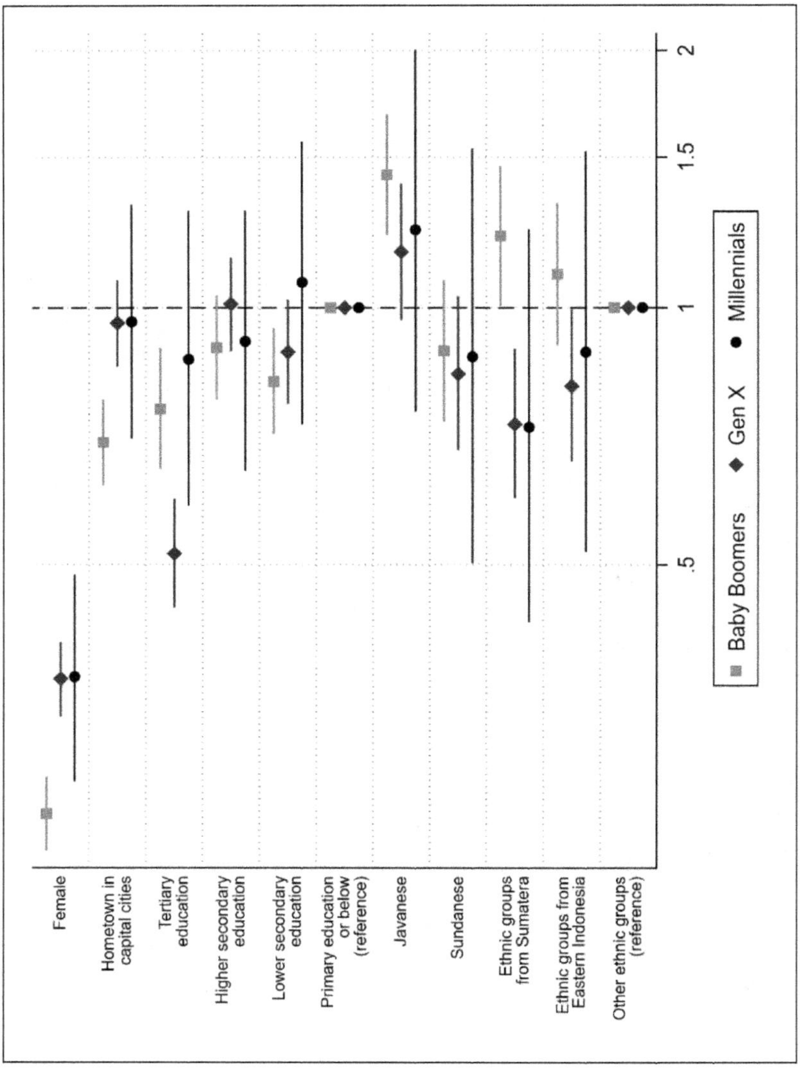

**FIGURE 1.6**
**Logistic Regression Estimates of First Migration by the Age of 25**

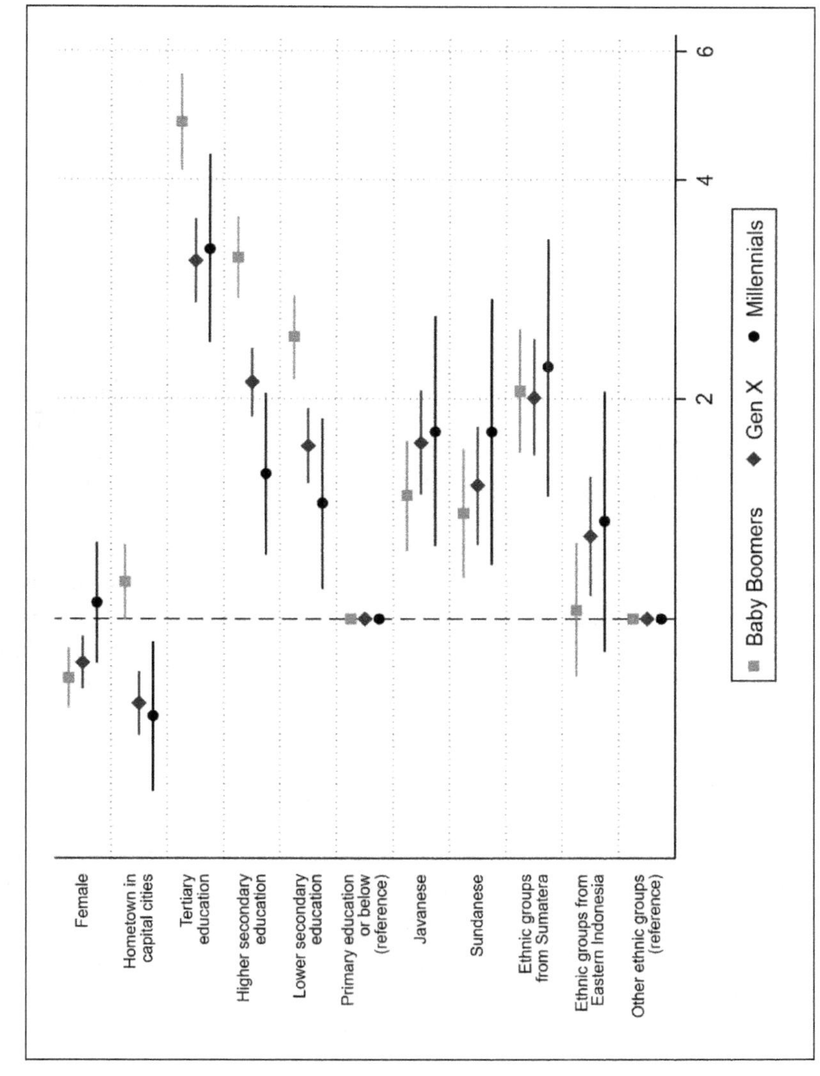

in their increased participation in higher education and the labour market (Afkar et al. 2020; Schaner and Das 2016). In the Indonesian context, while the issues of gender inequality persist, the gap between males and females in access to education and the labour market has been narrowing in recent years (Statistics Indonesia 2021c).

To get a better understanding of whether the onset of life course trajectories varies across birth cohorts, this study runs the Kaplan-Meier model to estimate the yearly hazards of entering into first marriage, entering into the labour force, and migrating for the first time across the birth cohorts. The yearly hazard of the first marital union by generation is presented in Figure 1.7.

The most noticeable difference between the cohorts can be observed in the high level of child marriage (below 15 years old) for the baby boomer cohort. The child marriage rate greatly decreased for Gen X and millennials. On the other hand, millennials show the highest probability of getting married after age 20. They still generally indicate a high tendency to be married by their mid-twenties, but there is an emerging pattern of postponement of marriage to later ages. A possible explanation for the shift in the average timing of first marriage by millennials is the longer years spent in school (Sundaram 2005; Utomo and Sutopo 2020). As explained in the earlier section, more than half of Indonesia's millennials attended senior high school and above, which is in contrast to the older generations. While the timing of the first marriage may have shifted, the younger generations tend to still follow the standard order of transition to adulthood by completing or terminating school before forming a family through marriage.

Moreover, earlier labour market entry might also influence delays in marriage by millennials. As shown in the previous Chi-square test, there is no significant association between getting married and entering the labour market at younger ages as millennials might enter the labour market but not get married before they hit 25 years of age. This situation implies that participation in the labour force could have the critical effect of delaying the age of marriage.

Figure 1.8 shows that the yearly probability of entering the labour force by the age of 25 is varied by generation. About a tenth of the population in each generation started to work during adolescence (below 15 years of age). Baby boomers have the highest likelihood of working from the initial years of young adulthood, while those from Gen X show

**FIGURE 1.7**
**Probability of Age at First Marriage by Generations**

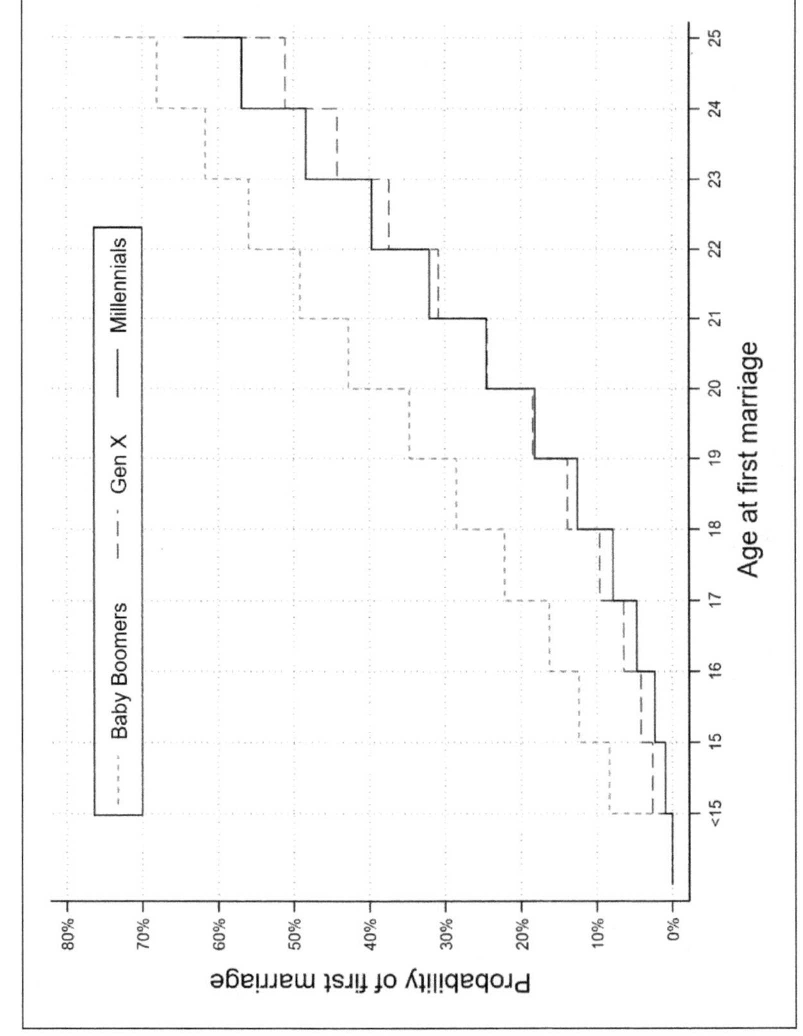

**FIGURE 1.8**
**Probability of Age at Labour Market Entry by Generations**

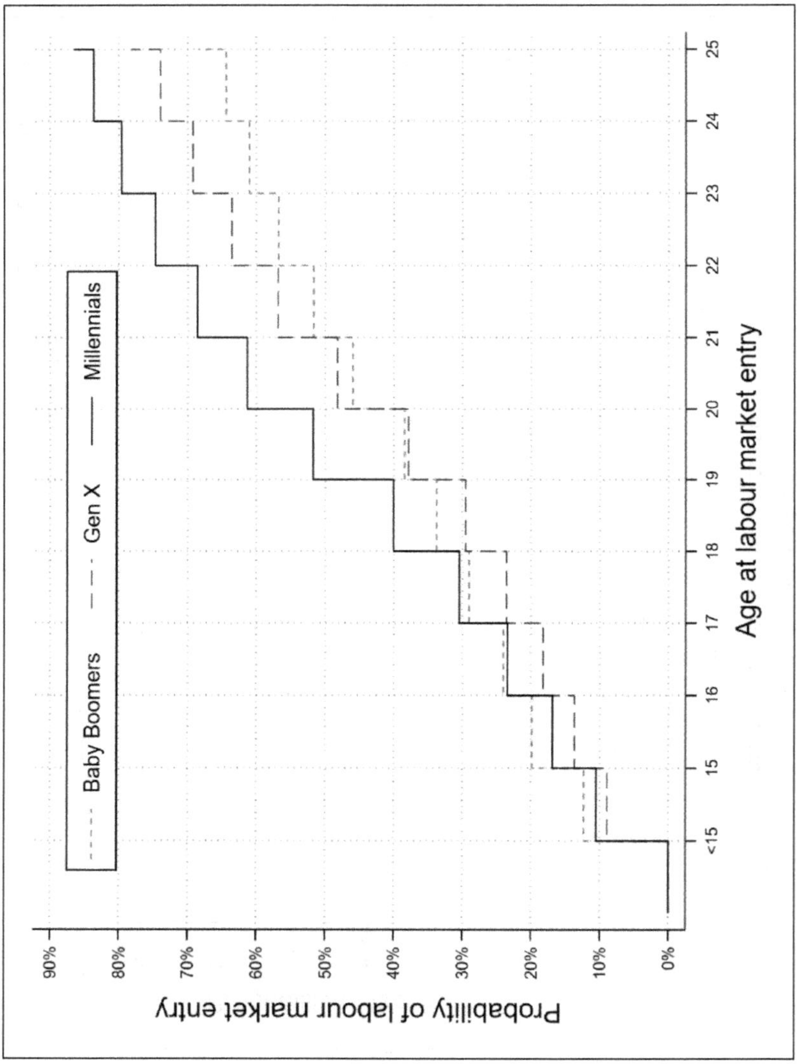

the least likelihood of entering the labour force in young adulthood. However, millennials soon catch up. They show an increasing likelihood of starting their employment trajectories between the ages of 18 to 19, with the likelihood of entering the labour force by that age being higher for millennials than for baby boomers and Gen X. This finding seems to corroborate the fact that millennials stay longer in school, which may delay their participation in the labour market, while at the same time, the rise of digital-based jobs provides opportunities for young adults to enter the labour market early.

Figure 1.9 captures the pattern of the yearly hazard of first migration by cohort. In general, at the age of 25, about four out of ten millennials and Gen X would have migrated at least once, while only about a third of baby boomers migrated at age 25. From the ages of 15 to 17, the migration rates are relatively similar for each cohort. However, the probability of migrating for the oldest cohort tends to only increase at a steady rate towards the end of the observed period. This pattern indicates the limited effect of life course transitions on migration by this generation (Bernard, Bell, and Charles-Edwards 2014). On the other hand, the probability of migrating progressively increases around 18–20 years for the younger cohorts, although the likelihood for those from Gen X is slightly lower than that for millennials. The progressive increase of first migration probability at these ages, particularly for the millennials, might be due to the contextual changes and structural incentives that have supported youth migration in recent decades. In the Indonesian context, easier access to information, rapid advances in the means of communication, and the development of transportation networks have had a critical effect on migration, allowing for more long-distance migration, as well as a more dispersed pattern of origin–destination in recent years (Malamassam 2022; Sukamdi and Mujahid 2015). Notably, rural areas in the eastern part of Indonesia have become increasingly important as destinations. The proportion of highly educated migrants who have moved towards this region has increased significantly between 2000 and 2010 (Malamassam 2022).

**FIGURE 1.9**
**Probability of Age at First Migration by Generations**

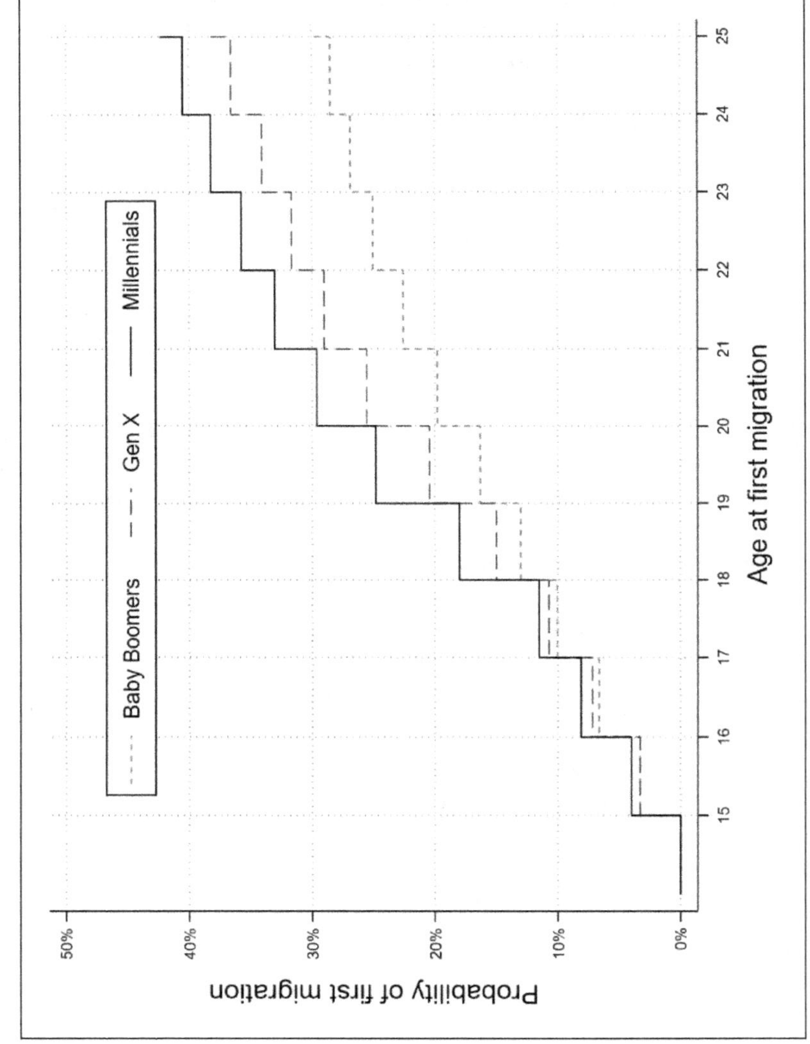

# CONCLUSION

This study focuses on generational comparisons of transition to adulthood events. The analysis of demographic dynamics by generations illustrates the expansion of education in Indonesia and progress in regional development. The remarkable variations in educational attainment across the generations have had critical effects on demographic behaviours over time. Also, the examination of generational differences in life course events illustrates the expansion of labour market opportunities and the improvement of regional connectivity in recent years.

This study fills the knowledge gap regarding the demographic aspects of generational differences in the Indonesian context. The more nuanced understanding of the transition to adulthood across generations that this research has sought to provide can serve as an important basis for population and human capital development since it provides insights into societal changes over time.

Due to data availability, the scope of this study is limited to the older millennial cohort. Further studies that explore the variations in life events of younger millennials, as well as the Gen Z cohort, would help to obtain deeper insights into the demographic dynamics of young adult Indonesians. Also, this study examined the life events of interest separately. A sequential analysis is needed to better understand the effect of generational differences on demographic behaviour.

**ANNEX 1.1**
**List of Indonesian Family Life Survey (IFLS) Questions Used for Analysis in This Study**

| *Variable* | *IFLS Question(s)* |
|---|---|
| Educational attainment | *Module DL*<br>What is the highest education level attended? |
| First marriage | *Module KW*<br>What is your current marital status?<br>How many times have you been married?<br>Which year did you [first] get married?<br>How old were you when your [first] marriage started? |
| Labour market entry | *Module TK*<br>When did you start working full-time for the first time?<br>What was your age when you started to work full-time for the first time? |
| First migration | *Module MG*<br>What is the name of your birthplace when you were born?<br>When you were 12 years old, did you live in the same place where you were born?<br>What was the name of the place where you lived when you were 12 years old?<br>Have you ever moved after the age of 12?<br>Have you ever moved across villages to live at the new location for more than 6 months?<br>What is the name of the destination?<br>When did you move to [destination]?<br>How old were you when you moved?<br><br>Note: This study only considered movement across districts as migration. Those who moved between villages in a district are considered as never having migrated. |

## Notes

1. Indonesia's 1974 Marriage Act was revised in 2019. Based on the revised act, the minimum age of marriage for Indonesians is 19 years for both male and female. This study refers to the initial version of the act since the focus is on millennials and older generations who were not subjected to the minimum age legislated by the revised act.
2. For the subsequent waves, IFLS attempted to re-interview all original respondents of the households in the first wave, including those who had moved house. In each wave, there was a significant increase in the number of households interviewed, the additional households being split-off households from the earlier waves. About 89 per cent of the original households in the first wave were re-interviewed in all subsequent waves. For the subsequent waves, the household retention rate was more than 90 per cent. In its fifth wave, a total of 16,931 households were interviewed and about 24 per cent of them were split-off/new households.

## References


Adioetomo, Sri Moertiningsih, Horst Posselt, and Ariane Utomo. 2014. *Youth in Indonesia*. The United Nations Population Fund (UNFPA) Monograph Series no. 2. https://indonesia.unfpa.org/sites/default/files/pub-pdf/BUKU_Monograph_No2_Youth_in_Indonesia_ENG_05_Low-res.pdf

Afkar, Rythia, Noah Yarrow, Soedarti Surbakti, and Rachel Cooper. 2020. "Inclusion in Indonesia's Education Sector: A Subnational Review of Gender Gaps and Children with Disabilities". Policy Research Working Paper no. 9282. Washington, DC: World Bank. https://openknowledge.worldbank.org/entities/publication/1eb18597-81de-5a0d-9391-f5a3b7619157

Aybek, Can. 2011. "Varying Hurdles for Low-Skilled Youth on the Way to the Labour Market". In *A Life-Course Perspective on Migration and Integration*, edited by Michael Windzio, Matthias Wingens, Helga de Valk, and Can Aybek, pp. 55–74. Dordrecht: Springer.

Bailey, Adrian J. 2009. "Population Geography: Lifecourse Matters". *Progress in Human Geography* 33, no. 3: 407–18. https://doi.org/10.1177/0309132508096355

Barro, Robert J., and Jong-Wha Lee. 2013. "A New Data Set of Educational Attainment in The World, 1950–2010". *Journal of Development Economics* 104 (September): 184–98. https://doi.org/10.1016/j.jdeveco.2012.10.001

Bell, Martin, and Salut Muhidin. 2009. "Cross-National Comparison of Internal Migration (Human Development Research Paper 2009/30)". Geneva: United National Development Programme. https://hdr.undp.org/system/files/documents//hdrp200930pdf.pdf

Bernard, Aude, Martin Bell, and Elin Charles-Edwards. 2014. "Life-Course Transitions and the Age Profile of Internal Migration". *Population and Development Review* 40, no. 2: 213–39. https://doi.org/10.1111/j.1728-4457.2014.00671.x

Berngruber, Anne, and Arne Bethmann. 2022. *Generational Patterns of Transitions into Adulthood across Europe—It's Complicated.* Survey of Health, Ageing and Retirement in Europe (SHARE) ERIC Working Paper Series 80, 2022. https://doi.org/10.17617/2.3386651

Biemann, Torsten, Anette Eva Fasang, and Daniela Grunow. 2011. "Do Economic Globalization and Industry Growth Destabilize Careers? An Analysis of Career Complexity and Career Patterns over Time". *Organization Studies* 32, no. 12: 1639–63. https://doi.org/10.1177/0170840611421246

Billari, Francesco C., and Aart C. Liefbroer. 2010. "Towards a New Pattern of Transition to Adulthood?". *Advances in Life Course Research* 15, nos. 2–3: 59–75. https://doi.org/10.1016/j.alcr.2010.10.003

Bjork, Christopher. 2005. *Indonesian Education: Teachers, Schools, and Central Bureaucracy.* New York: Routledge.

Duffy, Bobby. 2021. *The Generation Myth: Why When You're Born Matters Less Than You Think.* London: Hachette UK.

Elder, Glen H., Monica Kirkpatrick Johnson, and Robert Crosnoe. 2003. "The Emergence and Development of Life Course Theory". In *Handbook of The Life Course*, edited by Jeylan T. Mortimer and Michael J. Shanahan, pp. 3–19. Boston: Springer. https://doi.org/10.1007/978-0-306-48247-2_1

Frankenberg, E., and L. Karoly. 1995. "The 1993 Indonesian Family Life Survey: Overview and Field Report". Working Paper, RAND Corporation. https://www.rand.org/pubs/drafts/DRU1195z1.html

———, and D. Thomas. 2000. "The Indonesia Family Life Survey (IFLS): Study Design and Results from Waves 1 and 2". Working Paper, RAND Corporation. https://www.rand.org/well-being/social-and-behavioral-policy/data/FLS/IFLS.html

Frian, Antonio, and Fransiska Mulyani. 2018. "Millenials Employee Turnover Intention In Indonesia". *Innovative Issues and Approaches in Social Sciences* 11, no. 3: 90–111. https://doi.org/10.12959/issn.1855-0541.IIASS-2018-no3-art5

Ginsburg, Carren, Philippe Bocquier, Donatien Béguy, Sulaimon Afolabi, Karim Derra, Orvalho Augusto, Mark Otiende, Frank Odhiambo, Pascal Zabré, and Abdramane Soura. 2016. "Human Capital on The Move: Education as a Determinant of Internal Migration In Selected INDEPTH Surveillance Populations in Africa". *Demographic Research* 34, no. 30: 845–84. https://doi.org/10.4054/DemRes.2016.34.30

Gunawan, Joko, Yupin Aungsuroch, Mary L. Fisher, and Anna M. McDaniel. 2020. "Comparison of Managerial Competence of Indonesian First-Line Nurse

Managers: A Two-Generational Analysis". *Journal of Research in Nursing* 25, no. 1: 5–19. https://doi.org/10.1177/1744987119880237

Hobcraft, John, Jane Menken, and Samuel Preston. 1985. "Age, Period, and Cohort Effects In Demography: A Review". In *Cohort Analysis in Social Research,* edited by William M. Mason and Stephen E. Fienberg. New York: Springer. https://doi.org/10.1007/978-1-4613-8536-3_4

Hofäcker, Dirk, and Jana Chaloupková. 2014. "Patterns of Family Life Courses in Europe–between Standardisation and Diversity: A Cross-national Comparison of Family Trajectories and Life Course Norms in European Countries". *Comparative Population Studies* 39, no. 3: 559–86. https://doi.org/10.12765/CPoS-2014-11en

ILO (International Labour Organization). 2014. *National Legislation on Hazardous Child Labour*. October, 2014. International Programme on the Elimination of Child Labour (IPEC) and Fundamental Principles and Rights at Work (FPRW) Branch. https://www.ilo.org/ipecinfo/product/download.do?type=document&id=27090

Jones, Gavin W., Hasnani Rangkuti, Ariane Utomo, and Peter McDonald. 2016. "Migration, Ethnicity, and the Educational Gradient in the Jakarta Mega-Urban Region: A Spatial Analysis". *Bulletin of Indonesian Economic Studies* 52, no. 1: 55–76. https://doi.org/10.1080/00074918.2015.1129050

Kogan, Irena, Frank Kalter, Elisabeth Liebau, and Yinon Cohen. 2011. "Individual Resources and Structural Constraints in Immigrants' Labour Market Integration". In *A Life-Course Perspective on Migration and Integration*, edited by Michael Windzio, Matthias Wingens, Helga de Valk, and Can Aybek, pp. 75–100. Dordrecht: Springer. https://doi.org/10.1007/978-94-007-1545-5_4

Kudrna, George, Trang Le, and John Piggott. 2021. "Macro-Demographics and Ageing in Emerging Asia: The Case of Indonesia". Working Paper 2021/23, Australian Research Council of Excellence in Population Ageing Research (CEPAR). https://cepar.edu.au/sites/default/files/WP2021-32_Kudrna-et-al-2021.pdf

Malamassam, Meirina Ayumi. 2022. "Spatial Structure of Youth Migration in Indonesia: Does Education Matter?". *Applied Spatial Analysis and Policy* 15, no. 4: 1045–74. https://doi.org/10.1007/s12061-022-09434-6

Muhidin, Salut. 2018. "An Analysis of the Relationship Between Internal Migration and Education in Indonesia". UNESCO Digital Library. https://unesdoc.unesco.org/ark:/48223/pf0000266053

Mulder, Clara Helena. 1993. "Migration Dynamics: A Life Course Approach". PhD dissertation. Amsterdam: Thesis Publishers.

Nobles, Jenna, and Alison Buttenheim. 2008. "Marriage and Socioeconomic Change in Contemporary Indonesia". *Journal of Marriage and Family* 70, no. 4: 904–18. https://doi.org/10.1111/j.1741-3737.2008.00535.x

Pardede, Elda, and Salut Muhidin. 2006. "Life Course Stages and Migration

Behaviour of Indonesian Population: Evidence from The IFLS Data". Submitted for the Annual Meeting of the Population Association of America (PAA). https://paa2006.populationassociation.org/papers/60016

Permata, Meily Ika, Yanfitri Yanfitri, and Andry Prasmuko. 2019. "The Labor Shifting in Indonesian Labor Market". *Bulletin of Monetary Economics and Banking* 12, no. 3: 251–88. https://doi.org/10.21098/bemp.v12i3.373

Plane, David A., Christopher J. Henrie, and Marc J. Perry. 2005. "Migration Up and Down the Urban Hierarchy and Across The Life Course". *Proceedings of the National Academy of Sciences* 102, no. 43: 15313–18. https://doi.org/10.1073/pnas.0507312102

Qibthiyyah, Riatu, and Ariane J. Utomo. 2016. "Family Matters: Demographic Change and Social Spending In Indonesia". *Bulletin of Indonesian Economic Studies* 52, no. 2: 133–59. https://doi.org/10.1080/00074918.2016.1211077

RAND Corporation. n.d. "The Indonesian Family Life Survey (IFLS)". https://www.rand.org/well-being/social-and-behavioral-policy/data/FLS/IFLS.html

Rosser, Andrew. 2018. "Beyond Access: Making Indonesia's Education System Work". Lowy Institute, 21 February 2018. https://www.lowyinstitute.org/publications/beyond-access-making-indonesia-s-education-system-work

Saragih, Eva, Arry Widodo, and Budi Prasetyo. 2016. "Big City Millenial Workers In Indonesia and Factors Affecting Their Commitment to the Organisation". *Pertanika Journal of Social Science and Humanities* 24, (May): 47–58. https://doi.org/10.13140/RG.2.1.3222.2961

Schaner, Simone, and Smita Das. 2016. "Female Labor Force Participation In Asia: Indonesia Country Study". Economics Working Paper Series no. 474. Asian Development Bank (ADB), Manila. https://www.adb.org/sites/default/files/publication/180251/ewp-474.pdf

Schittenhelm, Karin. 2011. "Overcoming Barriers. Career Trajectories of Highly Skilled Members of the German Second Generation". In *A Life-Course Perspective on Migration and Integration*, edited by Michael Windzio, Matthias Wingens, Helga de Valk, and Can Aybek, pp. 101–19. Dordrecht: Springer. https://doi.org/10.1007/978-94-007-1545-5_4

Shanahan, Michael J. 2000. "Pathways to Adulthood in Changing Societies: Variability and Mechanisms in Life Course Perspective". *Annual Review of Sociology* 26 (August): 667–92. https://doi.org/10.1146/annurev.soc.26.1.667

Statistics Indonesia. 2017. *Perkawinan Usia Anak di Indonesia 2013 dan 2015 (Edisi Revisi).*

———. 2021a. "Penduduk Indonesia Menurut Provinsi 1971, 1980, 1990, 1995, 2000 Dan 2010". 2 December 2021. https://www.bps.go.id/statictable/2009/02/20/1267/jumlah-penduduk-hasil-sensus-penduduk-sp-dan-survei-penduduk-antar-sensus-supas-menurut-provinsi-1971---2015.html

———. 2021b. "Hasil Sensus Penduduk 2020". Berita Resmi Statistik No. 7/01/

Th.XXIV. https://www.bps.go.id/pressrelease/2021/01/21/1854/hasil-sensus-penduduk-2020.html

———. 2021c. *Kajian Penghitungan Indeks Ketimpangan Gender 2021*. https://www.bps.go.id/publication/2021/12/13/8d3f5b35393193b1cf1272a0/kajian-penghitungan-indeks-ketimpangan-gender-2021.html

Strauss, John, K. Beegle, Bondan Sikoki, A. Dwiyanto, Y. Herawati, and Firman Witoelar. 2004. "The Third Wave of the Indonesia Family Life Survey: Overview and Field Report". Working Paper, RAND Corporation.

———, Firman Witoelar, and Bondan Sikoki. 2016. "The Fifth Wave of the Indonesia Family Life Survey: Overview and Field Report Volume 1". RAND Corporation. https://www.rand.org/content/dam/rand/pubs/working_papers/WR1100/WR1143z1/RAND_WR1143z1.pdf

———, Firman Witoelar, Bondan Sikoki, and A.M. Wattie. 2009. "The Fourth Wave of the Indonesia Family Life Survey: Overview and Field Report". Working Paper, RAND Corporation.

Suharti. 2013. "Trends in Education in Indonesia". In *Education in Indonesia*, edited by Daniel Suryadarma and Gavin W. Jones, pp. 15–52. Singapore: ISEAS – Yusof Ishak Institute. https://doi.org/10.1355/9789814459877-007

Sukamdi, and Ghazy Mujahid. 2015. "Internal Migration in Indonesia". Jakarta: The United Nations Population Fund (UNFPA). https://indonesia.unfpa.org/sites/default/files/pub-pdf/FA_Isi_BUKU_Monograph_Internal_Migration_ENG.pdf

Sundaram, Aparna. 2005. "Modernization, Life Course, and Marriage Timing In Indonesia". PhD dissertation, University of Maryland, USA.

Suryadarma, Daniel, and Gavin W. Jones. 2013. "Meeting the Education Challenge". In *Education in Indonesia*, edited by Daniel Suryadarma and Gavin W. Jones, pp. 1–14. Singapore: ISEAS – Yusof Ishak Institute. https://doi.org/10.1355/9789814459877-006

Thomas, R. Murray. 1969. "Effects of Indonesian Population Growth on Educational Development, 1940–1968". *Asian Survey* 9, no. 7: 498–514. https://doi.org/10.2307/2642357

Ting, Hiram, Tze-Yin Lim, Ernest Cyril de Run, Hannah Koh, and Murni Sahdan. 2018. "Are We Baby Boomers, Gen X and Gen Y? A Qualitative Inquiry into Generation Cohorts in Malaysia". *Kasetsart Journal of Social Sciences* 39, no. 1: 109–15. https://doi.org/http://dx.doi.org/10.1016/j.kjss.2017.06.004

Uhlenberg, Peter. 1996. "Mutual Attraction: Demography and Life-Course Analysis". *The Gerontologist* 36, no. 2: 226–29. https://doi.org/10.1093/geront/36.2.226

Utomo, Ariane, and Oki Rahadianto Sutopo. 2020. "Pemuda, Perkawinan, dan Perubahan Sosial di Indonesia". *Jurnal Studi Pemuda* 9, no 2: 77–87. https://doi.org/10.22146/studipemudaugm.60144

Van Winkle, Zachary. 2018. "Family Trajectories Across Time and Space: Increasing

Complexity in Family Life Courses In Europe?". *Demography* 55, no. 1: 135–64. https://doi.org/10.1007/s13524-017-0628-5

———, and Anette Fasang. 2017. "Complexity in Employment Life Courses in Europe in the Twentieth Century—Large Cross-National Differences but Little Change Across Birth Cohorts". *Social Forces* 96, no. 2: 1–30. https://doi.org/10.1093/sf/sox032

Vidal, Sergi, and Katharina Lutz. 2018. "Internal Migration Over Young Adult Life Courses: Continuities and Changes Across Cohorts In West Germany". *Advances in Life Course Research* 36 (June): 45–56. https://doi.org/10.1016/j.alcr.2018.03.003

Virtanen, Pekka, Liudmila Lipiäinen, Anne Hammarström, Urban Janlert, Antti Saloniemi, and Tapio Nummi. 2011. "Tracks of Labour Market Attachment in Early Middle Age: A Trajectory Analysis over 12 Years". *Advances in Life Course Research* 16, no. 2: 55–64. https://doi.org/10.1016/j.alcr.2011.03.001

Warwick, Donald P. 1986. "The Indonesian Family Planning Program: Government Influence and Client Choice". *Population and Development Review* 12, no. 3: 453–90. https://doi.org/10.2307/1973219

World Bank. 2021. *Beyond Unicorns: Harnessing Digital Technologies for Inclusion in Indonesia.* 29 July 2021. Geneva: World Bank. https://www.worldbank.org/en/country/indonesia/publication/beyond-unicorns-harnessing-digital-technologies-for-inclusion-in-indonesia

# 2

# Millennials and Politics in Indonesia
## 2019 and Beyond

Kurniawati Hastuti Dewi and Ahmad Helmy Fuady

### ABSTRACT

*This chapter explores the involvement of Indonesian millennials in politics and investigates the potential for their rise to disrupt the hold of the existing political elites and introduce fresh political ideas, values and practices. The analysis distinguishes between two distinct paths in millennials' involvement in politics: rising through the political dynasty route and rising with no familial connections in politics. Millennials from political dynasties often rely on their family connections to secure positions of power, perpetuating the dominance of existing political elites and raising concerns about a political oligarchy. In contrast, millennials with no family background in politics rely on their entrepreneurial achievements or connections to religious and traditional leaders. These non-dynastic leaders offer an alternative perspective and the potential to challenge the established political order, inspiring voters and fostering a more diverse and democratic political landscape. However, significant challenges persist for millennials seeking political office. The centralized party system, where a small group of party elites control the recruitment process, presents obstacles to accessing grassroots networks. This creates a barrier to meaningful millennial participation in politics and the potential impact they can make. Creating an inclusive and democratic political environment that empowers millennials to positively shape the future of Indonesian politics requires addressing systemic challenges and preventing the domination of politics by entrenched elites and dynasties.*

## INTRODUCTION

Indonesia's most recent direct local elections (*pilkada langsung*) were held on 9 December 2020, amid the COVID-19 pandemic. Despite the pandemic, the election drew the highest voter turnout nationally, at 76.09 per cent, compared with previous direct local elections (Kompas 2021a). In addition to the complexity of holding elections amid the pandemic, the phenomenon that has received the most public attention is the emergence and victory of the millennial generation in running for regional head (*kepala daerah*) positions. Perludem (2021) noted that at least twenty elected regional heads and seventeen elected deputy regional heads were below 34 years of age, which means that 13.7 per cent of the regions have since been led by young millennials (those born between 1981 and 1996).

The rise of young millennials in Indonesia's local politics mirrors the wave of young millennials leading at the national level. A significant number of millennials are now in parliament as well as in the national government. At the 2019 general election, sixty-eight millennials were elected as members of the national parliament (Dewan Perwakilan Rakyat, or DPR for short), making up 11.8 per cent of the 575 members of the body. Political parties also always target millennials to increase their vote shares, and some even claim to be millennial parties. One example is the Indonesia Solidarity Party (Partai Solidaritas Indonesia, PSI), which was the initiative of a number of journalists and former activists in 2013 and offers a fresh vision of "no longer [being] hostage to old political interests, bad track records, historical legacies and bad images from previous parties" (Nowak 2021, p. 10). In addition, Joko Widodo (Jokowi) in his second term as president of Indonesia (2019–24), has appointed seven millennials as his special staffers (*Kompas*, 2 February 2021).

The phenomenon of millennials assuming political office or working for holders of political office, however, seems to contradict the general perception of millennials in the West, who are often reported to be apathetic about politics. Millennials are said to consider politics to be unethical and dirty. Zachara (2020) notes that millennials are reluctant voters, widely perceived as apolitical and non-ideological. Shames (2017) describes the reluctance of millennials to assume political office. The cost of assuming political power is considered too high, materially and in non-material terms, while the benefits and the likelihood of getting anything done are low. In addition, millennials have been labelled as the "Generation Me", with low empathy and lack of concern for others and little civic engagement, such as on social issues, government and politics (Twenge 2013). The low participation of young voters in elections is a matter of concern for many politicians, who are keen to determine how to gain their votes. Thus, there have been numerous studies on millennials and politics, most of which are related to their voting behaviours (Novak 2016; Sawyers 2020; LaCombe and Juelich 2019; Glover 2018; Brading 2017). In addition, the political aspirations of millennials are often expressed through social media. Therefore, many studies have been focused on the way millennials express themselves politically through social media and technology (see Glover 2018; Ida, Muhammad Saud, and Mashud 2020; Latif, Afandi, and Darmawan 2020; Prasetyanti and Prasetyo 2017; Udupa, Venkatraman, and Khan 2020).

Unlike previous studies on Indonesian millennials, this chapter analyses Indonesian millennials assuming political office or seeking political careers. It aims to understand whether the rise of millennial leaders in Indonesia can disrupt the existing political elites and bring in fresh political ideas, values and practices. Finally, it reflects on how this trend could bring new hope for Indonesia's politics and anticipate future development challenges. We argue that millennials are starting to rise in Indonesia's local and national politics. Many of them are part of political elites or dynasties, but some millennial leaders came from non-elite families with interesting paths towards entering politics. The existing political elites have been dominating politics and policymaking in Indonesia and tend to form political dynasties at the local and national levels (Aspinall and As'ad 2016; Buehler 2012; Dewi 2022; Purdey 2016). Millennials, as young generations, are expected to bring new hope to politics through their fresh values and ideas, with the assumption that the digital era opens up more opportunities (in terms of knowledge and networks) for them to enter politics. There is a glimmer of hope that they can disrupt the existing political elites and democracy in Indonesia.

## MILLENNIALS IN INDONESIA: A BRIEF OVERVIEW

Millennials generally refer to those who were born between 1981 and 1996 (Dimock 2019). Young voters are now significant actors in Indonesian politics. The 2020 population census shows that: (1) the Indonesian population is dominated by Generation Z (born between 1997 and 2012), comprising 74.93 million or 27.94 per cent of the total population of Indonesia; (2) the next largest generation is in its productive age, namely the millennials, comprising 69.38 million or 25.87 per cent of the population; (3) Generation X (born between 1965 and 1980), comprising 58.65 million or 21.88 per cent of the population, comes next; and (4) the smallest group represented in the population are the pre-boomers (born before 1945), comprising only 5.03 million or 1.87 per cent of the population (Jayani 2021). Millennials are sizeable in number; they are at a productive age, mature enough in politics, they vote and are being voted in.

In the larger picture of Southeast Asia, both millennials and Generation Z will make up 75 per cent of consumers in ASEAN by 2030, which indicates that they will be a major driving force behind the global economy (EDB Singapore 2021), given that ASEAN is the world's third most populous economy (World Economic Forum 2020). They drive changes in lifestyle, including digital-native behaviour, social network usage, consumption patterns, and youth culture (EDB Singapore 2021). As the first digital natives, the millennial generation exhibits familiarity with digital technology and social media networks. They came of age during advances in digital technology and online information. They also have large networks through the development of social media. Being apathetic to formal politics, they express their opinions, aspirations and anger through social media. They are well informed about socio-political conditions and are often involved in the production of information and misinformation.

When we discuss a generation and politics, it is important to take into account socio-political events that contributed to the formation of generational classifications. The socio-political events surrounding the formative years of a generation may shape their values and political preferences. The Greatest Generation (1900–24) is the generation that lived and grew up during the Great Depression and the Second World War; the Silent Generation (1925–45) is the generation known for working hard and keeping quiet because they grew up during the Dust Bowl and, in part, the Great Depression; baby boomers (1946–64) is the generation born after soldiers returned from the Second World War and created the post-demographic "baby boom"; and Generation X (1961–81) is the generation born after the Second World War baby boom (Zachara 2020; Rouse and Ross 2018). Interestingly, the millennial generation (1981–96) was named as such because it comprises the first generation who spent their formative years at the beginning of the new millennium and were not associated with a specific social or political situation.

The attribution of socio-political events to demographic generations is Western-biased. For a specific country or area, we should also consider its specific socio-political situation that may shape personal values and political preferences. In Indonesia, the term Generation of 1945 (*Angkatan 1945*) is assigned to the generation that grew up during the revolution and the early period of Indonesian independence; the Generation of 1966 (*Angkatan 1966*) refers to the generation that grew up during the socio-political and economic crisis at the end of what was known as the Old Order (the reign of Sukarno) and the beginning of the New Order (the Soeharto era); and the Generation of 1998 (*Angkatan 1998*) or the *Reformasi* generation is the generation that grew up during the Asian economic crisis and the reform period that ended the New Order. This generation of 1998 comprises both Generation X and millennials.

The term "generational" is basically about the formative years, particularly the youth period. Indonesia's youth are the main engine for turning points in the country's political history. First, during the youth pledge (*sumpah pemuda*) on 28 October 1928, Indonesian youths declared a united Indonesia as one country (Tanah Air Indonesia) and one nation (Bangsa Indonesia), with one shared language (Bahasa Indonesia). The Youth Pledge Day is considered the seed of Indonesian unity. Second, youths were involved in the Indonesian revolution as student soldiers (Tentara Pelajar Indonesia, or TPI). Indeed, the proclamation of Indonesian independence might not have happened without youth involvement. With a power vacuum imminent in the run-up to the Japanese surrender, a group of youths kidnapped and confined Sukarno and his number two, Muhammad Hatta, to a house in Rengasdengklok on 16 August 1945, made them write the independence proclamation, and had them declare it the next day. Third, by the end of the Old Order, youth and student movements held huge mass protests because of the economic and political crisis in the country. The big protest in 1965 led Indonesia to the New Order under Soeharto's presidency. Fourth, it was protests by the student movement in 1998 arising from the economic crisis, as well as corruption, collusion and nepotism (KKN), that ended Soeharto's presidency.

Millennials are part of the youth that has been the agent of social and political changes. They grew up amid a decisive and massive socio-political change, namely the *Reformasi* or reformation. *Reformasi* signified not only a regime change but also a change in the socio-political and economic orientation of the country. Some of the changes—real or perceived—include improved status of local governments vis-à-vis the central government, political control of the military, and less rampant corruption. These changes would certainly have shaped the personal values of Indonesian millennials.

Millennials tend to be swing voters and therefore are often wooed by political parties, unlike the older generations, which usually have strong preferences for one political party or the other. As youngsters, millennials tend to be rebellious and do not like the status quo. It is no wonder then that perceptions have hardened that millennial youths are a threat not only to national security but also to the dominant moral values. They have been systematically stigmatized as a "new enemy of the state" in post-New Order Indonesia, especially during the administration of Susilo Bambang Yudhoyono or SBY, as he is popularly known (Budiman et al. 2012).

Interestingly, millennials are today seen as an important generation to help solve Indonesia's development problems. On 21 November 2019, President Jokowi introduced seven millennials as special staff to the president to assist him in government. The seven millennials, aged 23 to 36, are expected to bring new ideas and solutions to the government. These special staffers are also expected to serve as a bridge between the president and young people, students, and the Indonesian diaspora across the world. According to President Jokowi, "These seven young people will be my discussion partners, daily, weekly, monthly, providing fresh, innovative ideas, so that we can look for new ways, ways that are out of the box, that jump to catch up with the progress of the country" (BPMI Setpres 2019).

The seven millennials, according to an official press release (BPMI Setpres 2019), are:

1. Adamas Belva Syah Devara, 29, the founder and chief executive officer (CEO) of Ruang Guru, an education start-up;
2. Putri Indahsari Tanjung Putri, 23, the CEO of Creativepreneur Event

Creator, and chief business officer of Kreavi, both companies related to the creative industry;

3. Andi Typhoon Garuda Putra Andi, 32, the CEO of a microfinance institution, PT Amartha;
4. Ayu Kartika Devi, 36, the founder and mentor of the Sabang Merauke social movement, which celebrates diversity;
5. Gracia Billy Mambrasar, 31, the CEO of the Kitong Bisa Foundation, which trains young people in soft skills, creative thinking and entrepreneurial acumen;
6. Angkie Yudistia, 32, the founder of Thisable Enterprise, a social enterprise for people with disabilities, a member of the Asia-Pacific Federation of the Hard of Hearing and Deafened, and a member of the International Federation of Hard of Hearing Young People; and
7. Aminuddin Ma'ruf Aminuddin, 33, the general chairperson of the General Board of the Indonesian Islamic Student Movement (PMII) for the 2014–16 period.

These millennial staffers are young people who can be said to be successful in their respective fields. They use technology to develop their business and social start-ups, which made them known as sociopreneurs. They have social concerns, which can be seen from the types of start-ups they founded. Their success in managing a business or social activities using technology seems to be the main consideration in their appointment.

Many doubt that these millennials will be able to play an effective role in voicing the aspirations of young groups or provide fresh ideas to overcome development challenges (*Kompas*, 22 November 2019). However, their appointment shows at the least that Jokowi does acknowledge the importance of the millennial group.

## MILLENNIALS AND POLITICAL PARTIES

Since millennials constitute the largest proportion of votes, political parties have always targeted them with a view to increasing their vote shares. According to *Kompas* (2 February 2021), young voters, mainly millennials and Generation Z, will constitute about 31.2 per cent of voters in the next general election in 2024. Therefore, many political parties compete to woo this demographic, claiming to be parties for young voters. In particular, the aforesaid PSI, which is led by young politicians such as Grace Natalie,

Tsamara Amany, and Raja Juli Antoni, declared itself a millennial party in the 2019 general elections (*IDN Times*, 5 April 2019).

However, gaining the trust and loyalty of millennials is not a simple task. Many surveys show that the level of trust in political parties is low. A survey by Lembaga Survei Indonesia (LSI) in June–July 2022 showed that political parties and parliament are the most untrustworthy institutions in Indonesia (LSI 2022). Millennials, who tend to be apolitical and non-ideological and have easy access to social and political information, generally have negative perceptions of political parties, which they associate with money politics and oligarchies.

Nevertheless, a political party is a key pathway to entering formal politics. It is political parties that nominate members of parliament at the local and national levels, as well as for presidential candidates. As noted by Aspinall and Berenschot (2019, p. 69), political parties remain important *gatekeepers*, with the power to nominate candidates in Indonesia's system of clientelism and patronage democracy. Even though direct local elections open up opportunities for independent candidates to be elected as heads of local government, political parties—particularly endorsement from the elite at their respective central boards—still hold the key ticket for successful contestation (Dewi and Raharjo 2020). Thus, joining a political party is considered a crucial step to assuming political office.

A classic channel for recruitment and regeneration in political parties is youth or student organizations. These include student movements, as well as the youth wings of civil society organizations and political parties. Among Indonesia's prominent youth and student organizations are:

- Himpunan Mahasiswa Islam (Islamic Students Association, HMI);
- Gerakan Mahasiswa Nasional Indonesia (Indonesian National Student Movement, GMNI);
- Persatuan Mahasiswa Islam Indonesia (Indonesian Islamic Students Association, PMII);
- GP Ansor (Ansor Youth Movement), the youth wing of Indonesia's largest Islamic organization, Nahdlatul Ulama;
- Muhammadiyah Youth, the youth wing of the second-largest Islamic organization, Muhammadiyah;
- Angkatan Muda Pembaharuan Indonesia (Indonesian Renewal Youth Force, AMPI), the youth wing of the Golkar party;

- Kader Muda Demokrat (Democratic Youth Cadre), the youth wing of the Democratic Party; and
- Gerakan Pemuda Ka'bah (Ka'bah Youth Movement), the youth wing of the United Development Party (PPP).

For political parties, youth organizations are important vehicles for maintaining the support of the youth as well as for political regeneration. Therefore, it is typical for political leaders in Indonesia to have learnt the ropes of politics within such student or youth organizations. For the youth, joining youth organizations is a crucial step towards a political career. Youth organizations are training grounds for youths to acquire organizational abilities and experiences, as well as networking opportunities, before joining a political party.

## MILLENNIAL MEMBERS OF PARLIAMENT

Many millennials have run for parliament and been elected. However, the number of millennials elected to political office is still limited. Our calculation, based on data from the General Election Commission (Komisi Pemilihan Umum, KPU), shows that 68 of the 575 members of parliament elected at the 2019 general election are millennials. This constitutes 11.8 per cent of the total, which is way below the proportion of millennials in Indonesia's population, i.e., 25.86 per cent. Thus, millennials are still underrepresented in parliament. Figure 2.1 shows the distribution of millennial members of parliament by province.

As can be seen in Figure 2.1, there are sixty-eight millennial members of parliament, coming from twenty provinces, while fourteen other provinces do not have millennial representatives in parliament. More than half of the sixty-eight millennial parliamentarians hail from provinces on Java Island. East, Central and West Java contributed the largest number of millennial members to parliament, with ten, nine and eight members, respectively. These are followed by Banten (six) and Papua (four). Table 2.1 shows millennial members of parliament by sex.

Table 2.1 indicates that there are forty-two (62 per cent) male and twenty-six (38 per cent) female millennials in parliament. Interestingly, 21.67 per cent of female members of parliament are millennials, while only 9.23 per cent of the male members of parliament are millennials. One of the possible explanations is the different ways that Indonesian voters

**FIGURE 2.1**
**Distribution of Millennial Members of Parliament by Province, 2019 General Election**

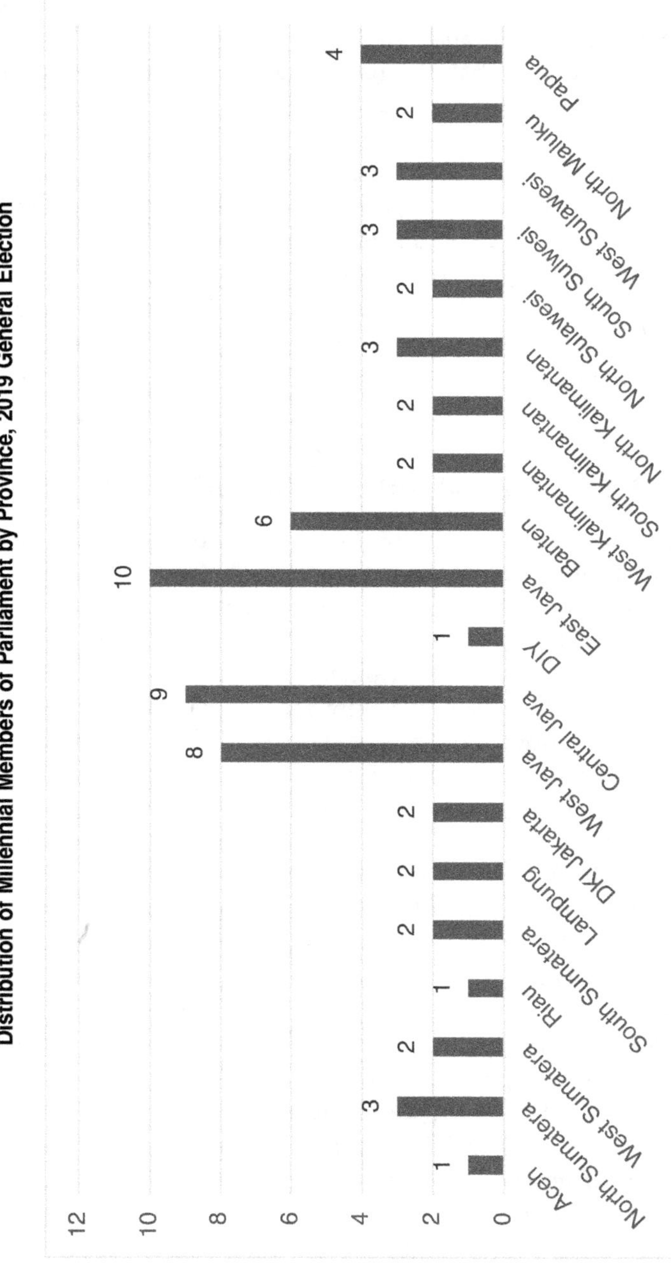


*Note:* Provinces without millennial members of parliament are not presented.
*Source:* Compiled from Election Commission (KPU).

**TABLE 2.1**
**Millennial Members of Parliament by Sex, 2019 General Election**

| | *Millennials* | *Total* | *% of Total* |
|---|---|---|---|
| Female | 26 | 120 | 21.67 |
| Male | 42 | 455 | 9.23 |

*Source:* Compiled from KPU data.

assess male and female candidates. Female candidates are judged by their appearance, so young female candidates are preferred to older ones. In male candidates, on the other hand, voters look for reliability, and mature male candidates are presumed to be more reliable than young male candidates. In other words, young female candidates are preferable to older ones, but this is not the case for young male candidates. Further research is needed to better understand the factors contributing to this trend and to explore how to increase the representation of millennials in Indonesian politics.

Table 2.2 shows millennial members of parliament by political party. Table 2.2 shows that the National Democratic Party (NasDem) has the largest proportion (16.95 per cent) of millennials in parliament, followed

**TABLE 2.2**
**Millennial Members of Parliament by Political Party, 2019 General Election**

| *Political Party* | *Millennials* | *Total* | *% of Total* |
|---|---|---|---|
| Demokrat | 7 | 54 | 12.96 |
| Geridra | 11 | 78 | 14.10 |
| Golkar | 9 | 85 | 10.59 |
| NasDem | 10 | 59 | 16.95 |
| PAN | 7 | 44 | 15.91 |
| PDI-P | 14 | 128 | 10.94 |
| PKB | 8 | 58 | 13.79 |
| PPP | 2 | 19 | 10.53 |
| PKS | 0 | 51 | 0.00 |
| Total | 68 | 576 | 11.81 |

*Source:* Compiled from KPU data.

by the National Mandate Party (PAN) (15.91 per cent), Gerindra (14.10 per cent), and the National Awakening Party (PKB) (13.79 per cent). The Indonesian Democratic Party of Struggle (PDI-P) has the largest number of millennials in parliament (fourteen), but this number constitutes only 10.94 per cent of its 128 members of parliament. Surprisingly, the Prosperous Justice Party (Partai Keadilan Sejahtera, PKS), which was born after the *Reformasi* era, does not have any millennials in parliament.

Many of the millennial members of parliament rose to public attention because of their wealth and elite backgrounds. Kumparan.com (2019) listed some examples of millennial parliamentarians who are affluent (both in terms of money and other assets) and come from elite families:

1. Puteri Komarudin (Golkar), daughter of Ade Komarudin (ex-speaker of DPR), Rp40 billion;
2. Farah Nahlia (PAN), daughter of Brigjen Fadil Imram (high official from the Indonesian national police, POLRI), Rp17 billion;
3. Hillary Brigitta (NasDem), daughter of Elly Engelbert Lasut (district head, Kepulauan Talaud) Rp9 billion;
4. Muhammad Rahul (Gerindra), son of Muhammad Natsir (member of DPR), Rp7 billion;
5. Bramantyo S. (Democratic Party), son of Gatot M. Suwondo (ex-President Director of Bank Negara Indonesia), Rp2.5 billion;
6. Rizki Natakusumah (Democratic Party), son of Dimyati Natakusumah (member of DPR), Rp1.9 billion;
7. Adrian Paruntu (Golkar), son of Christiany Paruntu (district head, North Minahasa), Rp1.6 billion;
8. Dyah Roro Esti (Golkar), daughter of Satya Widya Yudha (member of DPR), Rp1.2 billion;
9. Fachry Konggoasa (PAN), son of Kery Saiful Konggoasa (district head, Konawe), Rp400 million;
10. Arkana Akram (NasDem), son of Irianto Lambarie (governor of North Kalimantan), Rp198 million.

Joining political parties and getting elected to parliament is not easy in Indonesia, where political dynasties or families that have multiple members involved in politics are a prevalent phenomenon (Aspinall and As'ad 2016; Buehler 2012, 2013; Purdey 2016; Dewi 2022). This has made it difficult for millennials or any individual outside of established political families to enter the political arena or to break into politics as they may not have the same connections or the same level of support and resources as those from established political dynasties. Furthermore, the culture of nepotism and patronage in Indonesian politics can make it difficult for non-dynastic politicians to get a foothold in politics as they may not have the same level of support as those from political dynasties.

## MILLENNIALS IN LOCAL POLITICS

In the 2020 direct elections for various regional leadership positions, 9 gubernatorial positions, 225 district head positions and 37 other major positions were contested. Of the 738 pairs who participated in the elections, 77 pairs (about 10 per cent) included young millennial candidates. Out of these, 31 ran for regional head positions, and 46 for regional deputy head positions (Perludem 2021). In this section, the term "young millennials" refers to millennials aged below 34 years (born between 1986 and 1996) at the time of the 2020 elections.

The map in Figure 2.2 shows the distribution of young millennials elected as heads of regional government. According to Perludem (2021), twenty young millennials were elected as regional heads (sixteen district heads and four mayors), and seventeen were elected as deputy district heads. Young millennials were elected as heads of regional government in Java, Sumatra, Sulawesi and Kalimantan. No young millennials were elected as governor or deputy governor (see also Figure 2.3).

As for gender equality, only two young female millennials were elected as regional heads, namely, Dyah Hayuning Pratiwi (Purbalingga district) and Rezita Meylani Yopi (Indragiri Hulu district). Both of them are from political dynasties, the former being the daughter of the ex-district head and the latter being the wife of the ex-district head. No young female millennials were elected as regional deputy heads. This is an interesting development that bears further investigation, considering the general trend of increasing numbers of female political leaders elected since direct local elections were introduced in 2005 (Dewi 2015). Figure 2.3 shows elected pairs in the 2020 election.

## MILLENNIALS FROM POLITICAL DYNASTIES

According to Perludem (2021), thirteen of the twenty young millennials (or 65 per cent) who were elected as district heads and mayors have familial

**FIGURE 2.2**
**Distribution of Young Millennials Elected as Regional Heads in the 2020 Direct Local Elections**

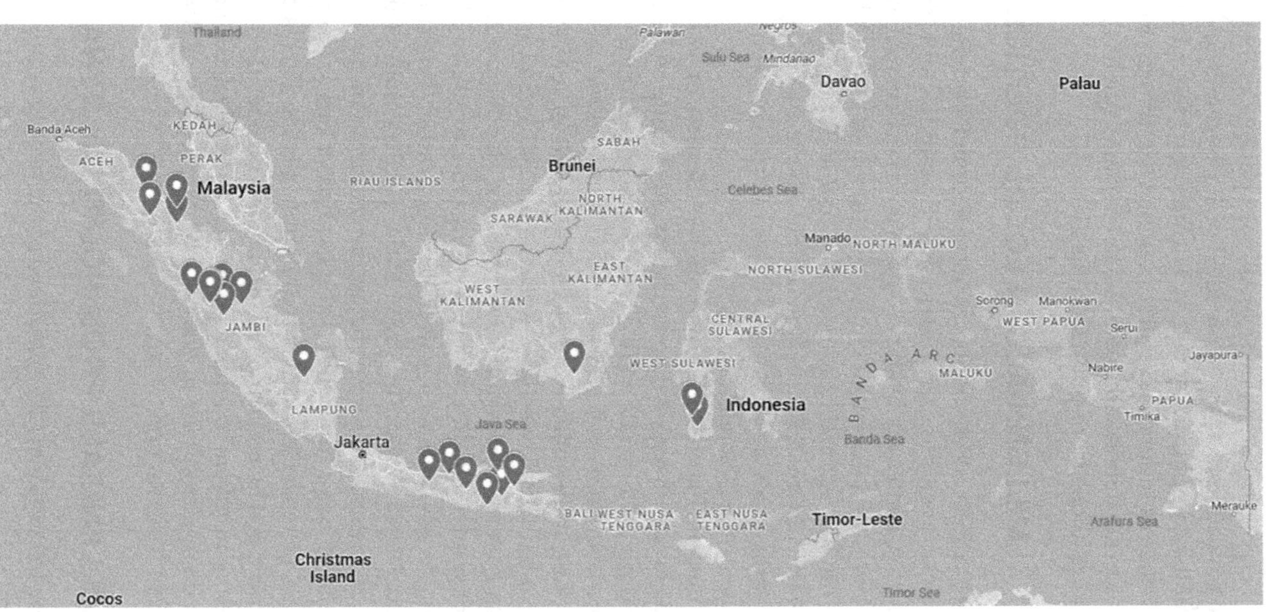

**FIGURE 2.3**
**Elected Pairs in the 2020 Direct Local Elections**

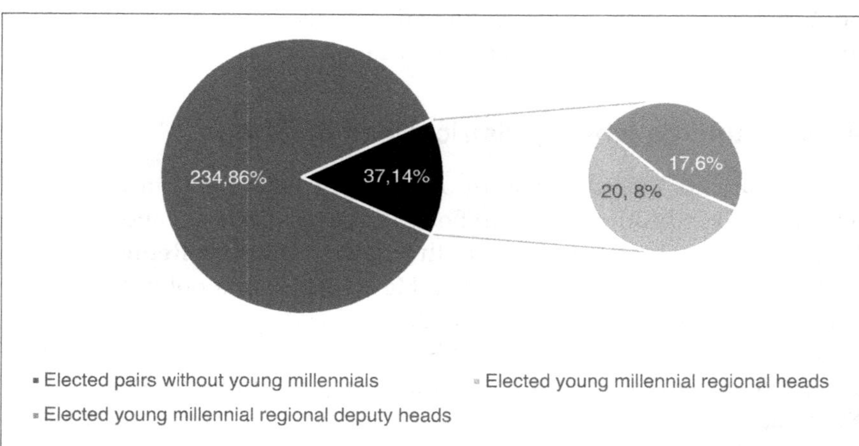


*Source:* Based on data from KPU and Perludem (2021).

ties to local and national political elites. They are sons, wives or sons-in-law of previous regional heads or other national political figures. Meanwhile, 59 per cent of the seventeen young millennials elected as regional deputy heads also have political ties with local and national political elites. They are sons, wives or in-laws of previous regional heads or national political elites, as can be seen in Table 2.3. Previous district heads who had already served for two terms and therefore can no longer compete in the election typically send their wives, sons, daughters or nephews to compete in local elections. Another trend is that of national political elites sending their family members to compete in local elections, such as Bobby, son-in-law of President Jokowi, who contested in Medan under the PDI-P ticket, and Hanindito, son of Pramono Anung, the secretary general of PDI-P.

For political dynasties, we use Mark R. Thompson's definition, which assesses the political histories of popular female national leaders in Asia and boldly uses the term "political dynasties" rather than familial ties as a key variable for female politicians in assuming political leadership (Thompson 2012, 2002). "Political dynasty" applies specifically to families that continuously maintain political and economic power over generations, such as Indira Gandhi's family in India, Benazir Bhutto's family in Pakistan, the Marcos family in the Philippines, and the Sukarno family in Indonesia.

Here, we follow Thompson's political dynasty definition as it may exert a strong influence on the political emergence of millennial (men and women) political leaders. Table 2.3 lists young millennials elected as regional heads (district heads or mayors) in the 2020 local elections.

## Adnan Purichta Ichsan, District Head of Gowa

Adnan Purichta Ichsan was born on 9 March 1986. He is in his second term as district head of Gowa in South Sulawesi (2016–21 and 2021–24). Earlier, he was a member of the South Sulawesi House of Representatives (2014–15), elected on a Golkar ticket. He comes from a political dynasty: his father, Ichsan Yasin Limpo, was district head of Gowa for two terms (2005–10 and 2010–15). Ichsan Yasin's older brother, Syahrul Yasin Limpo, preceded him as district head of Gowa, serving from 1994 to 2002. Syahrul Yasin later served as governor of South Sulawesi for two terms (2008–13 and 2013–18) and then as minister of agriculture (2019–23). Adnan's grandfather, Muhammad Yasin Limpo, who was born in Gowa, was a military officer who later founded the Golkar Party in South Sulawesi, which served as a launch pad for his family members to develop their political careers. Here we can see that the Limpo political dynasty started in Gowa with the grandfather, Muhammad Yasin Limpo, followed by the accession to power of his sons, Syahrul Yasin and Ichsan Yasin, and now Adnan following suit. The Limpo family is the most influential political dynasty in South Sulawesi.

In the 2015 local election, two members of the Limpo family competed in Gowa, namely, Adnan and his aunt, Tenri Olle Yasin Limpo. A total of five pairs of candidates competed in the election, in which Adnan and H. Abdul Rauf Mallaganni (the "Adnan–Kio" ticket) ran as independent candidates, while his aunt and Hairil Muin ran on the PPP and NasDem tickets, respectively. Eventually, Adnan and his running mate won the election with 41.65 per cent of the total vote and served for one term (2016–21), while his aunt and Hairil Muin got only 26.06 per cent of the vote.

Adnan's victory over his aunt, who comes from the same political dynasty, has been explained by Dewi (2018), who explored the gender and femininity aspects. The strategy that Adnan and his running mate adopted for winning the 2015 election offered a vision and mission for the improvement of free health services, continuing free education services, and

**TABLE 2.3**
**List of Young Millennials Elected as Heads of Region in the 2020 Direct Local Elections**

| *No.* | *Region* | *Name* | *Year of Birth* | *Sex* | *Political Connection* |
|---|---|---|---|---|---|
| 1. | Banjar | Saidi Mansur | 1987 | M | No |
| 2. | Kota Bukittinggi | Erman Safar | 1986 | M | No |
| 3. | Dharmasraya | Sutan Riska | 1989 | M | No |
| 4. | Gowa | Adnan Purichta Ichsan | 1986 | M | Son of Ichsan Yasin Limpo, district head, Gowa (2005–10; 2010–15) |
| 5. | Indragiri Hulu | Rezita Meylani Yopi | 1994 | F | Wife of Yopi Arianto, district head, Indragiri Hulu (2010–15; 2016–2021) |
| 6. | Kediri | Hanindhito Himawan | 1992 | M | Son of Pramono Anung, cabinet secretary (2015–current) |
| 7. | Kendal | Dico M. Ganinduto | 1990 | M | Son of Dito Ganinduto, member of parliament (2004–9; 2009–14) |
| 8. | Kuantan Singingi | Andri Putra | 1987 | M | Son of Sukarmis, district head, Kuantan Singingi (2006–11; 2011–16) |
| 9. | Labuhanbatu Utara | Hendri Yanto | 1988 | M | Son of Khairuddin Syah Sitorus, district head, Labuhanbatu Utara (2010–15; 2016–21) |
| 10. | Kota Medan | Muhammad Bobby Afif Nasution | 1991 | M | Son in-law of President Jokowi |
| 11. | Ogan Ilir | Panca Wijaya Akbar | 1991 | M | Son of Maswardi Yahya, deputy-governor of South Sumatera and younger brother of A.W. Noviandi, district head, Ogan Ilir (2016–17) |

| | | | | | |
|---|---|---|---|---|---|
| 12. | Pangkajene Kepulauan | Muhammad Yusran Lalogau | 1992 | M | Nephew of Syamsuddin A. Hamid, district head, Pangkajene Kepulauan (2010–15; 2016–21) |
| 13. | Purbalingga | Dyah Hayuning Pratiwi | 1987 | F | Daughter of Triyono Budi Sasongko, district head, Purbalingga (2000–5; 2006–10) |
| 14. | Samosir | Vandiko Tiotius Gultom | 1992 | M | No |
| 15. | Sidoarjo | Ahmad Muhdlor | 1991 | M | No |
| 16. | Sijunjung | Benny Dwifa Yusfir | 1986 | M | Son of Yuswir Arifin, district head, Sijunjung (2010–15; 2016–21) |
| 17. | Kota Surakarta | Gibran Rakabuming Raka | 1987 | M | Son of President Jokowi, who was mayor of Solo (2005–12) |
| 18. | Kota Tanjung Balai | M. Syahrial | 1988 | M | No |
| 19. | Trenggalek | Mochamad Nur Arifin | 1990 | M | No |
| 20. | Tuban | Aditya Halindra F. | 1992 | M | Son of Haeny Relawati Rini Widyastuti, district head, Tuban (2001–2006; 2006–2011) |

*Source:* Compiled from Perludem (2021), KPU, and other sources.

agricultural and road infrastructure development, with an annual allocation of 20 per cent from the regional revenue and expenditure budget (APBD); in fact, this vision and mission is a continuation of the policy pursued by his father, who was district head of Gowa for two terms earlier. Adnan's victory in the election was strongly influenced by the legacy of his father as the previous district head (Khaerah and Rusnaedy 2019).

Another interesting aspect behind Adnan's victory in the 2015 local election is the exploitation of his advantage as a young candidate. The networks of the Forum Komunikasi Putra Putri Purnawirawan dan Putra Putri TNI POLRI (Communication Forum for Indonesian Veterans' Children, or FKPPI) in South Sulawesi supported the Adnan-Kio ticket. FKPPI and its members helped to campaign for Adnan because he is part of the FKPPI's extended family, being the grandson of the late Colonel Muhammad Yasin Limpo, and his father, Ichsan Yasin Limpo, is the chairman of the advisory board of FKPPI in South Sulawesi (Rusyd, Ibrahim, and Amsir 2019, p. 38). FKPPI focused on wooing new voters by: (1) presenting Adnan as the ideal leader for Gowa by virtue of his being younger than the other candidates, (2) holding various youth activities such as a youth competition and installing billboards featuring Adnan in strategic places to increase his mindshare among voters (Rusyd, Ibrahim, and Amsir 2019, p. 38).

Adnan-Kio competed again in the 2020 direct local election. However, there were no competitors, and they drew 91.22 per cent of the votes, with the rest being empty ballots (*kotak kosong*).

## Muhammad Bobby Afif Nasution, Mayor of Medan

Muhammad Bobby Afif Nasution was born on 5 July 1991. His father, Erwin Nasution, is a high-level bureaucrat in an Indonesian plantation company. Bobby's family is an aristocratic family from Mandailing Natal Penyabungan Timur. A young entrepreneur, Bobby serves as deputy chairman of the central governing body for the Association of Young Indonesian Entrepreneurs (HIPMI, 2019–22). He was 30 years old when he won the 2020 direct local election in Medan. There were two pairs of candidates competing in that election. Bobby and his running mate, Aulia Rachman (jointly fielded by PDI-P, Gerindra, Golkar, NasDem, Hanura party, PAN, PSI, and PPP) won the election with 393,327 votes or 53.45 per cent of the valid votes, taking fifteen subdistricts, while the competing team fielded by PKS received only 342,580 votes or 46.55 per cent (six subdistricts).

Bobby's victory reinforced the domination of political dynasties in Indonesia. Bobby married the daughter of President Jokowi in 2017. Interestingly, other than the political association of Bobby with PDI-P, the political party with which Jokowi is associated, Bobby did not amplify his affiliation with his father-in-law during the campaign. This is because, during the 2014 and 2019 presidential elections, Jokowi polled poorly in Medan, compared with the other contenders. For example, in the 2014 presidential election, Jokowi and his running mate, Jusuf Kalla, were defeated in Medan, polling only 47.84 per cent, compared with the 52.16 per cent won by the Prabowo–Hatta ticket. Likewise, in the 2019 presidential election, Jokowi and his running mate, Ma'ruf Amin, obtained only 46.85 per cent of the vote in Medan, losing to the Prabowo–Sandi ticket, which won 53.15 per cent. For this reason, Bobby hardly used any photographs of Jokowi during his campaign and socialization (Kulsum 2022).

## Gibran Rakabuming Raka, Mayor of Surakarta

Gibran was born on 1 October 1987. He is the oldest son of President Jokowi. He is a young entrepreneur. Two teams competed in the 2020 direct local elections in Surakarta (popularly known as Solo): the team of Gibran Rakabuming Raka and Teguh Prakosa, and the team of Bagyo Wahyono and FX Supardjo ("Bajo"). Team Gibran–Teguh was nominated by PDI-P (the party that holds the majority of seats in Surakarta's upper house of parliament or DPRD), PAN, Golkar, Gerindra and PSI, while team Bajo competed as individuals. Gibran–Teguh won the election with a total of 225,451 or 86.5 per cent of the valid votes; the Bajo team obtained only 35,055 or 13.5 per cent of the valid votes (CNN Indonesia 2020).

Taruna Merah Putih (TMP) Surakarta, a wing of the PDI-P, focused on the millennial generation or novice voters in campaigning for the victory of team Gibran–Teguh in the 2020 election. "One of the things that we continue is *blusukan* [impromptu visits to the grassroots] activities", said the chairman of the Surakarta TMP, Her Suprabu, on 29 November 2020 (Antara 2020). TMP administrators in every sub-district and all urban villages (*kelurahan*) in Surakarta City continued to carry out this activity until 5 December 2020, the last day of the campaign.

## Rezita Meylani Yopi, District Head of Indragiri Hulu

Rezita Meylani Yopi was born in Indragiri Hulu, Riau, on 7 May 1994. She is the district head of Indragiri Hulu who set a record as the youngest female district head in Indonesia's history. When she ran for election as district head in 2020 she was just 26 years old. Her husband, Yopi Arianto, was the district head of Indragiri Hulu for two terms. He too set a record as Indonesia's youngest district head when he was first elected to office in 2010 at age 30. Rezita's running mate in the 2020 election was H. Junaidi Rachmat. Both were nominated by Golkar, NasDem and the Hanura party. The team beat the four other contesting teams with 50.356 per cent of the votes (Sani 2020).

In September 2021, two months after being sworn in as district head, Rezita inaugurated two new digital applications developed by the Village Community Empowerment Service, namely, BUNDA (to help small and medium businesses) and SIMPEL (to serve the Village Head Election Monitoring System process) that are meant to optimize services to the community (Asripilyadi 2021).

## Dyah Hayuning Pratiwi, District Head of Purbalingga

Dyah Hayuning Pratiwi was born in Jakarta on 11 April 1987. Before becoming district head of Purbalingga in Central Java, she was the district's deputy district head, serving alongside district head Tasdi. She and Tasdi had won in the 2015 direct local elections. However, in 2018, Tasdi was arrested by the Corruption Eradication Commission (KPK) for involvement in a bribery case, and Dyah replaced him as acting district head from 2018 to 2020.

Dyah is the daughter of Triyono Budi Sasongko and Raden Roro Ina Ratnawati. Triyono is a prominent figure, having been the district head of Purbalingga for two terms (2000–5 and 2005–10). Dyah's mother is the daughter of Raden Mas Subagio Wiryosaputro, who was the great-grandson of the seventh district head of Purbalingga (1883–99), Raden Tumenggung Dipokusumo V (*IDN Times*, 27 April 2022). Dyah finished high school in the prestigious SMAN 8 Jakarta in 2005. She then obtained a bachelor of economics from the University of Indonesia and another bachelor of economics from the University of Queensland, Australia.

Dyah's husband, Rizal Diansyah, is supportive of her work. He often accompanied her during various visits and activities when she was still serving as acting district head and played an important role in her campaign when she later ran in the 2020 election (*Banyumas Daily*, 16 February 2021).

Dyah competed along with her running mate, Sadono, in the 2020 election. The pair were nominated by PDI-P, Golkar, PAN and PKS. They won the election with 54.74 per cent of the votes and will serve the district of Purbalingga until 2026 (Fahmi 2020).

Dyah is the first woman to serve as district head of Purbalingga, and also at a young age. She has succeeded in decreasing Purbalingga's poverty rate, which continued to decline from 18.98 per cent in 2016 to 15.05 per cent in 2019, while the region's economic growth increased by 5.65 per cent in 2019 (*Banyumas Daily*, 16 February 2021). Like many from the millennial generation, she often shares her activities on social media, namely, Instagram. Dyah was keen to improve the human development index (HDI), notably by collaborating with universities and several other institutions such as the State Islamic University (UIN), which will build a university in Purbalingga, and the Muhammadiyah Islamic movement to build the Purbalingga Muhammadiyah Institute of Technology and Business (Nugroho 2021).

## MILLENNIALS WITHOUT POLITICAL CONNECTIONS

Interestingly, there are also young millennials who have been elected as heads of regions without being tied to a political dynasty. As can be seen from Table 2.3, there are seven young millennial heads of local government who are not part of political dynasties. They come from diverse family backgrounds, with parents who are business people, civil servants, heads of villages and clerics, to name a few professions. Mochamad Nur Arifin, district head of Trenggalek in East Java, for instance, comes from a family involved in business; Ahmad Muhdlor, district head of Sidoarjo, East Java, is the son of a cleric; and Sutan Riska, district head of Darmasraya, West Sumatra, is the son of a village head. In this section, we provide an interesting narrative of young millennial leaders who emerged in the 2020 direct local elections without being tied to a political dynasty, drawing on the example of Mochamad Nur Arifin, the district head of Trenggalek.

Mochamad Nur Arifin was born in Surabaya on 7 April 1990. He was the deputy head of the district of Trenggalek from 2015 to 2019. In an interview, Arifin said that in politics, there are *nasab* and *nasib*. *Nasab* refers to the bloodlines or familial ties of a candidate, while *nasib* or fate is related to things that can be changed. He said that since he did not come from a family of political elites or religious leaders, he had to change his *nasib* by working hard (*Kompas*, 29 March 2021). Arifin worked hard to build his business and social activism and became a successful businessman, a position that then eased his entry into politics. He runs a family business dealing with kitchen utensils, which he inherited from his father. His father migrated from his hometown in Trenggalek to Surabaya. In Surabaya, his father became a rickshaw driver and his mother was a household assistant (Ardianto 2018). Their lives improved after his father opened his kitchen utensils business (*Kompas*, 29 March 2021). Arifin is the oldest of three siblings. His father's death prompted Arifin, then 17 years old, to help his mother run the family business. The young Arifin was also a vocalist of the "Marsmellow", band, which had released many singles.

When Arifin returned later to Trenggalek to open a factory, he realized that his business could not provide employment for the many who needed work. As part of his company's corporate social responsibility programme, Arifin developed organic farming in his hometown, which then became his outlet for political networking. In 2015 he met Emil Dardak and agreed to join him for the 2015 direct local election in Trenggalek. The two men were supported by several parties, namely PDI-P, Gerindra, Golkar, Demokrat, PAN, Hanura and PPP. Winning the election by more than 76 per cent of the votes, Arifin became the youngest deputy district head in Indonesia. He was 25 years old then.

Being young and successful and possessing sufficient capital are important individual assets for contesting elections. Arifin did not join the youth wings of political parties or the youth wings of mass organizations before joining politics. However, once he became district head of Trenggalek in 2019, replacing Emil Dardak, who was elected deputy governor of East Java, he was inducted into PDI-P and was elected head of the party's local branch the same year. Arifin then stood for election as district head in the 2020 direct local election, with Syah Muhammad Natanegara as his running mate. The pair won 68.16 per cent of the votes (Detik.com 2021). As the elected district head, Arifin, together with Syah, has been focused on creating employment opportunities, such as helping to create 5,000 new women entrepreneurs.

## NEW STRATEGIES AND PROGRAMMES?

Several points should be noted about millennials assuming political office as heads of local government.

First, some candidates use the strategy of highlighting their dynastic connections to increase their electability, while others refrain from being publicly associated with a political dynasty as such a connection may disadvantage them. For example, Adnan Purichta Ichsan in Gowa boldly sought to ride on the success of his father, Ichsan Yasin Limpo, as the former district head of Gowa. Muhammad Bobby Afif Nasution in the city of Medan, on the other hand, refrained from amplifying his affiliation with his father-in-law, Jokowi, during his campaign. This was because in Medan Jokowi invariably lost votes to the other presidential contenders during the 2014 and 2019 presidential elections. In Solo, the public has known Gibran Rakabuming Raka as the son of Jokowi, and so Gibran's political and familial ties cannot be evaded.

Second, the strategy of most candidates is to utilize the narrative of being young leaders while also using youth groups in their political campaigns. For example, Adnan used and gained support from the South Sulawesi networks of the aforementioned FKPPI to support his candidacy. Similarly, Gibran in Surakarta was supported by TMP Surakarta, the PDI-P wing focused on the millennial generation or novice voters.

Third, nothing stands out so prominently in the narratives of these leaders as that of being millennial leaders. Similar to their predecessors, the millennial leaders on average pledge and implement populist programmes such as free schools and health, infrastructure development, compensation for the poor and support for Islamic religious leaders. The programmes that seem to set them apart from their predecessors are innovations in e-government services, for example, the creation of online application services. This is the case with Bobby in Medan, who made a breakthrough in the infrastructure sector that involves creating an electronic cataloguing system (e-catalogue) to accelerate infrastructure improvements and improve the quality and accuracy of workmanship. Similarly, Gibran has developed the Quick Response Surakarta Smart City programme to implement e-government services (see Surakarta.go.id 2021). Such e-governance services are not unique today because every local government in Indonesia aspires to provide them.

Fourth, what is interesting is that two female millennial leaders have launched more critical innovations. For example, Rezita in Indragiri Hulu introduced the BUNDA and SIMPEL applications. BUNDA helps small and medium enterprises (SMEs) with IT technology, whereas the SIMPEL application is used to monitor the Village Head Election System. Dyah in Purbalingga has focused on improving educational competence by building universities in the district. This effort perhaps is related to her higher education and foreign education background.

## CONCLUSION

By examining the backgrounds of millennial political leaders, this chapter has highlighted the two paths of millennials' involvement in Indonesian politics, namely the political dynasty route and the non-political dynasty route. The first part of the chapter highlights the fact that many of the millennials in politics are part of political dynasties. Political dynasties use their millennial scions to perpetuate their political domination. Young millennial leaders from dynastic backgrounds are the most common in Indonesian politics. They have political networks and financial resources, which enable them to compete in local elections. They can easily use the political networks of their family members, such as their husbands or fathers who had previously served as heads of local government. Coming from a family of political elites facilitated their access to the critical financial resources for winning elections. Moreover, young millennial leaders with political dynasty backgrounds can easily leapfrog the leadership ladder in political parties. They do not need to join student movements, the youth wings of political parties or the youth wings of mass organizations. With the power of their families behind them, they can be directly chosen as candidates for election. Such a trend is dangerous as it may contribute to the development of a political oligarchy.

On the other hand, some millennial leaders have taken the non-political dynasty route. They come from non-elite families but have interesting paths in entering politics, which gives a glimmer of hope that they can disrupt political elites and the nature of democracy in Indonesia. They are businessmen, sons of clerics, or from the families of traditional leaders. To rise in local politics, they use the youth wings of political parties or mass organizations and also showcase their business success, particularly as sociopreneurs. Being young and inspirational is a way of capturing voter attention and rising in politics.

For millennials to enter the political arena and disrupt the status quo is not an easy task. The recruitment process in Indonesian politics presents a major challenge in this regard. While there is hope for change, the centralized system of political parties, in which a handful of elites control the central boards of political parties, remains a problem. Approval from this elite group is needed to become candidates for legislative or district head elections. Not all millennials have access to such elite circles unless they come from political dynasties or have had long service records in political parties. This state of affairs creates difficulty for new and young millennials to enter the political arena and have meaningful impacts.

In sum, there is a wave of young millennials entering Indonesian politics at the local and national levels. Unfortunately, as this chapter has highlighted, those who come from political dynasties are the best placed to rise in politics. Conversely, those who do not have dynastic backgrounds need to have a record of extraordinary achievement (such as being successful entrepreneurs or inspirational activists) in order to be noticed and to successfully compete in elections. The authors believe that millennials can only make meaningful contributions to Indonesian politics and democracy if the country can avoid being hijacked by political elites and dynasties.

## References

Antara. 2020. "Begini Cara Kampanye Pendukung Gibran Jelang Masa Tenang Pilkada Solo". *Tempo.co,* 29 November 2020. https://pilkada.tempo.co/read/1409910/begini-cara-kampanye-pendukung-gibran-jelang-masa-tenang-pilkada-solo

Ardianto, Robi. 2018. "Kisah Cak Ipin, Anak Tukang Becak Yang Jadi Bupati Termuda". Alinea International (Indonesia), 27 October 2018. https://www.alinea.id/politik/-b1U759eNQ

Aspinall, Edward, and Muhammad Uhaib As'ad. 2016. "Understanding Family Politics: Successes and Failures of Political Dynasties in Regional Indonesia". *South East Asia Research* 24, no. 3: 420–35. https://doi.org/10.1177/0967828X16659571

———, and Ward Berenschot. 2019. *Democracy for Sale: Elections, Clientelism, and the State in Indonesia*. Ithaca: Cornell University Press. http://www.jstor.org/stable/10.7591/j.ctvdtphhq

Asripilyadi. 2021. "Bupati Rezita Meylani Luncurkan Dua Aplikasi Baru". *Riau.antaranews.com*, 21 September 2021. https://riau.antaranews.com/berita/237801/bupati-rezita-meylani-luncurkan-dua-aplikasi-baru

Brading, Ryan. 2017. "Taiwan's Millennial Generation: Interests in Polity and Party Politics". *Journal of Current Chinese Affairs* 46, no. 1: 131–66. https://doi.org/10.1177/186810261704600106

*Banyumas Daily*. 2021. "Dyah Hayuning Pratiwi, Bupati Perempuan Pertama Purbalingga". 16 February 2021. https://banyumasdaily.com/2021/02/26/dyah-hayuning-pratiwi-bupati-perempuan-pertama-purbalingga/ (accessed 11 July 2022).

Budiman, Manneke, Narendra Yuka, P. Mangoenkoesoemo, Ayu Indah Wardani, and Nila Ayu Utami. 2012. "New Enemy of the State: Youth in Post-New Order Indonesia". In *Youth Future Agents of Change or Guardians of Establishment?* edited by Wilhelm Hofmeister. Singapore: Konrad-Adenauer Stiftung.

Buehler, Michael. 2012. "Angels and Demons". *Inside Indonesia*, 22 April 2012. http://www.insideindonesia.org/angels-and-demons-2

———. 2013. "Married with Children". *Inside Indonesia*, 20 July 2013. https://www.insideindonesia.org/married-with-children

BPMI Setpres (Bureau of Press, Media and Information, Presidential Secretariat, Indonesia). 2019. "Presiden Jokowi Kenalkan 7 Milenial Sebagai Staf Khusus Baru". 21 November 2019. https://www.presidenri.go.id/siaran-pers/presiden-jokowi-kenalkan-7-milenial-sebagai-staf-khusus-baru

CNN Indonesia. 2020. "Hasil Rekapitulasi KPU, Gibran Jadi Wali Kota Solo Berikutnya".16 December 2020. https://www.cnnindonesia.com/nasional/20201216185450-32-583103/hasil-rekapitulasi-kpu-gibran-jadi-wali-kota-solo-berikutnya

*Detik.com*. 2021. "KPU Tetapkan M Nur Arifin Sebagai Bupati Trenggalek Terpilih". *Detik News*, 22 January 2021. https://news.detik.com/berita-jawa-timur/d-5344984/kpu-tetapkan-m-nur-arifin-sebagai-bupati-trenggalek-terpilih

Dewi, Kurniawati Hastuti, 2015. *Indonesian Women and Local Politics: Islam, Gender and Networks in Post-Suharto Indonesia*. Singapore: NUS Press and Kyoto University Press. https://doi.org/10.2307/j.ctv1nth4c

———. 2018. "Gender Risk and Femininity: Personal Political Branding of Female Politicians in the Strong Political Dynasty Feature of South Sulawesi". *Jurnal Studi Pemerintahan* 9, no. 4: 533–58. https://doi.org/10.18196/jgp.9489

———, ed. 2022. *Gender and Politics in Post-Reformasi Indonesia: Women Leaders within Local Oligarchy Networks*. Singapore: Springer. https://doi.org/10.1007/978-981-19-1734-9

———, and Sandy Nur Ikfal Raharjo. 2020. *Pola Kandidasi dan Kebijakan Responsif Gender Perempuan Kepala Daerah di Indonesia*. Jakarta: Yayasan Pustaka Obor Indonesia bekerja sama dengan Pusat Penelitian Politik (P2P), Lembaga Ilmu Pengetahuan Indonesia. https://politik-brin-go-id.translate.goog/buku/pola-kandidasi-kebijakan-responsif-gender-perempuan-kepala-daerah-di-indonesia/?_x_tr_sl=id&_x_tr_tl=en&_x_tr_hl=en&_x_tr_pto=sc

Dimock, Michael. 2019. "Defining Generations: Where Millennials End and Generation Z Begins". Pew Research Center, 17 January 2019. https://www.pewresearch.org/fact-tank/2019/01/17/where-millennials-end-and-generation-z-begins

Economic Development Board (EDB), Singapore. 2021. "Decoding the Asian Millennial", 23 June 2021. https://www.edb.gov.sg/en/business-insights/insights/decoding-the-asian-millennial.html

Fahmi, M. Iqbal. 2020. "Hasil Akhir Rekapitulasi KPU Purbalingga, Tiwi-Dono 54,74 Persen, Oji-Jeni 45,26 Persen". *Kompas,* 15 December 2020. https://regional.kompas.com/read/2020/12/15/19384621/hasil-akhir-rekapitulasi-kpu-purbalingga-tiwi-dono-5474-persen-oji-jeni-4526?page=all

Glover, Elesia. 2018. *"The Role of Social Media in Millennial Voting and Voter Registration"*. PhD dissertation. *Walden Dissertations and Doctoral Studies* 5339.

Ida, Rachmah, Muhammad Saud, and Musta'in Mashud. 2020. "An Empirical Analysis of Social Media Usage, Political Learning, and Participation among Youth: A Comparative Study of Indonesia and Pakistan". *Quality and Quantity* 54, no. 4: 1285–97. https://doi.org/10.1007/s11135-020-00985-9

*IDN Times*. 2019. "Serba-Serbi PSI, Partai Para Millennials Di Pemilu 2019". 5 April 2019. https://www.idntimes.com/news/indonesia/denisa-tristianty/serba-serbi-psi-partai-para-millennial-di-pemilu?page=all

———. 2022. "Profil Dyah Hayuning Pratiwi Bupati Purbalingga". 27 April 2022. https://jateng.idntimes.com/news/jateng/bandot-arywono/profil-dyah-hayuning-pratiwi-bupati-purbalingga

Jayani, Dwi Hadya. 2021. "Proporsi Populasi Generasi Z Dan Milenial Terbesar Di Indonesia". Databoks. 24 May 2021. https://databoks.katadata.co.id/datapublish/2021/05/24/proporsi-populasi-generasi-z-dan-milenial-terbesar-di-indonesia

Khaerah, Nur, and Zaldi Rusnaedy. 2019. "Push, Pass, Pull Political Marketing Adnan Purichta Ichsan-Abdul Rauf Mallagani Pada Pemilihan Kepala Daerah di Kabupaten Gowa 2015". *Jurnal of Government* 4, no. 2: 125: 116–31.

*Kompas*. 2019a. "Menilik Latar Belakang Pendidikan 7 Staf Khusus Milenial Jokowi". 11 November 2019. https://www.kompas.com/tren/read/2019/11/22/133115365/menilik-latar-belakang-pendidikan-7-staf-khusus-milenial-jokowi?page=all

———. 2019b. "Staf Khusus Milenial Jokowi, antara Kebutuhan atau Ornamen Politik?". 22 November 2019. https://www.kompas.com/tren/

read/2019/11/22/180500065/staf-khusus-milenial-jokowi-antara-kebutuhan-atau-ornamen-politik-?page=all#page2

———. 2021a. "KPU: Partisipasi Pemilih Dalam Pilkada 2020 Paling Tinggi Sejak 2014". 2 February 2021. https://nasional.kompas.com/read/2021/02/02/14195231/kpu-partisipasi-pemilih-dalam-pilkada-2020-paling-tinggi-sejak-2014?page=2

———. 2021b. "BEGINU S2 Eps4: Mochamad Nur Arifin, 30 Tahun, Dua Kali Bupati Trenggalek Yang Hilang Di London". 29 March 2021. https://www.youtube.com/watch?v=vDrr4nmWbpI

Kulsum, Kendar Umi. 2022. "Tokoh: Walikota Medan Bobby Nasution". *Kompaspedia,* 22 April 2022.

*Kumparan.com*. 2019. "Mengenal Anggota DPR Milenial". *Kumparan NEWS,* 12 October 2019. https://kumparan.com/kumparannews/mengenal-anggota-dpr-milenial-1s2T8xcr6zr

LaCombe, Scott J., and Courtney Juelich. 2019. "Salient Ballot Measures and the Millennial Vote". *Politics and Governance* 7, no. 2: 198–212. https://doi.org/10.17645/pag.v7i2.1885

Latif, Enjang Abdul, Idrus Afandi, and Cecep Darmawan. 2020. "The Role of Social Media as a Means of Political Literacy of Millennials in the 2019 Presidential Elections Process (A Case Study in Garut Regency)". *Journal of International Conference Proceedings* 3, no. 1: 81–95. https://doi.org/10.32535/jicp.v2i4.783

Lembaga Survei Indonesia (LSI). 2022. "Survei Nasional Persepsi Publik terhadap Penegakan Hukum, Tugas Lembaga-Lembaga Hukum, dan Isu-isu Ekonomi". 24 July 2022. https://www.lsi.or.id/post/rilis-survei-lsi-24-juli-2022

Novak, Alison. 2016. *Media, Millennials, and Politics: The Coming of Age of the Next Political Generation*. Pennsylvania: Lexington Books.

Nowak, Nurman. 2021. *Youth, Politics and Social Engagement in Contemporary Indonesia*. Jakarta: Friedrich-Ebert Stiftung. https://library.fes.de/pdf-files/bueros/indonesien/18249.pdf

Nugroho. 2021. "Tanpa 100 Hari Kerja, Ini 7 Program Bupati-Wabup Purbalingga". *Gatra.com,* 4 March 2021. https://www.gatra.com/news-505327-politik-tanpa-100-hari-kerja-ini-7-program-bupati-wabup-purbalingga.html

Perludem. 2021. "Catatan Awal Tahun Perludem: Refleksi 2020, Teropong 2021 Pelaksanaan Demokrasi di Tengah Pandemi dan Arah Demokrasi ke Depan". 10 January 2021. http://perludem.org/2021/01/10/catatan-awal-tahun-perludem-refleksi-2020-teropong-2021-pelaksanaan-demokrasi-di-tengah-pandemi-dan-arah-demokrasi-ke-depan

Prasetyanti, Retnayu, and Sisman Prasetyo. 2017. "Generasi Millennial Dan Inovasi Jejaring Demokrasi Teman Ahok". *Jurnal Polinter* 3, no. 1. http://journal.uta45jakarta.ac.id/index.php/polhi/article/view/756/516

Purdey, Jemma. 2016. "Political Families in Southeast Asia". *South East Asia Research* 24, no. 3: 319–27. https://doi.org/10.1177/0967828X16659027

Rouse, Stella, and Ashley Ross. 2018. *The Politics of Millennials: Political Beliefs and Policy Preferences of America's Most Diverse Generation*. Michigan: University of Michigan. https://doi.org/10.3998/mpub.9526877

Rusyd, A.M.I., Ibrahim, and Achmad A. Amsir. 2019. "Peran Organisasi FKPPI Dalam Keterpilihan Adnan Purictha Yasin Limpo Pada Pilkada Serentak 2015 di Kabupaten Gowa". *VOX POPULI* 2, no. 1 (June 2019): 38.

Sani, Abdullah. 2020. "Raih 50.356 Suara, Istri Bupati Inhu Kalahkan Jenderal Polisi & Jagoan UAS di Pilkada". *Merdeka*, 17 December 2020. https://www.merdeka.com/politik/raih-50356-suara-istri-bupati-inhu-kalahkan-jenderal-polisi-amp-jagoan-uas-di-pilkada.html

Sawyers, Delaina L. 2020. "Gender and Millennial Support for Women Political Leaders". PhD dissertation, *Walden Dissertations and Doctoral Studies* 8138. https://scholarworks.waldenu.edu/dissertations/8138

Shames, Shauna. 2017. *Out of the Running: Why Millennials Reject Political Careers and Why It Matters*. New York: NYU Press.

*Surakarta.go.id*. 2021. "Kembangkan Quick Response Solo Smart City, Gibran Ingin Integrasi Big Data Segera Terwujud". 30 March 2021. https://surakarta.go.id/?p=19056

Thompson, Mark R. 2002. "Female Leadership of Democratic Transitions in Asia". *Pacific Affairs* 75 (Winter): 535–55. https://doi.org/10.2307/4127345

———. 2012. "Asia's Hybrid Dynasties". *Asian Affairs* 43, no. 2: 204–20. https://doi.org/10.1080/03068374.2012.682366

Twenge, Jean M. 2013. "The Evidence for Generation Me and Against Generation We". *Emerging Adulthood* 1, no. 1: 11–16. https://doi.org/10.1177/2167696812466548

Udupa, Sahana, Shriram Venkatraman, and Aasim Khan. 2020. "'Millennial India': Global Digital Politics in Context". *Television and New Media* 21, no. 4: 343–59. https://doi.org/10.1177/1527476419870516

World Economic Forum. 2020. "Future of Consumption in Fast-Growth Consumer Markets: ASEAN". Insight Report, June 2020. https://www3.weforum.org/docs/WEF_Future_of_Consumption_in_Fast_Growth_Consumer_Markets_ASEAN_2020.pdf

Zachara, Małgorzata. 2020. "The Millennial Generation in the Context of Political Power: A Leadership Gap?". *Leadership* 16, no. 2: 141–62. https://doi.org/10.1177/1742715019885704

# 3

# Progressive Yet Powerless
## The State of Indonesia's Progressive Youth Organizations in the Post-Authoritarian Era

Muhammad Fajar, An Nisa Astuti and
Carolus Bregas Pranoto

**ABSTRACT**

*The contemporary youth-led movements and protests in the Global North and South have rekindled the popular image of youths as agents of change. Indonesia is no exception, as Indonesian millennials have taken the initiative to push progressive agendas, especially after the fall of the authoritarian regime in 1998. This development has been tracked meticulously by various scholars whose works have raised hopes that the involvement of Indonesian millennials in politics will have positive impacts. Contrary to their views, however, we argue that Indonesian millennials need a stronger organizational foundation to play the role of driver of progressive agendas. Based on an online survey involving 206 progressive youth organizations in Indonesia and 82 semi-structured interviews, we found that although some of these organizations have managed to establish basic organizational mechanisms (statutes, annual plans, evaluation mechanisms), they are still not well connected to potential social bases, especially in university campuses and in provinces other than those where they are based. The absence of a broad social base potentially undermines their social justice agendas since an agenda without strong social support comes across to political elites and policymakers as mere empty bluster. We contend that our study contributes to conversations on the role of Indonesian youth in politics and the Indonesian youth social movement in the post-authoritarian era.*

## INDONESIAN YOUTHS AS AGENTS OF CHANGE

History often portrays youths as agents of change. Such an image stems from their involvement in critical moments such as large-scale protests, regime changes or revolutions. As youths have been at the centre stage of these moments throughout historical periods, every generation tends to produce its own narratives of how heroic youths spark social change.

The millennial generation is not an exception. Born between the early 1980s and late 1990s, the millennial generation witnessed pivotal social disruptions in which they carried on the struggle for gender equality, civil liberty, environmental justice and racial justice, reproducing the popular narrative of youths as agents of change. As they grow into adolescence and consume information through multiple social media platforms, they realize that when their freedom and basic rights are undermined, they must take up the baton for transforming their society. Combined with wanting to redress society's economic grievances, millennials seek transformations of the existing political and social order that they find repressive and impeding their hopes for a better future. Thus, in the 2010s, the period in which most became adolescents, millennials participated in social disruptions such as the Arab Spring (2011), the March for Our Lives in the United States (2018), the Hong Kong student protests (2019–20), the Thai student demonstrations (2020–21) and the Myanmar student protests (2021–22). Through these moments, millennials expressed their grievances towards authorities whom they felt were shackling them and abusing the population. These events show that millennials' capacity for disrupting the existing order is considerable when the conditions for their emergence are ripe.

Popular perception also touts Indonesian millennials for their role as agents of change. Historically, Indonesia has been familiar with the valiant image of youths. Since the colonial era, the belief in the historical role of youths as change agents has endured (Lee 2011b). The term *angkatan* (generation) inscribes youth-driven historic moments in public memory, popularizing the *angkatan* of 1945, 1966, 1978 and 1998. Indonesian millennials are no anomaly. The 2019 civil society and student protests against controversial bills discussed by the Indonesian Parliament revived the image of Indonesian youths (millennials and Generation Z) as a potent political force. Although the protests only succeeded in postponing the passing of the controversial bills (Janti 2022), the sea of youths gathered on 24–30 September 2019 raised the hope that millennials and Generation Z could accomplish the unfinished struggle of the 1998 student activists. A researcher captures such a hope: "Now millennials are just rising but will be shining. Keep the light sparkling young people and steal the stage" (Fathurrahman 2020).

Indonesian studies scholars have piggybacked on the emergence of Indonesian youth activism following the fall of the authoritarian regime in 1998 and the opening of political space to produce a plethora of works (Afrianty 2012; Arifianto 2019; Azca 2011; Beta 2019; Chaplin 2018; Kailani 2012; Lee 2011a; Nilan 2017; Nisa 2013, 2018; Prihatini 2018; Rijal 2020; Sastramidjaja 2019; Suyanto, Sirry, and Sugihartati 2022). Fewer restrictions on voicing political aspirations and the freedom to establish mass organizations have encouraged young Indonesians to set up formal and informal organizations to promote both conservative and progressive agendas. The growth of studies on Indonesian youths in the post-authoritarian era aligns with the public hype surrounding Indonesian millennials.

Going against current hopes that Indonesian millennials have the capacity to drive social change and the academic hype about Indonesian youths and millennials, we adopt the organizational approach in the social movement literature to argue that Indonesian millennials have a shaky foundation for driving the progressive agenda. From an online survey we conducted with 206 progressive youth organizations and 82 semi-structured interviews with progressive youth activists from 82 organizations, we infer that although some of these organizations have managed to establish basic organizational mechanisms (i.e., statutes, annual plans, evaluation mechanisms), Indonesia's progressive millennials are still not well connected to potential social bases, a shortcoming that could undermine their struggle for social justice agenda. The absence of a broad and deep social base, especially in university campuses and other provinces, potentially delegitimizes their agendas since an agenda without strong social support only comes across as a mere bluster to political elites and policymakers. Due to such weaknesses, progressive youth activists still struggle to successfully propel the progressive agenda in the Indonesian political arena.

Our inquiry also improves the existing studies on Indonesian youth movements. We observe that these studies have focused too much on individuals as the unit of analysis (Azca 2011; Nilan 2017; Prihatini 2018); drawn too many examples from Muslim conservative youth organizations (Afrianty 2012; Arifianto 2019; Azca 2011; Beta 2019; Chaplin 2018; Kailani 2012; Nisa 2013, 2018; Rijal 2020); and focused mainly on student movements in universities (Afrianty 2012; Arifianto 2019; Chaplin 2018; Lee 2011b; Nilan 2017; Sastramidjaja 2019; Suyanto Sirry and Sugihartati 2022).

Our study improves the existing studies in several ways. *First,* we emphasize social movement organizations instead of individual activists to deduce the capacity of Indonesian millennials to promote the progressive agenda. By stressing their organizational infrastructure, namely, the sector they represent, their institutional character, networks and resources, we underscore the importance of organizations as the backbone of activism since individual activism without organizational bases is unsustainable (Edwards and Marullo 1995). *Second,* we focus on progressive youth organizations since examining only Muslim conservative youth organizations discounts the role of progressive youth organizations in contemporary Indonesian politics (Nilan and Wibowanto 2021; Ridwan and Wu 2018). *Third,* we widen our lens to examine progressive youth organizations outside university campuses. Against some scholars' focus on student movements, we argue that explaining the state of Indonesian youth politics through the lens of university student movements obscures the influential roles played by civil society organizations outside universities in supporting student movements (Aspinall 2005). Due to the lack of experience and resources to escalate their pressure, student movements often receive assistance from civil society organizations. The latter act as mobilizing structures (McAdam et al. 1996, p. 3), supplying networks, material support and knowledge to mobilize broader adherents. Thus, examining progressive youth organizations outside university campuses permits us to understand better the embeddedness of student movements in civil society that determines their power.

Our study yields the following contributions. *First,* it provides a bird's eye view of the landscape of Indonesian progressive youth organizations, some of them driven by millennials. Our study could be the first step in building a more comprehensive view of Indonesian youth activism. *Second,* our study foregrounds the organizational approach in the literature on Indonesian youth politics. This approach offers a fresh perspective to inspect the organizational bases of Indonesian progressive youth movements instead of stressing the individual level of analysis (Azca 2011; Nilan 2017; Prihatini 2018). Bringing the organizational analysis into the literature allows us to understand how activists muster the organizational power that, in turn, determines their capacity to propel their agendas forward. *Third,* our quantitative and qualitative approaches intervene in the existing studies that heavily utilize the qualitative approach (but see Parker et al. 2018; Prihatini 2018). We contend that incorporating both methods could generate richer data and a fresher view of Indonesia's progressive youth organizations.

## ORGANIZATIONAL APPROACH

The organizational approach in social movement studies, which this chapter adopts, is a merger between social movement and organizational literature. Initially, in the 1960s and 1970s, both bodies of literature took different tracks of inquiry. However, after those periods, some social movement scholars started incorporating insights from organizational literature to shed light on new theoretical problems in social movements. These scholars employ concepts drawn from organizational literature to understand, for instance, how social movements impact firms' behaviour (Dubuisson-Quellier 2013; Georgallis 2017; King 2008; Soule 2012), how social movement organizations adapt to changing environments (Clemens 1997; Minkoff 1999; Soule and King 2008); and how the organizational tactics of social movement diffuse (Edwards 2014; Soule 1997; Strang and Soule 1998; Wang and Soule 2012). These scholars concur that organizational studies have provided a new avenue to inspect the organizational aspects of social movements, regardless of their agenda.

In line with the organizational approach in social movement literature, *first,* we employ "social movement organizations" (SMOs) instead of "social movements" as our unit of analysis. SMOs are formal organizations that associate themselves with a social movement (or a countermovement) that seeks to implement a certain agenda (McCarthy and Zald 1977, p. 1218). Social movements, on the other hand, are collective actions that combine "(1) campaigns of collective claims on targeted authorities; (2) an array of claim-making performances including special-purpose associations, public meetings, media statements, and demonstrations; (3) public representations of the cause's worthiness, unity, numbers, and commitment" (Tilly 2004, p. 7). SMOs are the constituents of a social movement that set the movement's goal. By focusing on SMOs, we can understand the strengths and weaknesses of social movements through the way they prioritize issues, establish organizational structures, build networks and garner resources.

*Second*, taking Indonesian progressive youths as a partial representation of Indonesian millennials, we define progressive youths based on a combination of criteria: the definition by Dibley and Ford (2019) of "progressives" as people who struggle for a society that is "open and inclusive, treats all citizens with respect, and provides them with equal access to civil and political rights"; and Indonesia's 2009 Youth Law's definition of youth as an age category spanning 16 to 30 years of age (Ministry of Youth and Sport 2009). Combining these two definitions, we selected for study youth-led SMOs *or* SMOs that advocate equal access for Indonesian youths to civil, political, economic, cultural or social rights.

*Third*, we focus on the roles of the organizational sector, levels of institutionalization, networks, and resources to assess the change-making capacity of Indonesia's progressive youth movement organizations. These variables underpin SMOs' activities such as framing, mobilizing resources and weaving connections with potential allies. "Sector" refers to the configuration of social movements in a particular time and place (McCarthy and Zald 1977). "Institutionalization" refers to the formation of the solid structure of an organization (Staggenborg 2013). In this research, we focus on basic organizational features: statutes, annual plans and evaluation mechanisms. We argue that these three elements are necessary for solidifying the structure of an organization. "Network" is a set of nodes connected by ties based on specific criteria (Diani and McAdam 2003). We examine the network from an SMO's capacity to develop chapters across provinces and campuses. "Resource" refers to material resources such as money and people (Alinsky 1971). Money allows activists to organize protests, press conferences and seminars. Meanwhile, people are the core power of social movements to increase their bargaining power *vis-à-vis* their targets. We focus on how progressive youth organizations gather potential members.

We argue that these four variables are handy in unpacking the capacity of Indonesian progressive youth movements. Focusing on the sector improves our understanding of the key issues that progressive youths wrestle with. As a label, "progressive" is a big church with many denominations. Variegating them based on sectors in which they are active should inform us of the configuration of Indonesian progressives across different sectors. Understanding the institutionalization of Indonesian progressive youth organizations allows us to perceive the organizational structure that underpins the advocacy of the progressive agenda. Such knowledge is necessary to go beyond the discussion of Indonesian progressive groups that tends to centre more on their ideologies (Nilan 2015, 2021; Nilan and Wibowanto 2021). Examining the network uncovers the potential capacity of progressive youth organizations to mobilize people across provinces. Understanding the network exposes the capacity of progressive groups to coordinate and garner potential support for their agendas. Lastly, examining resources assists us in answering the fundamental question: how strong are Indonesian progressive youth organizations? Posing the question brings the discussion of organizational power to the centre of our analysis.

## METHOD

Our study rested on an online survey and semi-structured online interviews, which were conducted from July to November 2021. We sent our survey, which consisted of 33 questions, to 310 organizations. Of these, we achieved a response rate of 66.45 per cent, with 206 organizations completing the survey. We developed the list of organizations by adopting a snowball method until the study period ended. Following our definition of progressive youth SMOs, our cases were youth-led organizations *or* non-youth-led organizations that promote equal access for Indonesian youths to civil, political, economic, cultural or social rights. To verify whether an organization was youth-led we were guided by the age of its leader. To ascertain the progressive stance of an organization, we inspected its visions, missions and agenda, as available on its website or social media. Our database identified organizations across seven sectors: gender equality, political education, religion and minority groups, environment, urban, labour, and mental health. Ten of the organizations (5 per cent) that we targeted were established before the fall of Soeharto in 1998, and 196 (95 per cent) emerged in the post-authoritarian era. The average age of these organizations was 7.7 years. We composed the survey questions from the four key variables.

The semi-structured interviews were based on the list of organizations collected during the survey. From 206 organizations, we interviewed 82 progressive youth activists representing 80 progressive youth organizations that participated in the survey and 2 progressive youth activists representing 2 organizations outside the survey. The selected informants represent each of the 7 sectors identified from the survey. We utilized semi-structured interviews to give some nuance to our quantitative findings (Table 3.1). However, the interviews alone cannot represent the broader trends uncovered through the quantitative findings. We have used pseudonyms for all informants quoted in this chapter.

The social backgrounds of our 82 informants are varied. Their parents' jobs represent a mix of professions, from the state to the private sectors: 41.3 per cent of our informants' fathers work in the private sector, 28.8 per cent have a career in the public sector, 2.5 per cent are retirees, and 27.5 per cent did not disclose their fathers' occupations; on the mothers' side, 36.3 per cent of our informants' mothers work in the private sector, 20 per cent work in the public sector, 12.5 per cent are stay-at-home mothers, and 31.3 per cent of our informants did not inform us about their mothers' jobs. Our informants were enrolled in different majors during their college years. As many as 40 per cent of our informants have social science backgrounds, followed by arts and humanities (13.8 per cent), law (12.5 per cent), science, technology, engineering, and mathematics (10 per cent), education (6.3 per cent), and vocational (1.3 per cent).

## FINDINGS AND DISCUSSION

Our focus is to describe the state of Indonesian progressive youth organizations through four organizational variables: sector, institutionalization, network, and resource. We present our quantitative data in each variable and relate it to some of our qualitative findings.

### Sector

Our data shows that some sectors are more populated by Indonesian progressive youth organizations than others. Progressive youth

**TABLE 3.1**
**Organizations Covered in Survey and Interviews**

| *Organization* | *Sector* | *Year Established* | *Base* | *Membership* |
|---|---|---|---|---|
| The Centre for Human Rights Study — The Islamic University of Indonesia (Pusat Studi Hak Asasi Manusia — Universitas Islam Indonesia) | Political education | 2011 | Yogyakarta | Run by 25 staff members; no registered members |
| Voice of Youth | Religious and minority groups | 2019 | East Java | Run by 14 staff members; no registered members |
| The Women Workers (Perempuan Pekerja) | Labour | 2009 | Central Java | Run by 4 staff members; no registered members |
| Peace Leader Indonesia | Religious and minority groups | 2014 | East Java | Run by 5 staff members; 200 registered members |
| The Hysteria Collective (Kolektif Histeria) | Urban | 2004 | Central Java | Run by 4 staff members; 11 registered members |
| The Indonesian Youth Confucian Generation (Gemaku) | Religious and minority groups | 2000 | Jakarta | Run by 15 staff members; 1,000 registered members |
| The Congress Alliance of Indonesian Labour Unions (Kongres Aliansi Serikat Buruh Indonesia, KASBI) | Labour | 2009 | Jakarta | Run by 9 staff members; 1,000 registered members |
| The Progressive Student Union of the University of Indonesia (Serikat Mahasiswa Progresif Universitas Indonesia, Semar-UI) | Political education | 2013 | West Java | Run by 7 staff members; 68 registered members |
| The Cross Religion Youth Forum (Forum Pemuda Lintas Agama, Formula) | Religious and minority groups | 2019 | West Java | Run by 9 staff members; 20 registered members |

organizations are concentrated in two sectors: gender equality (35 per cent) and political education (23.8 per cent), comprising more than half of our cases (Figure 3.1). Gender equality was a prominent issue even before the fall of Soeharto's "New Order" regime (Blackburn 1999; Khanis 2013). The struggle of activists in the 1970s and 1980s to push the gender empowerment agenda has contributed to the formation of activist networks that underpin contemporary gender activism in Indonesia. These networks provide knowledge, resources and repertoires for progressive youth activists to advance their activism.

A similar argument is valid for the political education sector. The opposition against the New Order regime has left a legacy of political education repertoires that persists until today, particularly the use of study clubs as a means of organizing. After the New Order regime issued the Ministry of Education and Culture Regulation 156/1978 on the Normalization of Campus Life (NKK/BKK), which, among other things, decreed the dissolution of student governments on Indonesian campuses, student activism faded. Nonetheless, Indonesian students in the 1980s established study groups as a safe space for their activism. In the study groups, Indonesian students learnt radical political discourses such as Marxism and feminism, which boosted their activism and opposition to

**FIGURE 3.1**
**Breakdown of Organizations Surveyed by Sector**

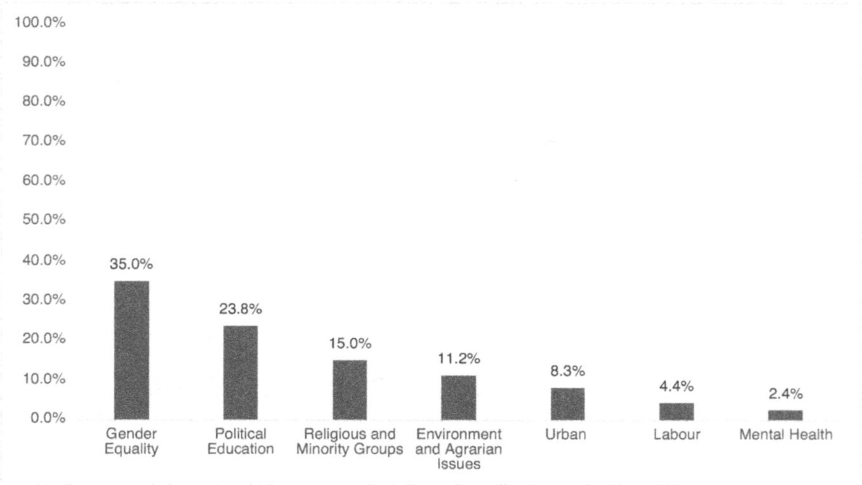

the authoritarian regime. The centrality of study groups for contemporary Indonesian progressive youth activism perseveres, with progressive youth activists utilizing study groups as a platform for politically educating their fellows. Avi of the Centre for Human Rights Study at the Islamic University of Indonesia affirms the centrality of the old study group networks that have facilitated his path towards activism:

> If someone asks me what my organizational affiliation is, I say I am with Rode 610. People usually just call it Rode. But, the legal organization is the Yogyakarta Study Forum Circle. So, this Rode is actually united in Jogja [Yogyakarta]. From the 1960s until now, Jogja is still the epicentre of various movements in Indonesia, and this Rode is one of them … the system is very egalitarian, I don't have to say "Sir", "Ma'am"; even the oldest are called by their names ... also their educational culture, where you try to understand things not only from one perspective ... Rode 610 consists of multiple perspectives and ideology. (Avi, 28 years old, male, online interview, 21 November 2021).

Avi's experience shows that Rode 610 functioned as a stepping stone for his activism early in his college days. His interest in the study group was driven by the organization's egalitarianism and the educational tradition that incorporates multiple perspectives from different ideologies. The emphasis on egalitarianism suggests that members do not prioritize age as a decisive factor in interactions. Thus, the organization provides a safe space for them to learn and gain knowledge from old and new members. Meanwhile, the diversity of perspectives arising from the different ideologies espoused by the members exposed him to the opportunity to gain social capital and the networks necessary for his organizing work and activism in the future.

The tendency to treat the organization as a stepping-stone and safe space applied not only to the gender and political education sectors but also to the less dominant sectors such as religion and minority groups (15 per cent), environment and agrarian (11.2 per cent), urban (8.3 per cent), labour (4.4 per cent), and mental health (2.4 per cent). For new members, organizations serve as a free space to discuss issues and express their identities. Organizations also allow members to share their grievances safely with each other and consolidate their views collectively. Banur's experience in joining Voice of Youth affirms the function of an organization as a free space to discuss issues and express identity:

> Voice of Youth has been operating for almost three years; it was founded in January 2019. I just joined in its second year, basically on the organization's first anniversary ... In my second year, I felt comfortable and had freedom of speech and a safe space to discuss many things, especially [about] identity and [sexual] orientation. It was comfortable to find a new family with a similar vision, path and colour ... What matters is that our friends of the gender minority can live peacefully, not stigmatized, away from stereotypes. That itself already amazes me very much. (Banur, 23 years old, male, online interview, 8 October 2021)

## Institutionalization

Our data also shows that 53.9 per cent of the total cases have no statutes (Figure 3.2). Formulating a statute can be a challenging task. It requires members of SMOs to negotiate and align their different visions about the future direction of their organization. Committing to a statute may force members of social movements to compromise their interests. Due to such challenges, developing a statute may require time and resources for an organization, especially for a new collective aiming to be a formal organization.

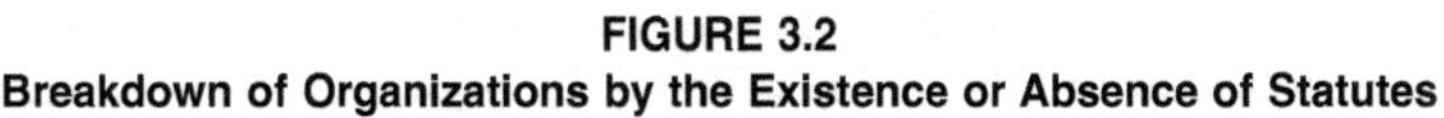

**FIGURE 3.2**
**Breakdown of Organizations by the Existence or Absence of Statutes**

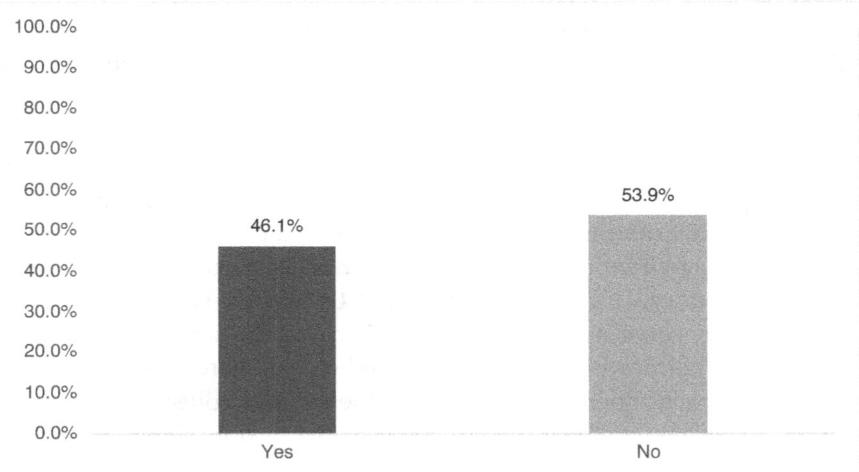

Assessing the presence of an annual programme of action, we found that 69.4 per cent of the organizations surveyed already have an annual programme (Figure 3.3). This shows that Indonesia's progressive youth organizations generally may not have a problem formulating an annual plan. Planning should not be a problem for progressive youth activists since their experience in student organizations has taught them how to plan activities annually. However, this does not imply that progressive youth activists are astute in long-term planning. Long-term planning usually involves planning activities and programmes for one to three years. Such planning differs from annual planning, which usually aims to fulfil short-term organizational objectives. These plans also often adapt to donor objectives instead of an organization's long-term objectives.

Utilizing evaluation capacity as an indicator, we discovered that 74.3 per cent of progressive youth organizations have a basic capacity to evaluate their activities (Figure 3.4). This capacity is important because SMOs must critically evaluate their daily activities' contribution to attaining

**FIGURE 3.3**
**Breakdown by the Existence or Absence of Annual Programmes**

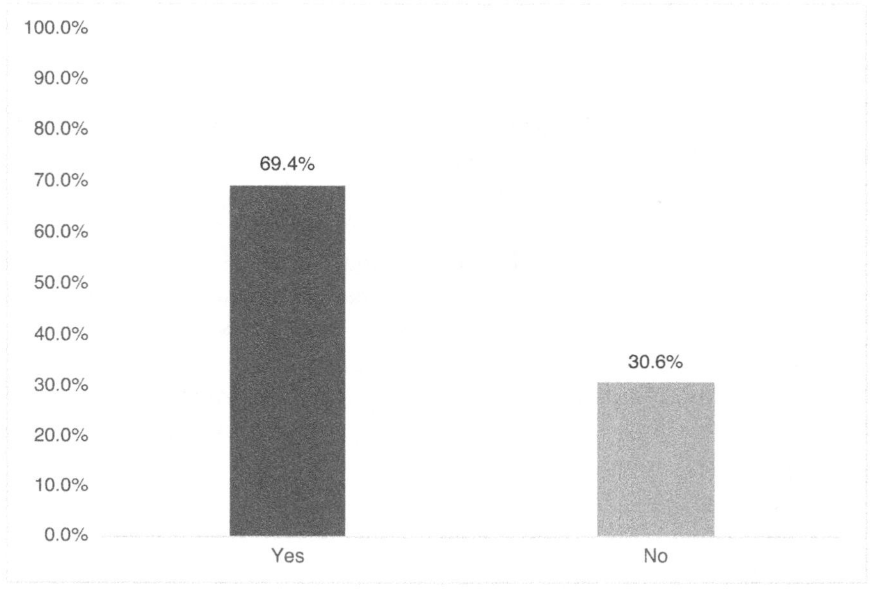

**FIGURE 3.4**
**Breakdown by the Existence or Absence of Evaluation Mechanisms**

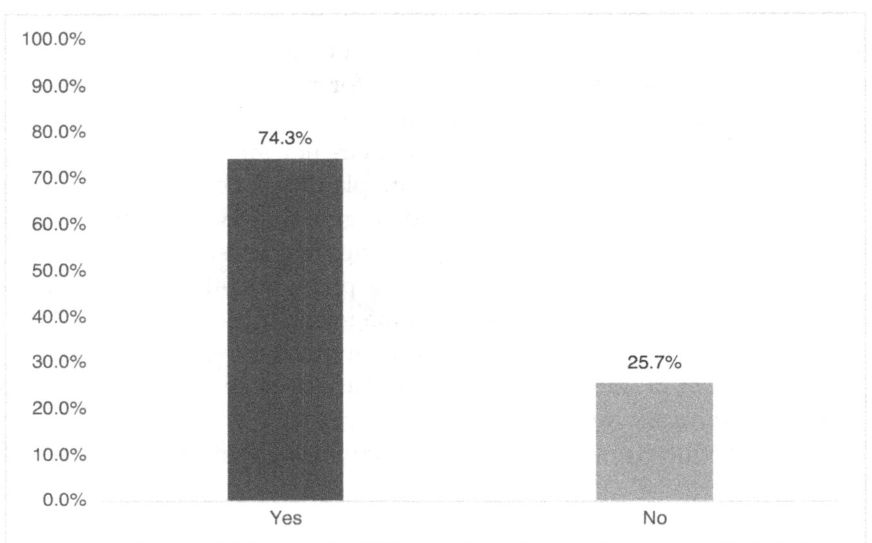


organizational goals. Without a mechanism for critical evaluation, SMOs are prone to orthodoxy (Zald and Ash 1966). Orthodoxy emerges when organizational ideologies and goals are taken for granted and become ossified. When ideologies and goals turn thus into dogmas, organizations would uncritically apply strategies and tactics to achieve their objectives. Having an evaluation mechanism in place would remedy such a tendency as failed strategies and blind organizational goals can be jettisoned.

Although more than half of our cases have basic organizational features (i.e., statutes, annual plans and evaluation mechanisms), they still lack other organizational characteristics of professional organizations. For instance, our further inquiry revealed that progressive youth activists have struggled to build a clear division of labour among organization members. A clear division of labour entails the allocation of members into positions based on their experience and expertise. Yesa of the Women Workers highlights such a problem in her organization:

> The weakness is that our organization's members are unclear; they just tag along, right? I want us to have a solid structure in the future; someone will be the general coordinator, the advocacy coordinator, and another

> member will be the public relations coordinator. That is how I want it. Currently, it is [still] a collective; we do not force them to work. Because this is a collective, we work together … It is just that I want it to be more structured so that we can divide the tasks. That is our weakness now; we do not have a clear structure yet. (Yesa, 28 years old, female, online interview, 14 October 2021)

Yesa's experience affirms that establishing a firm organizational structure is an uphill struggle. Most of the progressive youth activists maintain a "collective culture", which creates a dilemma. On the one hand, such a culture projects the romanticism of working together without a clear division of labour, prioritizing togetherness as the main goal. On the other hand, the collective culture risks the emergence of the free rider problem. This means that certain members would carry out fewer tasks and burden other members to accomplish important tasks. Such shirking of responsibility could create friction among members due to the uneven work allocation. This could set back the initial formative steps of establishing an organization.

Another problem highlighted by the progressive youth activists surveyed and interviewed is the organization's dependence on its leaders. The over-reliance on founders acts as a disincentive for activists to build organizational mechanisms since an organization would rely solely on the leader to develop the organization. Widyo of Peace Leader Indonesia highlights this argument:

> The first weakness of the community is that it depends on the leader ... The challenge lies in the leader, so once the leader leaves, that is the end of the organization. Regeneration is not good from this point of view. (Widyo, 30 years old, male, online interview, 2 October 2021).

Widyo's account suggests knowledge, resources and skills are often embedded in the leader instead of being institutionalized as organizational mechanisms and procedures. He warns that Indonesia's progressive youth organizations could fall into the trap of personalistic leadership. With personalistic leadership, an organization bets its survival on the hand of the leader since the leader dictates the direction of the organization. Such domination could impede institutionalization since an organization lives in a dynamic environment, and one person's view could not be sufficient to navigate the organization in a changing environment.

Our interviews also suggest that the durability of an organization does not guarantee its level of institutionalization. A progressive youth organization can survive for a long period, but may not yet be able to institutionalize firmly its workings so that there are clear organizational structures and procedures. Yesa of the Women Workers, for instance, laments her organization's inability to establish a more structured division of labour although it has been in existence since 2009. Existing for twelve years does not seem to pressure Yesa's organization to create a clear division of labour. Another example is the Hysteria Collective. Established in 2004, it advocates a more equal and sustainable ecosystem for art workers. Although it has been around for seventeen years, its members are still struggling to set up a stable organization. Azam of the Hysteria Collective narrates:

> What often impedes [our organization's work] is the turnover rate. Hysteria's membership is fluid; there is a core team and a volunteer team. Each year there are always personnel changes, and, thus, we have to adjust our vision, making our work less effective. Financially, our collective has not also been stable. Sometimes we struggle just to pay rent and electricity. (Azam, 34 years old, male, online interview, 6 October 2021).

Maintaining staff commitment under a condition of scarce resources also could compromise the continuity of an organization's vision (the issue of resources will be discussed further below). The lack of resources forces an organization to rely on staff who have to divide their time between different commitments. If the staff are not permanent, then it would be left to temporary staff to carry out the organization's progressive vision. However, temporary staff are not likely to have a sense of connection to an organization that cannot promise permanency and would lower their expectations. Thus, these staff would lack commitment to the organization's progressive vision and contribute less to its continuity. In such circumstances, asking a part-time staff member to formulate consistent and robust plans is unrealistic. This view is shared by Dawud of the Indonesian Youth Confucian Generation (Gemaku), a twenty-one-year-old organization promoting religious tolerance. Dawud opines thus:

> From a member's point of view, it will be hard for them to be fully active [in the organization]. Gemaku is struggling to formulate a [organizational] design and ensure the continuity of our vision in the future because the members have their own work [outside the organization]. That

> makes [our organization] not their top priority, and they see it more as an opportunity to kill their time. (Dawud, 39 years old, male, online interview, 10 October 2021)

## Networks

We found that 72.3 per cent of Indonesia's progressive youth organizations reside in Java (Figure 3.5). This trend is not surprising. Java has better infrastructures than other areas in Indonesia, thanks to decades of Java-centric economic development. The abundant endowment of resources and infrastructures provides fertile soil for organizations to grow since 48 per cent of public and private universities reside in Java, creating a steady stream of potential activists for youth organizations (Central Bureau of Statistics 2021). However, the abundance of resources in Java signals the inequality of resources between Java-based and non-Java-based progressive youth organizations. Non-Java-based organizations often face arduous challenges in establishing an organization.

Our data also shows that most of the organizations (77.7 per cent) do not have cross-provincial branches (Figure 3.6). This indicates their weak organizational capacity to coordinate activities across different geographical locations. The absence of cross-provincial networks could affect their capacity for pressuring the government. In crucial moments such as when massive protests are needed to challenge government policies, broad and deep cross-provincial networks could draw protest participants better than narrow and shallow networks. Mobilizations based on broad and deep cross-provincial networks could yield bigger protests that could increase their credibility and in turn their effectiveness in achieving their demands. Ulvana of the Congress of Alliance of Indonesian Labour Unions compares the capacity of his organization's network to draw support from Java and outside Java:

> Membership in each region is not evenly distributed, not balanced. So, most [members] are located in, for example, a new city, a big industrial city, [such as] Tangerang. In Jakarta, there are not too many. When we organize demonstrations in Jakarta, we mobilize from Tangerang, Bogor, Bekasi, Karawang and Purwakarta, from Subang and West Java ... We lack such a capacity in Sumatra, Kalimantan and Sulawesi. The network is small and spatially sparse ... That is our challenge to organize in the regions which are located far, far apart. (Ulvana, 42 years old, male, online interview, 24 October 2021)

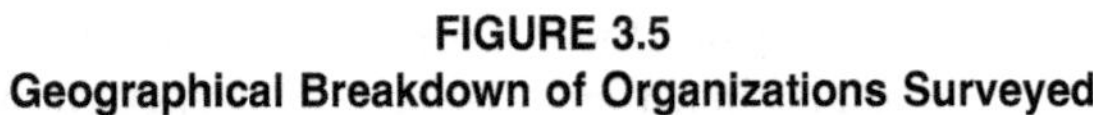

**FIGURE 3.5**
**Geographical Breakdown of Organizations Surveyed**

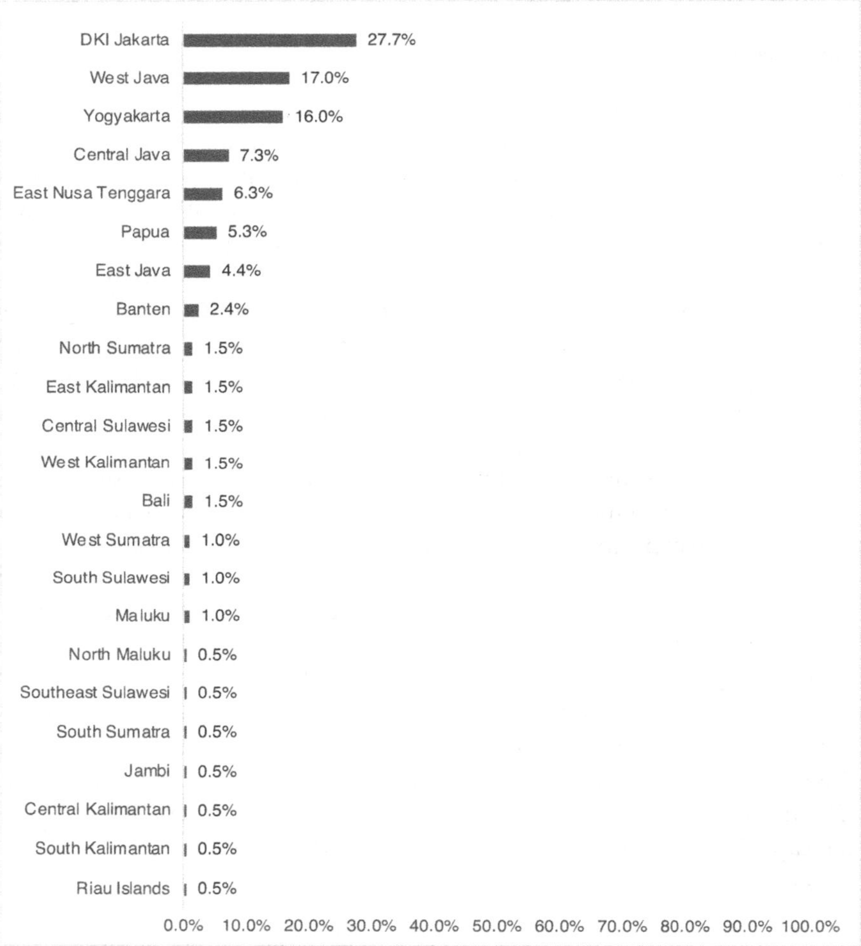

|  |  |
|---|---|
| DKI Jakarta | 27.7% |
| West Java | 17.0% |
| Yogyakarta | 16.0% |
| Central Java | 7.3% |
| East Nusa Tenggara | 6.3% |
| Papua | 5.3% |
| East Java | 4.4% |
| Banten | 2.4% |
| North Sumatra | 1.5% |
| East Kalimantan | 1.5% |
| Central Sulawesi | 1.5% |
| West Kalimantan | 1.5% |
| Bali | 1.5% |
| West Sumatra | 1.0% |
| South Sulawesi | 1.0% |
| Maluku | 1.0% |
| North Maluku | 0.5% |
| Southeast Sulawesi | 0.5% |
| South Sumatra | 0.5% |
| Jambi | 0.5% |
| Central Kalimantan | 0.5% |
| South Kalimantan | 0.5% |
| Riau Islands | 0.5% |

0.0% 10.0% 20.0% 30.0% 40.0% 50.0% 60.0% 70.0% 80.0% 90.0% 100.0%

Ulvana's experience shows the limited cross-provincial connectivity of an Indonesian progressive youth organization. Despite being an established organization with membership at the regional level, Ulvana's organization still faces difficulty in mobilizing people from their provincial bases to join protests in Jakarta. Such conditions will be more challenging for progressive youth organizations that are mostly centred in Java and do not have any

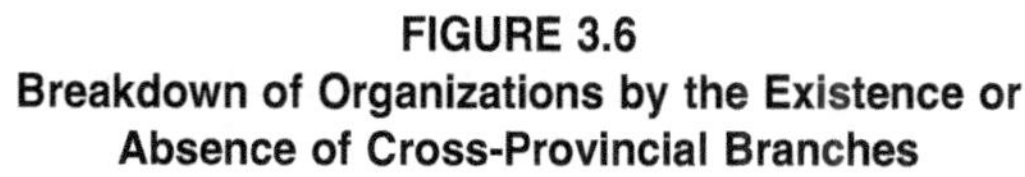

**FIGURE 3.6**
**Breakdown of Organizations by the Existence or Absence of Cross-Provincial Branches**

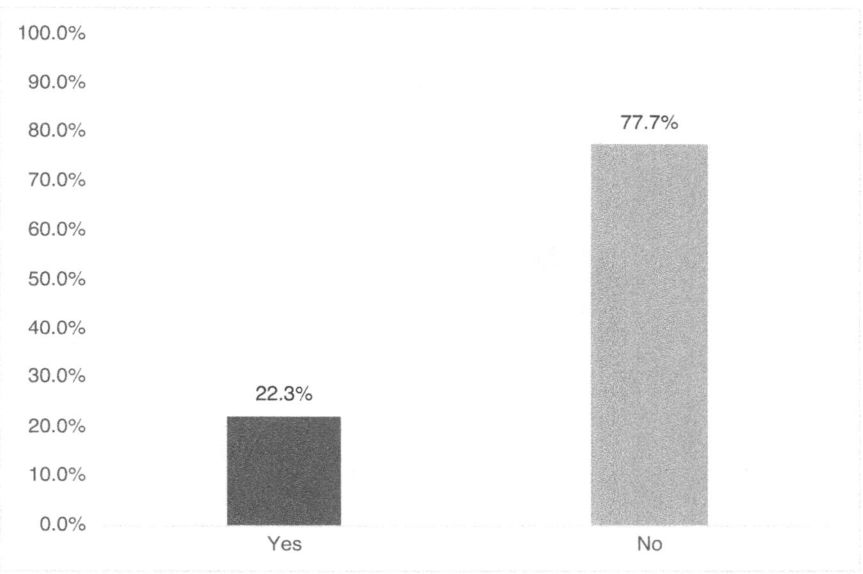


provincial network. The lack of a cross-provincial network and limited organizational capacity to mobilize people across geographical locations highlight the structural problem that affects not only newly founded organizations but also established ones.

## Resources

Regarding resources, our data shows several key trends. *First,* half of the progressive youth organizations have registered members (53.4 per cent) (Figure 3.7). The size of organizational membership varies from as few as two to a whopping 100,000. Registered members are important for organizations since numbers indicate social movement power (DeNardo 1985). A large membership allows a social movement organization to diversify its activities and networks by utilizing strong support from its members. Furthermore, numbers reflect power in the eyes of political elites. A widely supported social movement agenda signals credibility to political

**FIGURE 3.7**
**Breakdown by Number of Registered Members**

elites. If political elites hold such perceptions, they will take the agenda seriously and concede to the demands of the social movement organization (Andrews 2001, p. 76). No social movement agenda is passable without substantial support from political elites (Stearns and Almeida 2004).

We also found that 88.8 per cent of the progressive youth organizations we studied do not have networks on Indonesian campuses (Figure 3.8). Our data suggests a disconnect between Indonesian progressive organizations and student movements. Without networks on campuses, progressive organizations would not have the infrastructure to mobilize campus students. Such a weakness is unfortunate since campus students have much free time to participate in activism and therefore are potential resources to be mobilized (Altbach 1989). They usually reside near each other, allowing intense interactions for organizing purposes (Altbach 1970). Free time and close geographical proximity are assets for starting collective action.

**FIGURE 3.8**
**Breakdown by Existence or Absence of Campus Branches**

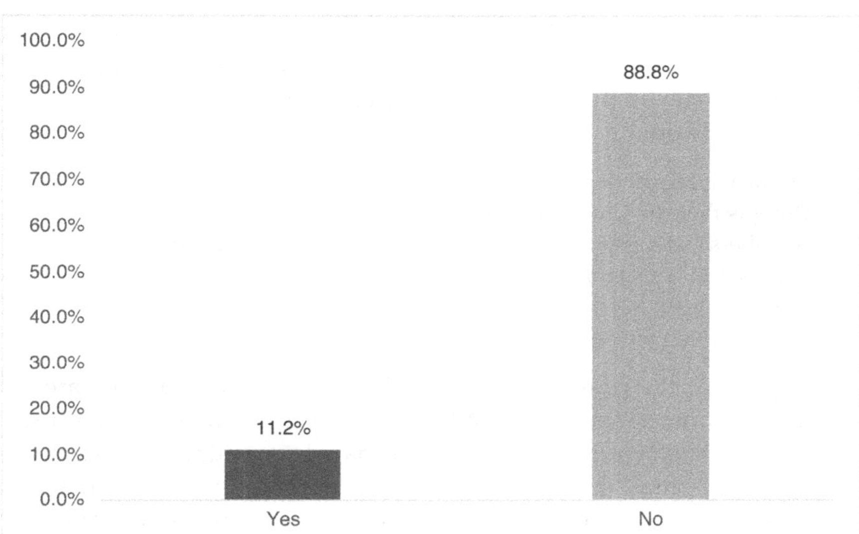


Furthermore, the lack of provincial and campus networks indicates that Indonesia's progressive youth activists have not prioritized the mobilization of people as the source of their power. We argue that such a stance is determined by their perception of power. In politics, power often stems from the possession of money or a large number of people (Alinsky 1971). Both types of resources are equally significant. With money, activists can invest in, for instance, educating new members through workshops. Moreover, a large membership base would increase the credibility of an organization's agenda in the eyes of political elites. Nonetheless, Indonesian progressive youth activists do not perceive power as deriving from money or people. They believe that power emanates from other sources, as exemplified by Tirtamaya of the Progressive Student Union of the University of Indonesia (Semar-UI):

> It is more about bonding, so we all share the same goals for the welfare of the people and the liberation of the oppressed people. Because we all share the same goals, we are both against a government without a clear vision, which oppresses the people, so we are all united because we

> share the same goal. I think it is a great source of strength for Semar-UI. (Tirtamaya, female, 22 years old, online interview, 4 October 2021)

Another informant, Sofie of the Cross Religion Youth Forum, also mentioned commitment and leadership as sources of power for her organization instead of money or people. As an activist in religion and minority issues, she elaborates thus:

> I think it is about commitment. Funding is always available. The important thing is that the Cross Religion Youth Forum does not have permanent members, so those who want to take an active part are welcome. Leadership is also important. Because we coordinate with the leader. But she also depends on us, whether we want to take action. (Sofie, 30 years old, female, online interview, 4 October 2021)

We argue that the resources mentioned by Tirtamaya and Sofie are not tangible resources such as people or money but intangible resources such as bonding between members and shared commitment. Tirtamaya's organization may have committed members but lacks financial resources, while the opposite is true for Sofie's organization. Although both organizations may continue to thrive, these informants have also highlighted how such conditions make the running of their respective organizations precarious. However, Tirtamaya has reflected on her recent engagement to strengthen the organization's financial resources. The recent waves of mass protests in 2021 served as a lesson for her to think about the means of developing her organization's financial capacity to support its members:

> When we [joined] the 2021 mass action, [our members] were caught. We then thought about how futile it is for us since the police have upgraded themselves while we continue to stay this way, being easily rounded up ... It is like we are repeating the same thing over and over again, so we thought like we were fools. So, in the end, if we desire social change, we have to first strengthen our base, by which we have to first strengthen our own economy. Now, I am still learning how to achieve this. (Tirtamaya, female, 22 years old, online interview, 4 October 2021)

## CONCLUSION

Reflecting on the case of Indonesian progressive youth organizations, we opine that the organizational variables above are mutually reinforcing in shaping the powerlessness of these youth movements. Thus, the progressive segment of Indonesian millennials still has a formidable task to advance their agendas since the lack of organizational infrastructure (i.e., institutionalization, networks, and resources) would undermine their objectives. This state of affairs is troubling since progressive Indonesian forces have never been key players in Indonesian politics. Even after the fall of the authoritarian regime, progressive agendas such as redistributive politics have never been endorsed by policymakers as their main policy agendas (Warburton et al. 2021). Without strong progressive youth movements that serve to socialize and train future Indonesian progressives, the future of the progressive agenda in Indonesia is bleak.

Our study improves the existing literature on Indonesian youth movements both conceptually and methodologically. Conceptually, our study shifts the lens of inquiry from the individual level of analysis used in previous studies. As we studied progressive activism, we realized that unpacking the organizational underpinning of such activism allows us to understand better the organizational structure that determines the power of Indonesian progressive youth organizations. Such an approach also assists us in revisiting the heroic depiction of Indonesian progressive millennials and Indonesian youths that should be revised. Instead of ascribing to Indonesian youths the role of agents of change, treating the strength of Indonesian youth movements as an empirical question is more productive in opening various avenues of investigation. The organizational approach in examining Indonesian progressive youths is one among other possibilities in such inquiry. Methodologically, combining quantitative and qualitative data not only helps to reveal the organizational elements of Indonesian progressive youth organizations but also the experience of progressive youth activists in navigating their organizations. The quantitative data provides an overview of progressive youth organizations, particularly their organizational infrastructure, while the qualitative data uncovers the individual experiences of steering their organizations. Combining both data should be an alternative strategy for further studying Indonesian youth movements.

The findings of our study suggest that Indonesia's progressive youth organizations should practise the basics of organization building. The basics include establishing a solid organizational structure that can effectively distribute work among the organization's members, based on experience and expertise. A solid organizational structure is necessary for anticipating the complex tasks and challenges that arise as an organization grows. Furthermore, progressive youth organizations should expand their organizational networks and membership to increase the leverage and credibility of their agendas. Expanding membership requires developing chapters in other regions, including potential pockets of support such as universities. Progressive youth activists can also expand their memberships by initiating long-term education programmes that cultivate future generations of activists for their organizations. The struggle for social justice often outlives the activists who endorse such an agenda. Thus, designing social movement education that can constantly supply progressive youth organizations with members is necessary for realizing the social justice agenda in the future.

## Acknowledgement

The research for this chapter was funded by the Kurawal Foundation. We are grateful for insightful comments and feedback from participants of the International Conference on Millennial Disruptions, 15–16 August 2022, organized by the ISEAS – Yusof Ishak Institute. Rahardhika Arista Utama, Sabina Satriyani Puspita and Yoes C. Kenawas also provided constructive feedback on the early draft of the chapter. We extend our appreciation to Andika N. Perkasa, Carolina Retmawati, Christina Pakpahan, Nadira R. Chairani and Nadlirotul Ulfa for their invaluable assistance during the data collection phase.

## References

Afrianty, Dina. 2012. "Islamic Education and Youth Extremism in Indonesia". *Journal of Policing, Intelligence and Counter Terrorism* 7, no. 2: 134–46. https://doi.org/10.1080/18335330.2012.719095

Alinsky, Saul D. 1971. *Rules for Radicals: A Practical Primer for Realistic Radicals.* New York: Vintage.

Altbach, Philip G. 1970. "The International Student Movement". *Journal of Contemporary History* 5, no. 1: 156–74. https://doi.org/10.1177/002200947000500111

———. 1989. "Perspectives on Student Political Activism". *Comparative Education* 25, no. 1: 97–110. https://doi.org/10.1080/0305006890250110

Andrews, Kenneth T. 2001. "Social Movements and Policy Implementation: The Mississippi Civil Rights Movement and the War on Poverty, 1965 to 1971". *American Sociological Review* 66, no. 1 (February): 71–95. https://doi.org/10.2307/2657394

Arifianto, Alexander R. 2019. "Islamic Campus Preaching Organizations in Indonesia: Promoters of Moderation or Radicalism?". *Asian Security* 15, no. 3: 323–42. https://doi.org/10.1080/14799855.2018.1461086

Aspinall, Edward. 2005. *Opposing Suharto: Compromise, Resistance, and Regime Change in Indonesia*. California: Stanford University Press. https://www.sup.org/books/title/?id=5947

Azca, Muhammad Najib. 2011. "After Jihad: A Biographical Approach to Passionate Politics in Indonesia". PhD dissertation, University of Amsterdam.

Beta, Annisa R. 2019. "Commerce, Piety and Politics: Indonesian Young Muslim Women's Groups as Religious Influencers". *New Media & Society* 21, no. 10: 2140–59. https://doi.org/10.1177/14614448198387

Blackburn, Susan. 1999. "Women and Citizenship in Indonesia". *Australian Journal of Political Science* 34, no. 2: 189–204. https://doi.org/10.1080/10361149950362

Central Bureau of Statistics. 2021. "Number of Universities, Lecturers, and Students (Public and Private) under the Ministry of Research, Technology, and High Education/Ministry of Education and Culture by Province, 2021". Central Bureau of Statistics. Accessed 10 November 2021. https://www.bps.go.id/indikator/indikator/view_data_pub/0000/api_pub/cmdTdG5vU0IwKzBFR20rQnpuZEYzdz09/da_04/1accessed%20on%20November%2010

Chaplin, Chris. 2018. "Salafi Activism and the Promotion of a Modern Muslim Identity: Evolving Mediums of Da'wa amongst Yogyakartan University Students". *South East Asia Research* 26, no. 1: 3–20. https://doi.org/10.1177/0967828X177524

Chen, Jonathan, and Emirza Adi Syailendra. 2014. "Old Society, New Youths: An Overview of Youth and Popular Participation in Post-Reformasi Indonesia". RSIS Working Paper, No. 269. Singapore: Nanyang Technological University. https://dr.ntu.edu.sg/handle/10220/19846

Clemens, Elisabeth S. 1997. *The People's Lobby: Organizational Innovation and the Rise of Interest Group Politics in the United States*, 1890–1925. Illinois: University of Chicago Press.

DeNardo, James. 1985. *Power in Numbers: The Political Strategy of Protest and Rebellion*. New Jersey: Princeton University Press.

Diani, Mario, and Doug McAdam. 2003. "Introduction: Social Movements, Contentious Actions, and Social Networks 'from Metaphor to Substance'?". In *Social Movements and Networks: Relational Approaches to Collective Action*, edited by Mario Diani and Doug McAdam, pp. 1–18. Oxford: Oxford University Press.

Dibley, Thushara, and Michele Ford. 2019. "Introduction: Social Movements and Democratization in Indonesia". In *Activists in Transition: Progressive Politics in Democratic Indonesia*, edited by Thushara Dibley and Michele Ford, pp. 1–21.

Ithaca: Cornell University Press. https://ses.library.usyd.edu.au/bitstream/handle/2123/28632/Postprint_Introduction%20Social%20Movements%20and%20Democratization%20in%20Indonesia.pdf?sequence=1

Dubuisson-Quellier, Sophie. 2013. "A Market Mediation Strategy: How Social Movements Seek to Change Firms' Practices by Promoting New Principles of Product Valuation". *Organization Studies* 34, no. 5–6: 683–703. https://doi.org/10.1177/0170840613479227

Edwards, Bob, and Sam Marullo. 1995. "Organizational Mortality in a Declining Social Movement: The Demise of Peace Movement Organizations in the End of the Cold War Era". *American Sociological Review* 60, no. 6: 908–27. https://doi.org/10.2307/2096432

Edwards, Gemma. 2014. "Infectious Innovations? The Diffusion of Tactical Innovation in Social Movement Networks, the Case of Suffragette Militancy". *Social Movement Studies* 13, no. 1: 48–69. https://doi.org/10.1080/14742837.2013.834251

Fathurrahman, Izzan. 2020. "Millennials: Rise and Shine". *Jakarta Post*, 7 January 2020. https://www.thejakartapost.com/academia/2020/01/07/millennials-rise-and-shine.html

Georgallis, Panayiotis. 2017. "The Link between Social Movements and Corporate Social Initiatives: Toward a Multi-Level Theory". *Journal of Business Ethics* 142, no. 4: 735–51. https://doi.org/10.1007/s10551-016-3111-0

Hamayotsu, Kikue. 2011. "Beyond Faith and Identity: Mobilizing Islamic Youth in a Democratic Indonesia". *Pacific Review* 24, no. 2: 225–47. https://doi.org/10.1080/09512748.2011.560960

Janti, Nur. 2022. "Fractured Student Movement Losing Power to Effect Change". *Jakarta Post*, 21 May 2022. https://www.thejakartapost.com/indonesia/2022/05/20/fractured-student-movement-losing-power-to-effect-change.html

Kailani, Najib. 2012. "Forum Lingkar Pena and Muslim Youth in Contemporary Indonesia". *RIMA: Review of Indonesian and Malaysian Affairs* 46, no. 1: 33–53. https://doi.org/10.3316/ielapa.984332214396280

Khanis, Suvianita. 2013. "Human Rights and the LGBTI Movement in Indonesia". *Asian Journal of Women's Studies* 19, no. 1: 127–38. https://doi.org/10.1080/12259276.2013.11666145

King, Brayden G. 2008. "A Political Mediation Model of Corporate Response to Social Movement Activism". *Administrative Science Quarterly* 53, no. 3: 395–421. https://doi.org/10.2307/27749273

Lee, Doreen. 2011a. "Images of Youth: On the Iconography of History and Protest in Indonesia". *History and Anthropology* 22, no. 3: 307–336. https://doi.org/10.1080/02757206.2011.595003

Lee, Doreen. 2011b. "Styling the Revolution: Masculinities, Youth, and Street Politics in Jakarta, Indonesia". *Journal of Urban History* 37, no. 6: 933–951. https://doi.org/10.1177/0096144211410

McAdam, Doug, and W. Richard Scott. 2005. "Organizations and Movements". In *Social Movements and Organization Theory*, edited by Gerald F. Davis, Doug McAdam, W. Richard Scott and Mayer Zald. New York: Cambridge University Press. https://doi.org/10.1017/CBO9780511791000

———, John D. McCarthy, and Mayer N. Zald. 1996. "Introduction: Opportunities, Mobilizing Structures, and Framing Processes—Toward a Synthetic, Comparative Perspective on Social Movements". In *Comparative Perspectives on Social Movements: Political Opportunities, Mobilizing Structures, and Cultural Framings*, edited by Doug McAdam, John D. McCarthy and Mayer N. Zald. New York: Cambridge University Press. https://doi.org/10.1017/CBO9780511803987.002

McCarthy, John D., and Mayer N. Zald. 1977. "Resource Mobilization and Social Movements: A Partial Theory". *American Journal of Sociology* 82, no. 6: 1212–41.

Minkoff, Debra C. 1999. "Bending with the Wind: Strategic Change and Adaptation by Women's and Racial Minority Organizations". *American Journal of Sociology* 104, no. 6: 1666–703.

Ministry of Youth and Sports, Indonesia. 2009. "Indonesia's Law No. 40 of 2009 on Youth". Ministry of Youth and Sports: Department of Youth Affairs.

Nilan, Pam. 2015. "Discourses of Non-Formal Pedagogy in Two Youth-Oriented Indonesian Environmental NGOs". *Asian Social Science* 11, no. 21: 162–73. https://doi:10.5539/ass.v11n21p162

———. 2017. "The Ecological Habitus of Indonesian Student Environmentalism". *Environmental Sociology* 3, no. 4: 370–80. https://doi.org/10.1080/23251042.2017.1320844

———. 2021. "Muslim Youth Environmentalists in Indonesia". *Journal of Youth Studies* 24, no. 7: 925–40. https://doi.org/10.1080/13676261.2020.1782864

———, and Gregorius Ragil Wibowanto. 2021. "Challenging Islamist Populism in Indonesia through Catholic Youth Activism". *Religions* 12, no. 6: 395. https://doi.org/10.3390/rel12060395

Nisa, Eva F. 2013. "The Internet Subculture of Indonesian Face-Veiled Women". *International Journal of Cultural Studies* 16, no. 3: 241–55. https://doi.org/10.1177/1367877912474534

———. 2018. "Creative and Lucrative Da'wa: The Visual Culture of Instagram amongst Female Muslim Youth in Indonesia". *Asiascape: Digital Asia* 5, no. 1–2: 68–99. https://doi.org/10.1163/22142312-12340085

Parker, Lyn, Kelsie Prabawa-Sear, and Wahyu Kustiningsih. 2018. "How Young People in Indonesia See Themselves as Environmentalists: Identity, Behaviour, Perceptions and Responsibility". *Indonesia and the Malay World* 46, no. 136: 263–82. https://doi.org/10.1080/13639811.2018.1496630

Prihatini, Ella S. 2018. "Indonesian Young Voters: Political Knowledge and Electing Women into Parliament". *Women's Studies International Forum* 70 (2018): 46–52. https://doi.org/10.1016/j.wsif.2018.07.015

Ridwan, Rinaldi, and Joyce Wu. 2018. "Being Young and LGBT, What Could Be Worse?' Analysis of Youth LGBT Activism in Indonesia: Challenges and Ways Forward". *Gender & Development* 26, no. 1: 121–38. https://doi.org/10.1080/13552074.2018.1429103

Rijal, Syamsul. 2020. "Following Arab Saints: Urban Muslim Youth and Traditional Piety in Indonesia". *Indonesia and the Malay World* 48, no. 141: 145–68. https://doi.org/10.1080/13639811.2020.1729540

Sastramidjaja, Yatun. 2019. "Youth 'Alienation' and New Radical Politics: Shifting Trajectories in Youth Activism". In *Continuity and Change after Indonesia's Reforms: Contributions to an Ongoing Assessment*, edited by Max Lane, pp. 238–62. Singapore: ISEAS – Yusof Ishak Institute. https://doi.org/10.1355/9789814843232-013

Sebastian, Leonard C., Jonathan Chen, and Emirza Adi Syailendra. 2014. "Pemuda Rising: Why Indonesia Should Pay Attention to Its Youth". RSIS Monograph no. 29. Singapore: Nanyang Technological University. https://www.rsis.edu.sg/rsis-publication/idss/pemuda-rising-why-indonesia-should-pay-attention-to-its-youth/#.ZDjlaHZBzrd

Skrentny, John D. 2006. "Policy-Elite Perceptions and Social Movement Success: Understanding Variations in Group Inclusion in Affirmative Action". *American Journal of Sociology* 111, no. 6: 1762–815. https://doi.org/10.1086/499910

Soule, Sarah A. 1997. "The Student Divestment Movement in the United States and Tactical Diffusion: The Shantytown Protest". *Social Forces* 75, no. 3: 855–82. https://doi.org/10.2307/2580522

———. 2012. "Social Movements and Markets, Industries, and Firms". *Organization Studies* 33, no. 12: 1715–33. https://doi.org/10.1177/0170840612464610

——, and Brayden G. King. 2008. "Competition and Resource Partitioning in Three Social Movement Industries". *American Journal of Sociology* 113, no. 6: 1568–610. https://doi.org/10.1086/587152

Staggenborg, Suzanne. 2013. "Institutionalization of Social Movements". In *The Wiley-Blackwell Encyclopedia of Social and Political Movements*, edited by David A. Snow, Donatella Della Porta, Bert Klandermans, and Doug McAdam. New Jersey: Wiley-Blackwell. https://doi.org/10.1002/9780470674871

Stearns, Linda Brewster, and Paul D. Almeida. 2004. "The Formation of State Actor-Social Movement Coalitions and Favorable Policy Outcomes". *Social Problems* 51, no. 4: 478–504. https://doi.org/10.1525/sp.2004.51.4.478

Strang, David, and Sarah A. Soule. 1998. "Diffusion in Organizations and Social Movements: From Hybrid Corn to Poison Pills". *Annual Review of Sociology* 24 (1998): 265–90.

Suyanto, Bagong, Mun'im Sirry, and Rahma Sugihartati. 2022. "Pseudo-Radicalism and the De-Radicalization of Educated Youth in Indonesia". *Studies in Conflict & Terrorism* 45, no. 2: 153–72. https://doi.org/10.1080/1057610X.2019.1654726

Tilly, Charles. 2004. *Social Movements, 1768–2004*. Colorado: Paradigm Publishers. https://doi.org/10.4324/9781315632063

Wang, Dan J., and Sarah A. Soule. 2012. "Social Movement Organizational Collaboration: Networks of Learning and the Diffusion of Protest Tactics, 1960–1995". *American Journal of Sociology* 117, no. 6: 1674–722. https://doi.org/10.1086/664685

Warburton, Eve, Burhanuddin Muhtadi, Edward Aspinall, and Diego Fossati. 2021. "When Does Class Matter? Unequal Representation in Indonesian Legislatures". *Third World Quarterly* 42, no. 6: 1252–75. https://doi.org/10.1080/01436597.2021.1882297

Zald, Mayer N., and Roberta Ash. 1966. "Social Movement Organizations: Growth, Decay and Change". *Social Forces* 44, no. 3: 327–41. https://doi.org/10.2307/2575833

# 4

# Indonesia's Millennials and Gen Zs

## Are They Financially (Il)literate?

Ibrahim Kholilul Rohman, Raka Rizky Fadilla, Kevin Bagas Ksatria and Feisal Nadhirrahman

**ABSTRACT**

*Indonesia's population increasingly comprises younger age groups. This segment of the population is currently exposed to and becoming the target consumer market for the rapid development of multiple new financial products in the past decade or so, a consequence of the digital revolution and relentless technological innovation. One question that arises amid this development is: are Indonesia's younger generations financially illiterate or are they so literate that they become less risk-averse in managing their portfolios? This study involved conducting a survey of 142 participants, mostly students at the University of Indonesia. It distinguishes financial awareness from financial ownership and associates these two variables with different age groups. The study finds that there are differences in awareness (or literacy) and ownership of financial products among different age groups. Those from Generation Y have higher awareness about most financial products, including the high-risk asset types such as cryptocurrencies and non-fungible tokens, than the Generation X, but they tend to buy the less risky asset types, except insurance products. Although higher financial awareness is associated with higher financial ownership, this study also shows a significantly weaker relationship between awareness and the level of ownership of financial products for Gen Z compared with Gen X. It indicates that Gen Z youths, despite being generally more knowledgeable of various financial products, do not necessarily own more of these products.*

## INTRODUCTION

Based on the population census of 2020, Indonesia's population is dominated by those from Generation Z. Applying the categorization of generational cohorts used by the Pew Research Center (2019),[1] about 74.93 million or 27.94 per cent of Indonesia's population represent Generation Z; 69.38 million or 25.87 per cent represent Generation Y (millennials) and 58.65 million or 21.88 per cent represent Generation X (BPS 2020). As young generations dominate the population, it bears raising the question of how they perceive financial products that have become intrinsically intertwined with technology and digitalization today.

Financial inclusion has generally been more pervasive among the younger generations, namely Gen Y and Gen Z. Indonesia's Otoritas Jasa Keuangan (Financial Service Authority, or OJK) has developed the Financial Literacy Index, which gauges financial understanding and literacy among Indonesians. OJK's 2019 survey shows that Indonesia's younger population achieved a score of 44–47 per cent—a higher score compared with the score of 38.03 per cent for all age groups on average (OJK 2020). This means that 4–5 out of 10 young people understand the concept of financial instruments, compared with fewer than 4 out of 10 people nationally.

While this finding comes as good news, the younger generations in Indonesia are facing challenges in managing their cash flows and making sound judgements on how to select financial products to buy. Most young graduates in their early working careers are saddled with exorbitant travel and accommodation costs, especially those working around the central business district.[2] At the same time, they are often involved in high-risk investment decisions involving financial technology, such as peer-to-peer (p2) lending, pay later, cryptocurrency, non-fungible tokens (NFTs), online shadow banking and related digital finance outlets.[3]

Indonesia's Commodity Futures Trading Regulatory Agency (CoFTRA) shows that 7.5 million Indonesians performed cryptocurrency transactions in 2021, an increase of 87.5 per cent compared with 2020 when the number of people making such transactions was only about 4 million. Demographically, most of them are young. In terms of transaction values, cryptocurrency transactions reached Rp478.5 trillion as of July 2021, equivalent to 6 per cent of Bank Indonesia's total money supply as of November 2021. However, the striking fact revolves around the volume of cryptocurrency transactions in 2021, which increased by 636.15 per cent from 2020.

Another new phenomenon among the younger generations is the interest shown in NFTs, which are unique digital objects validated by a digital encryption technology known as blockchain. Enthusiasm for NFTs has particularly been escalating in Indonesia owing to the "Ghozali effect". A young man named Ghozali took daily selfie photos during the period 2017–21 and sold them as NFTs, with an accumulated trading value that reached 284 Ethereum—a unit of cryptocurrency—equivalent to about US$930.000 by the end of 2022.

This study is aimed at examining whether Indonesia's younger generations are more financially illiterate or are so literate that they become less risk-averse when buying financial products. By employing a simple regression analysis using the ordinary least squares (OLS) method, this study investigates how Indonesia's younger generations perceive different types of financial products compared with the older generations. The study is based on survey data collected from 142 respondents.

The next section of the chapter reviews some existing studies, which mostly discuss the behaviours of young generations in various countries in making financial product choices. The third section lays out the data collection methodology and regression model specifications for this research. The fourth section discusses the findings and then draws inferences from the data. The concluding section delves into the policy implications of this study.

## LITERATURE REVIEW

With the ubiquity of technologies, there are fewer barriers to entry into financial markets. Technology has brought about non-conventional financial products, such as cryptocurrencies, NFTs and peer-to-peer lending, which coexist with the more conventional ones such as savings, time deposits and bonds. Driven by low barriers to entry and exciting new products, youths start to make financial decisions at a much earlier age compared with previous generations. This is the reason why financial literacy among the youth becomes even more important (Lusardi, Mitchell, and Curto 2009).

Despite being an important topic, "financial literacy" has become an umbrella term discussed without any standard definition (Remund 2010). This research adopts the definition developed by the Organization for Economic Co-operation and Development (OECD), which interprets financial literacy as: "knowledge and understanding of financial concepts and risks, and the skills, motivation and confidence to apply such knowledge and understanding in order to make effective decisions across a range of financial contexts, to improve the financial well-being of individuals and society, and to enable participation in economic life" (OECD 2014). Under this conceptual framework, a financially literate person is one who has "good" financial knowledge and understanding when taking financial decisions.

Financial knowledge is also used as a synonym for financial literacy. How knowledgeable someone is about finance is usually judged by his/her understanding of the concepts of simple interest, compounding interest, the time value of money, the impact of inflation on price levels and investment returns, savings, investment and borrowing (Huston 2010; OECD INFE 2011). Some studies highlight more advanced concepts such as risk diversification (Lusardi, Mitchell, and Curto 2009). Consequently, an individual with a higher level of financial literacy is assumed to have a better understanding of the concept of risks that would lead him/her to make more informed decisions in selecting riskier assets, such as high-return stocks, for their asset portfolios (Van Rooij, Lusardi, and Alessie 2011).

The role of financial literacy in determining financial asset portfolios is inconclusive. On the one hand, as a case study in China shows, people/households with higher financial literacy tend to delegate at least part of their portfolio management to experts and invest in mutual funds (Chu et al. 2017). On the other hand, it is also found in other studies that people with higher financial literacy seek less financial advice and hence choose less risky investment products (Kramer 2016).

## FINANCIAL LITERACY OF THE YOUTH

Today's young generations are involved in financial decisions earlier in life, compared with the older generations. However, studies explaining the position of youth in the financial literacy map diverge. In Australia, it is found that youths aged 18–24 tend to have the lowest to the middle level of financial literacy, and the gains in financial literacy are obtained as someone gets older (Worthington 2006). Henager and Cude (2016) show that short-term and long-term financial participation improves with age. Looking at youths only, Lusardi, Mitchell, and Curto (2009) report that only one-third of young adults in the United States possess basic knowledge of interest rates, inflation and risks.

As the spectrum of finance is wide, the level of understanding can vary depending on the topics. In Nepal, a study found that while youths have good numeracy levels and understand banking-related topics, their understanding of topics related to taxes, financial statements and insurance is limited (Thapa and Nepal 2015). A case study involving students at Padjajaran University, Indonesia, found that students tend to lack basic numeracy as far as investment, insurance and credit are concerned (Nidar and Bestari 2012).

From the theoretical perspective, financial literacy is linked to several factors such as cognitive ability and educational attainment (Lusardi 2003; Cole et al. 2009). Gender and racial backgrounds are also among the determining factors, with females tending to have more limited knowledge of personal finances compared with males (Chen and Volpe 2002). The financial backgrounds of parents also play a major role. Lusardi, Mitchell, and Curto (2009) find that youths whose parents are better educated own more stocks and savings instruments as well as pension funds. These parents may influence their kids to become more financially literate. Thus, the role of family is important in the early formation of a financial mindset (Gudmunson and Danes 2011).

## THE YOUTH AND CHOICE OF INVESTMENT

There is a common view that youths tend to have lower financial knowledge while also tending towards owning riskier investment types. One way to verify this view is by observing the risk appetite of the younger generations with regard to alternative investments that entail high price volatility, such as cryptocurrency. In Japan (Fujiki 2020) and in the United States (Auer and Tercero-Lucas 2021), it has been found that cryptocurrency investors are likely to be younger and better educated and have higher financial literacy. In other words, being young increases the likelihood of owning cryptocurrency. This phenomenon is in line with the fact that younger people are more risk-loving compared with older people, who tend to be more conservative or risk-averse concerning asset ownership (Albert and Duffy 2012). Moreover, Auer and Tercero-Lucas (2021) find that a person's level of digital skills is an important factor behind cryptocurrency ownership. This might increase the likelihood of youth owning cryptocurrency since many of them are "digital natives".

However, studies arguing that cryptocurrency investors are most likely to be financially literate could be challenged. Kim, Hanna, and Lee (2022) find that cryptocurrency investors tend to be overconfident, indicating that financial literacy is not always a good determinant of cryptocurrency ownership. The recent crypto craze is fuelled by youths seeking quick and higher returns, which is a similar driving force that motivates an individual to make transactions in the stock market (Kezdi and Willis 2011).

But, as one study shows, investors in bitcoin, a major cryptocurrency in terms of transaction volume, tend to have higher "fear of missing out" (FOMO) traits, compared with stock investors and non-investors (Kim et al. 2020). This means bitcoin investors are afraid to miss out on potential gains, as experienced by their peers and those in their social networks. This FOMO trait may prompt illiterate and inexperienced investors to invest in cryptocurrencies without proper financial backgrounds and understanding of this new form of investment. Even more concerning, investing in technology-backed financial assets such as bitcoin and other cryptocurrency assets requires a basic understanding of the blockchain technology that underpins cryptocurrencies, an area of knowledge that is found to be neglected by many youths (e.g., Sabarwal 2022).

## DATA AND METHODOLOGY

This study aims to understand the relationship between age and financial awareness and ownership. It involved conducting an online survey, which was distributed through Google Forms and drew responses from 142 respondents. The survey was conducted during the period of May–June 2022, and the data has been used in Nadhirrahman (2022).

### Financial Awareness and Ownership

This study assigns two dependent variables: financial awareness and financial ownership. Financial awareness indicates knowledge of financial products, while financial ownership is the ownership of financial products currently available in the market. Financial awareness was determined through a self-reporting question: "Do you know the following financial assets?". Financial ownership was determined through a self-reporting question: "Do you own the following financial assets?". We developed indices as a proxy for both financial awareness and financial ownership by adding up all financial products known or owned (respondent knows about/has a particular financial product = 1; and respondent does not know about/does not have a particular financial product = 0). The highest financial index representing awareness or ownership is 11. This is the case where a respondent knows or owns all 11 financial assets in the questionnaire: savings, deposits, stocks, bonds, property, pension funds, insurance, mutual funds, gold, cryptocurrencies and NFTs.

## Gen X, Gen Y and Gen Z

We classified our respondents into three generations based on the aforementioned Pew Research study: Gen X are those born between 1965 and 1980; Gen Y were born between 1981 and 1996; and Gen Z were born in 1997 or later.

## Control Variables

We employed several covariates as control variables, including demographic variables representing residential area (urban = 1; rural = 0), gender (male = 1; female = 0) and the number of household members. We used income as an additional covariate and divided the respondents into four groups based on monthly income: those earning less than Rp2 million; those earning Rp2–4.99 million; those earning Rp5–9.99 million; and, lastly, those earning Rp10–19.99 million.

## Empirical Strategy

We used the OLS method in the following model specification:

$$Y_i = \alpha + \beta X_i + \gamma_i Control_i + \varepsilon_i$$

where $Y_i$ stands for the financial awareness or financial ownership of individual i, $X_i$ represents a dummy for Gen Y and Gen Z, taking Gen X as the base dummy, $Control_i$ stands for control variables, and $\varepsilon_i$ is an error term distributed under normal distribution.

To obtain an analysis of the correlation between each generation and awareness and ownership of the types of assets, we used logistic regression, with the same control variables as the main model.

## RESULTS AND DISCUSSION

### Descriptive Statistics

The sample was dominated by Gen Y representatives, those living in urban areas, males, those from households with an average of 3–4 persons, and those earning Rp5–9.99 million. We found that, on average, the respondents have knowledge of 6–7 financial products, but only own 3–4 financial products out of eleven financial products. We noted that Gen Z is the most informed group of respondents about different types of financial instruments (Appendix 4.1). Savings is the most well-known product while NFTs is the least known product. The same pattern is seen in the ownership of financial products. Based on this survey, the newer the financial product, the smaller the proportion of respondents who know about and own the product. See Table 4.1.

### Main Results

Column 1 of Table 4.2 shows the results for the dependent variable representing financial awareness, while column 2 shows the results for financial ownership. In summary, this study indicates that Gen Y has higher financial awareness than Gen X. Also, people living in urban areas have higher financial awareness than those living in rural areas. Meanwhile, there is no evidence of a relationship between age and financial ownership. However, financial ownership is associated with income levels as the sole determining factor, with those with higher incomes being more likely to own financial products.

A summary of these results is presented in the table in Appendix 4.1 while Appendix 4.2 captures these results in the form of a graph.

**TABLE 4.1**
**Descriptive Statistics**

| *Variables* | *Obs* | *Mean* | *Std. Dev.* | *Min* | *Max* |
|---|---|---|---|---|---|
| *Dependent Variables* | | | | | |
| Financial Awareness Index | 142 | 6.289 | 3.344 | 1 | 11 |
| Financial Ownership Index | 142 | 3.352 | 1.932 | 1 | 10 |
| Awareness of Savings Accounts | 142 | .972 | .166 | 0 | 1 |
| Awareness of Time Deposits | 142 | .782 | .415 | 0 | 1 |
| Awareness of Obligations | 142 | .521 | .501 | 0 | 1 |
| Awareness of Mutual Funds | 142 | .739 | .44 | 0 | 1 |
| Awareness of Bonds | 142 | .585 | .495 | 0 | 1 |
| Awareness of Gold | 142 | .697 | .461 | 0 | 1 |
| Awareness of Property | 142 | .556 | .499 | 0 | 1 |
| Awareness of Crypto | 142 | .324 | .47 | 0 | 1 |
| Awareness of Insurance | 142 | .528 | .501 | 0 | 1 |
| Awareness of Pension Funds | 142 | .423 | .496 | 0 | 1 |
| Awareness of NFTs | 142 | .162 | .37 | 0 | 1 |
| Ownership of Savings Account | 142 | .965 | .185 | 0 | 1 |
| Ownership of Time Deposits | 142 | .268 | .444 | 0 | 1 |
| Ownership of Obligations | 142 | .12 | .326 | 0 | 1 |
| Ownership of Mutual Funds | 142 | .514 | .502 | 0 | 1 |
| Ownership of Bonds | 142 | .204 | .405 | 0 | 1 |
| Ownership of Gold | 142 | .479 | .501 | 0 | 1 |
| Ownership of Property | 142 | .254 | .437 | 0 | 1 |
| Ownership of Crypto | 142 | .085 | .279 | 0 | 1 |
| Ownership of Insurance | 142 | .282 | .451 | 0 | 1 |
| Ownership of Pension Funds | 142 | .169 | .376 | 0 | 1 |
| Ownership of NFTs | 142 | .014 | .118 | 0 | 1 |
| *Generation* | | | | | |
| Gen X | 142 | .155 | .363 | 0 | 1 |
| Gen Y | 142 | .739 | .44 | 0 | 1 |
| Gen Z | 142 | .106 | .308 | 0 | 1 |
| *Demographic Characteristics* | | | | | |
| Urban | 142 | .775 | .419 | 0 | 1 |
| Male | 142 | 0.592 | 0.493 | 0 | 1 |
| Number of Household Members | 142 | 3.732 | 1.439 | 0 | 9 |
| *Income* | | | | | |
| Less than Rp2,000,000 | 142 | .112 | .317 | 0 | 1 |
| Rp2,000,000–Rp4,999,999 | 142 | .126 | .333 | 0 | 1 |
| Rp5,000,000–Rp9,999,999 | 142 | .485 | .501 | 0 | 1 |
| Rp10,000,000–Rp19.999,999 | 142 | .190 | .393 | 0 | 1 |
| More than Rp20,000,000 | 142 | .084 | .279 | 0 | 1 |

**TABLE 4.2**
**Main Results**

| *Variables* | *(1) Financial Awareness Index* | *(2) Financial Ownership Index* |
|---|---|---|
| *Generation* | | |
| Gen Y | 1.926** | 0.410 |
| | (2.02) | (0.72) |
| Gen Z | 0.605 | 0.430 |
| | (0.50) | (0.65) |
| *Demographic Characteristics* | | |
| Urban | 1.488** | 0.428 |
| | (2.23) | (1.13) |
| Male | –0.0245 | –0.207 |
| | (–0.04) | (–0.59) |
| Number of Household Members | 0.273 | 0.0643 |
| | (1.32) | (0.59) |
| *Income* | | |
| Rp2,000,000–Rp4,999,999 | 0.566 | 0.552 |
| | (0.46) | (1.33) |
| Rp5,000,000–Rp9,999,999 | 0.0242 | 1.586*** |
| | (0.02) | (4.19) |
| Rp10,000,000–Rp19,999,999 | 1.096 | 2.254*** |
| | (0.97) | (4.18) |
| More than Rp20,000,000 | 1.908 | 2.835*** |
| | (1.21) | (3.67) |
| _cons | 2.190 | 1.046 |
| | (1.25) | (1.21) |
| *N* | 142 | 142 |

*Notes:* Bootstrapped with 100 repetitions. Robust standard error is in parentheses.
*** statistically significant at 1 per cent level, ** at 5 per cent level, * at 10 per cent level.

## Financial Awareness of Each Financial Product

We investigated the same questions on awareness and ownership for each financial product using logistic regressions. Table 4.3 shows the results of the marginal effect of age on awareness of eleven different financial products. We observed that compared with Gen X, Gen Y has significantly higher awareness of mutual funds, stocks, gold, cryptocurrencies and NFTs. On the other hand, compared with Gen X, Gen Z has a significantly higher

**TABLE 4.3**
**Regression of Financial Awareness of Each Financial Product**

| *Variables* | *(1) Savings Accounts* | *(2) Time Deposits* | *(3) Bonds* | *(4) Mutual Funds* | *(5) Stocks* | *(6) Gold* | *(7) Property* | *(8) Crypto* | *(9) Insurance* | *(10) Pension Funds* | *(11) NFTs* |
|---|---|---|---|---|---|---|---|---|---|---|---|
| Gen Y | 0.0954 | 0.208 | 0.238 | 0.530*** | 0.331** | 0.345*** | 0.0165 | 0.202** | –0.195 | 0.00596 | 0.149** |
| | (1.59) | (1.51) | (1.58) | (3.65) | (2.49) | (2.72) | (0.11) | (2.12) | (–1.43) | (0.04) | (2.24) |
| Gen Z | 0.0184 | 0.0940 | 0.229 | 0.398* | 0.255 | 0.304* | –0.258 | 0.0547 | –0.416** | –0.235 | 0.162 |
| | (0.28) | (0.57) | (1.11) | (1.83) | (1.21) | (1.66) | (–1.30) | (0.38) | (–2.36) | (–1.36) | (1.26) |
| _cons | 0.785*** | 0.202 | –0.146 | –0.126 | 0.142 | 0.148 | 0.542** | –0.0933 | 0.736** | 0.267 | –0.267* |
| | (6.90) | (0.85) | (–0.52) | (–0.51) | (0.60) | (0.67) | (2.27) | (–0.44) | (2.36) | (0.97) | (–1.76) |
| Controls | Yes | Yes | Yes | Yes | Yes | Yes | Yes | Yes | Yes | Yes | Yes |
| *N* | 142 | 142 | 142 | 142 | 142 | 142 | 142 | 142 | 142 | 142 | 142 |

*Notes:* Bootstrapped with 100 repetitions. All regression results are controlled by demographic and income characteristics of the sample (see Appendix 4.4). Robust standard error is in parentheses.

*** statistically significant at 1 per cent level, ** at 5 per cent level, * at 10 per cent level.

awareness of mutual funds and gold, but less awareness of insurance products.

### Financial Ownership of Each Financial Product

We also observed a link between age and financial ownership by using logistic regressions. This analysis is shown in Table 4.4 with the marginal effect of the regression, where the dependent variable is financial ownership and reported in columns 1–11, based on the type of assets. Compared with Gen X, those from Gen Y own more mutual funds, bonds and gold but fewer properties and insurance products. Compared with Gen X, those from Gen Z own more bonds.

### Young Generation and Financial Awareness

Furthermore, we included interaction variables of financial awareness and age. Table 4.5 and Appendix 4.6 show the results of the analysis. Although there is a significant and positive relationship between financial awareness and financial ownership, this relationship is weaker for Gen Z compared with Gen X. Another way to interpret the finding is that compared with Gen X, those from Gen Z, despite having higher financial awareness, own fewer financial products.

## DISCUSSION

From the analysis, we found that Gen Y has accumulated greater financial awareness than Gen X and Gen Z. However, higher financial awareness does not determine whether those from Gen Y own certain financial products (Appendix 4.1). For example, even though those from Gen Y know more about cryptocurrencies and NFTs than Gen X do, they prefer to spend their money on lower-risk financial products, such as mutual funds, bonds and gold, but not insurance products.

This finding also shows a significantly weaker relationship between awareness and the level of ownership of financial products for Gen Z compared with Gen X. It indicates that Gen Z youths, despite being generally more knowledgeable of various financial products, do not necessarily own more of these products.

**TABLE 4.4**
**Regression of Financial Ownership of Each Financial Product**

| *Variables* | *(1) Savings Account* | *(2) Time Deposits* | *(3) Bonds* | *(4) Mutual Funds* | *(5) Stocks* | *(6) Gold* | *(7) Property* | *(8) Crypto* | *(9) Insurance* | *(10) Pension Funds* | *(11) NFTs* |
|---|---|---|---|---|---|---|---|---|---|---|---|
| Gen Y | 0.0647<br>(0.92) | 0.0355<br>(0.29) | –0.0315<br>(–0.35) | 0.457***<br>(4.23) | 0.208*<br>(1.72) | 0.244**<br>(1.97) | –0.301**<br>(–1.99) | 0.0685<br>(0.66) | –0.253*<br>(–1.85) | –0.0863<br>(–0.74) | 0.00411<br>(0.34) |
| Gen Z | 0.0550<br>(0.71) | 0.0317<br>(0.22) | 0.192<br>(1.28) | 0.242<br>(1.34) | 0.304**<br>(2.04) | 0.109<br>(0.51) | –0.287<br>(–1.49) | 0.00699<br>(0.07) | –0.181<br>(–0.99) | –0.0432<br>(–0.35) | 0.0000304<br>(0.00) |
| _cons | 0.769***<br>(4.74) | –0.135<br>(–0.71) | 0.0223<br>(0.17) | –0.437**<br>(–2.33) | –0.244<br>(–1.07) | –0.0121<br>(–0.05) | 0.615**<br>(2.22) | –0.0612<br>(–0.56) | 0.343*<br>(1.71) | 0.182<br>(0.99) | 0.00279<br>(0.08) |
| Controls | Yes | Yes | Yes | Yes | Yes | Yes | Yes | Yes | Yes | Yes | Yes |
| *N* | 142 | 142 | 142 | 142 | 142 | 142 | 142 | 142 | 142 | 142 | 142 |

*Notes:* All regression results are controlled by demographic and income characteristics of the sample (see Appendix 4.5). Robust standard error is in parentheses.

*** statistically significant at 1 per cent level, ** at 5 per cent level, * at 10 per cent level.

**TABLE 4.5**
**Heterogeneity Analysis**

| *Variables* | *(1)* *Financial Ownership* |
|---|---|
| Gen Y * Financial Awareness | –0.141<br>(–1.23) |
| Gen Z * Financial Awareness | –0.392**<br>(–2.23) |
| _cons | 1.018**<br>(2.24) |
| *N* | 142 |

*Notes:* Bootstrapped with 100 repetitions. The regression results are controlled by Gen Y, Gen Z and financial awareness variables (see Appendix 4.6). Robust standard error is in parentheses.

*** statistically significant at 1 per cent level, ** at 5 per cent level, * at 10 per cent level.

However, there is a more conclusive finding here that the younger generations tend to have less knowledge and ownership of insurance products. Insurance products are basically aimed at covering future losses and mitigating risks. For the younger population, this consideration may not be among their current priorities in asset ownership due to time preference (Reimers et al. 2009; Tanaka, Camerer, and Nguyen 2010; Zelinsky, 2021).

## CONCLUSION AND RECOMMENDATIONS

This study provides a general understanding of how decisions in selecting financial products are related to age. It shows that Gen Y is the most knowledgeable among all generations about financial products. However, despite their knowledge of risky products, young people tend to choose less risky financial products, such as mutual funds, stocks and gold, but not insurance products.

For policymakers, this study may provide an understanding of how to deepen the population's financial awareness by targeting different age groups. The young generations that comprise the largest proportion of the population in Indonesia perceive financial instruments differently in comparison with the older generation. Innovation is necessary so that financial products can be tailored to the younger generations. The financial sector could implement what is known as third-degree price discrimination strategies, which recognize that the price elasticity of demand differs across age groups; in other words, different age groups have different willingness to pay a particular price for a product.

This study corroborates the significance of Indonesia's omnibus law in regulating the financial sector. Under the new law, known as the Financial Sector Development and Reinforcement (P2SK) Bill (Law number 4, 2022), especially Chapter XVI, the products of financial innovation such as cryptocurrency will be put under the supervision of the Financial Service Authority (OJK) to allow closer monitoring of the possible price/ value fluctuations. Such monitoring is considered critical especially since the buying and selling of cryptocurrencies by the younger generations is often driven by FOMO, instead of a solid understanding of the economic fundamentals of these products.

This study has some limitations though. Apart from the small sample size bias, the range of the sample is narrow as most of the respondents were university students. However, the study provides a comprehensive account of investment choices by this particular demographic to better understand the association—or lack of association—between the level of awareness and ownership of various financial assets.

# APPENDICES

## APPENDIX 4.1
## Summary Statistics of Each Generation

| *Variables* | *Gen X* | *Gen Y* | *Gen Z* |
|---|---|---|---|
| Mean of Financial Awareness Index | 5.364 | 4.448 | 5.6 |
| Mean of Financial Ownership Index | 2.136 | 3.105 | 2.8 |

## APPENDIX 4.2
## Pattern of the Understanding of Financial Products

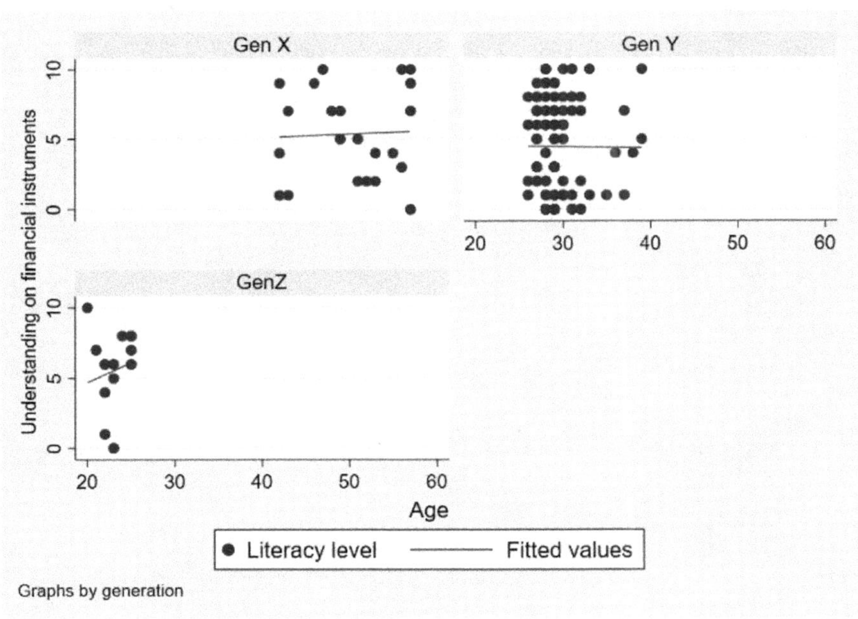

**APPENDIX 4.3**
**The Literacy-Ownership Gap**

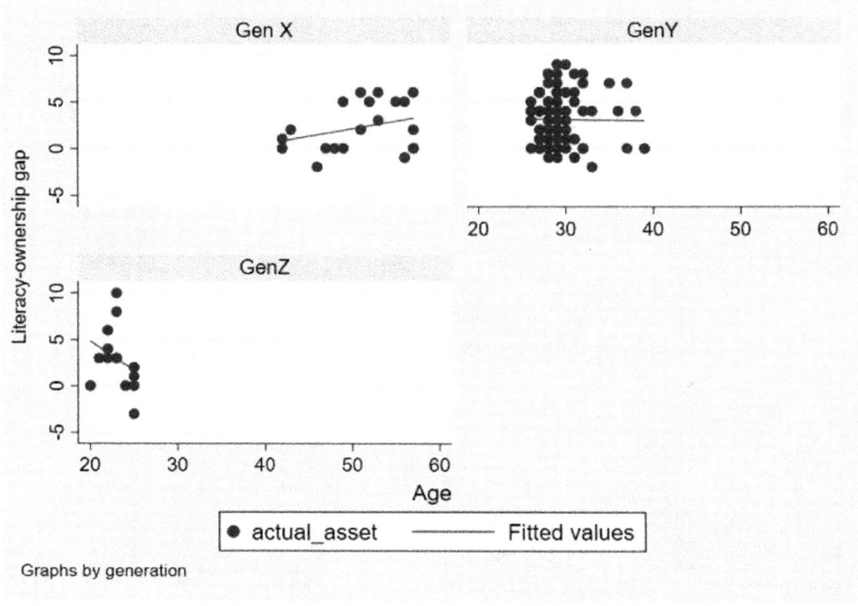

**APPENDIX 4.4**
**Regression of Financial Awareness of Each Financial Product**

| *Variables* | *(1) Saving Account* | *(2) Time Deposits* | *(3) Bond* | *(4) Mutual Fund* | *(5) Stock* |
|---|---|---|---|---|---|
| *Age Generation* | | | | | |
| Gen Y | 0.0954 | 0.208 | 0.238 | 0.530*** | 0.331*** |
| | (1.39) | (1.55) | (1.50) | (3.71) | (2.61) |
| Gen Z | 0.0184 | 0.0940 | 0.229 | 0.398** | 0.255 |
| | (0.27) | (0.52) | (1.28) | (2.05) | (1.40) |
| *Demographic Characteristics* | | | | | |
| Urban | 0.0631 | –0.00138 | 0.0544 | 0.152* | 0.126 |
| | (1.54) | (–0.01) | (0.49) | (1.74) | (1.23) |
| Male | 0.00410 | –0.0155 | –0.0364 | –0.0394 | 0.0312 |
| | (0.16) | (–0.21) | (–0.38) | (–0.56) | (0.35) |
| Number of Household Members | 0.0123 | 0.0617** | 0.0481 | 0.0264 | 0.0230 |
| | (1.39) | (2.38) | (1.55) | (1.04) | (0.82) |
| *Income* | | | | | |
| Rp2,000,000–Rp4,999,999 | –0.00481 | 0.287** | 0.298* | 0.247 | –0.0513 |
| | (–0.09) | (1.99) | (1.73) | (1.51) | (–0.29) |
| Rp5,000,000–Rp9,999,999 | 0.0760 | 0.132 | 0.196 | 0.220 | 0.0171 |
| | (1.49) | (0.82) | (1.16) | (1.24) | (0.09) |
| Rp10,000,000–Rp19,999,999 | –0.00289 | 0.438** | 0.448* | 0.672*** | 0.303 |
| | (–0.03) | (2.28) | (1.67) | (2.88) | (1.53) |
| More than Rp20,000,000 | 0.0175 | 0.181 | 0.304** | 0.219 | –0.101 |
| | (0.41) | (1.18) | (2.10) | (1.36) | (–0.64) |
| _cons | 0.785*** | 0.202 | –0.146 | –0.126 | 0.142 |
| | (6.56) | (0.90) | (–0.64) | (–0.57) | (0.70) |
| *N* | 142 | 142 | 142 | 142 | 142 |

*Notes:* All regression results are controlled by demographic and income characteristics of the sample. Robust standard error is in parentheses.

*** statistically significant at 1 per cent level, ** at 5 per cent level, * at 10 per cent level.

| *(6) Gold* | *(7) Property* | *(8) Cryptocurrency* | *(9) Insurance* | *(10) Pension Fund* | *(11) NFT* |
|---|---|---|---|---|---|
| 0.345** | 0.0165 | 0.202* | −0.195 | 0.00596 | 0.149*** |
| (2.42) | (0.11) | (1.77) | (−1.33) | (0.04) | (2.66) |
| 0.304 | −0.258 | 0.0547 | −0.416*** | −0.235 | 0.162 |
| (1.49) | (−1.27) | (0.37) | (−2.67) | (−1.55) | (1.39) |
| 0.172* | 0.0418 | 0.249*** | 0.224** | 0.240** | 0.167*** |
| (1.70) | (0.43) | (2.79) | (2.16) | (2.46) | (3.28) |
| −0.0165 | −0.0466 | 0.0580 | 0.00347 | 0.0355 | −0.00256 |
| (−0.17) | (−0.52) | (0.76) | (0.04) | (0.43) | (−0.04) |
| 0.0292 | 0.0438 | 0.0197 | −0.0178 | −0.00288 | 0.0296 |
| (1.14) | (1.63) | (0.65) | (−0.48) | (−0.09) | (1.35) |
| 0.0199 | 0.0255 | 0.0469 | −0.00739 | 0.117 | 0.118 |
| (0.12) | (0.12) | (0.27) | (−0.04) | (0.72) | (0.96) |
| 0.258 | −0.164 | −0.109 | −0.0827 | −0.000902 | 0.0228 |
| (1.44) | (−0.76) | (−0.70) | (−0.40) | (−0.01) | (0.23) |
| 0.323 | −0.0701 | −0.133 | −0.179 | 0.0740 | 0.0350 |
| (1.58) | (−0.33) | (−0.66) | (−0.77) | (0.37) | (0.27) |
| −0.0706 | −0.241 | −0.0457 | −0.210 | −0.0996 | 0.0701 |
| (−0.41) | (−1.34) | (−0.34) | (−1.37) | (−0.68) | (0.80) |
| 0.148 | 0.542** | −0.0933 | 0.736** | 0.267 | −0.267** |
| (0.62) | (1.97) | (−0.40) | (2.48) | (1.06) | (−2.10) |
| 142 | 142 | 142 | 142 | 142 | 142 |

**APPENDIX 4.5**
**Regression of Financial Ownership of Each Financial Product**

| *Variables* | *(1) Savings Accounts* | *(2) Time Deposits* | *(3) Bonds* | *(4) Mutual Funds* | *(5) Stocks* |
|---|---|---|---|---|---|
| *Age Generation* | | | | | |
| Gen Y | 0.0647 | 0.0355 | –0.0315 | 0.457*** | 0.208* |
| | (0.88) | (0.31) | (–0.40) | (4.37) | (1.66) |
| Gen Z | 0.0550 | 0.0317 | 0.192 | 0.242 | 0.304* |
| | (0.70) | (0.22) | (1.25) | (1.53) | (1.73) |
| *Demographic Characteristics* | | | | | |
| Urban | 0.0275 | –0.120 | –0.0244 | 0.211** | 0.208** |
| | (0.49) | (–1.41) | (–0.30) | (2.29) | (2.43) |
| Male | –0.00390 | –0.0638 | –0.0490 | –0.0196 | 0.0612 |
| | (–0.14) | (–0.80) | (–0.93) | (–0.26) | (0.71) |
| Number of Household Members | 0.00734 | 0.0461* | –0.0116 | 0.0514* | 0.0164 |
| | (0.54) | (1.73) | (–0.66) | (1.69) | (0.65) |
| *Income* | | | | | |
| Rp2,000,000–Rp4,999,999 | 0.0905 | 0.482*** | 0.217** | 0.210 | 0.0857 |
| | (0.81) | (4.29) | (2.13) | (1.60) | (0.74) |
| Rp5,000,000–Rp9,999,999 | 0.0920 | 0.0612 | 0.113 | 0.0762 | 0.0425 |
| | (0.70) | (0.78) | (1.31) | (0.53) | (0.30) |
| Rp10,000,000–Rp19,999,999 | 0.0774 | 0.344** | 0.236* | 0.425** | 0.152 |
| | (0.56) | (2.06) | (1.89) | (2.08) | (0.89) |
| More than Rp20,000,000 | 0.123 | 0.417*** | 0.239*** | 0.325*** | –0.0627 |
| | (1.21) | (4.76) | (2.65) | (2.72) | (–0.54) |
| _cons | 0.769*** | –0.135 | 0.0223 | –0.437** | –0.244 |
| | (4.38) | (–0.69) | (0.16) | (–2.43) | (–1.38) |
| *N* | 142 | 142 | 142 | 142 | 142 |

*Notes:* All regression results are controlled by demographic and income characteristics of the sample. Robust standard error is in parentheses.

*** statistically significant at 1 per cent level, ** at 5 per cent level, * at 10 per cent level.

| *(6) Gold* | *(7) Property* | *(8) Cryptocurrency* | *(9) Insurance* | *(10) Pension Funds* | *(11) NFTs* |
|---|---|---|---|---|---|
| 0.244* | –0.301** | 0.0685 | –0.253** | –0.0863 | 0.00411 |
| (1.76) | (–2.02) | (0.71) | (–2.03) | (–0.72) | (0.26) |
| 0.109 | –0.287 | 0.00699 | –0.181 | –0.0432 | 0.0000304 |
| (0.55) | (–1.54) | (0.08) | (–1.15) | (–0.33) | (0.00) |
| | | | | | |
| 0.000602 | –0.0267 | 0.0733 | 0.0773 | 0.0240 | –0.0229 |
| (0.01) | (–0.28) | (1.42) | (0.87) | (0.38) | (–0.60) |
| –0.0459 | –0.0561 | 0.0139 | –0.0676 | 0.00630 | 0.0179 |
| (–0.52) | (–0.78) | (0.27) | (–0.82) | (0.08) | (1.36) |
| 0.0404 | –0.0201 | –0.00574 | –0.0299 | –0.0295 | –0.000545 |
| (1.35) | (–0.73) | (–0.33) | (–1.26) | (–1.14) | (–0.17) |
| | | | | | |
| 0.199 | 0.236 | 0.139** | 0.355*** | 0.203** | 0.0365 |
| (1.24) | (1.26) | (2.04) | (2.94) | (2.04) | (1.00) |
| 0.133 | –0.116 | 0.0440 | 0.152 | –0.0434 | –0.00173 |
| (0.79) | (–0.64) | (0.68) | (1.24) | (–0.73) | (–0.13) |
| 0.564*** | 0.248 | 0.0710 | 0.361* | 0.341* | 0.0151 |
| (2.79) | (1.05) | (0.60) | (1.92) | (1.92) | (0.93) |
| 0.149 | –0.0628 | 0.0262 | 0.245*** | 0.167** | 0.0194 |
| (0.91) | (–0.40) | (0.57) | (3.23) | (2.48) | (0.85) |
| –0.0121 | 0.615** | –0.0612 | 0.343** | 0.182 | 0.00279 |
| (–0.05) | (2.24) | (–0.52) | (2.06) | (1.10) | (0.06) |
| 142 | 142 | 142 | 142 | 142 | 142 |

## APPENDIX 4.6
## Heterogeneity Analysis

| *Variables* | *(1)*<br>*Financial Ownership* |
|---|---|
| Gen Y * Financial Awareness | –0.141<br>(–1.30) |
| Gen Z * Financial Awareness | –0.392**<br>(–2.32) |
| Financial Awareness | 0.440***<br>(4.19) |
| Gen Y | 0.452<br>(0.89) |
| Gen Z | 1.323<br>(1.50) |
| _cons | 1.018**<br>(2.01) |
| *N* | 142 |

*Notes:* Bootstrapped with 100 repetitions. The regression results are controlled by Gen Y, Gen Z and financial awareness variables. Robust standard error is in parentheses. *** statistically significant at 1 per cent level, ** at 5 per cent level, * at 10 per cent level.

## Notes

1. Kim Parker and Ruth Igielnik, "On the Cusp of Adulthood and Facing an Uncertain Future", Pew Research Center, 14 May 2020, https://www.pewresearch.org/social-trends/2020/05/14/on-the-cusp-of-adulthood-and-facing-an-uncertain-future-what-we-know-about-gen-z-so-far-2/
2. "Susahnya Jadi Anak Indekos di Jakarta, Mau Irit Tapi Sulit: Millennial", *Kumpuran.com*, 3 May 2018, https://kumparan.com/millennial/susahnya-jadi-anak-indekos-di-jakarta-mau-irit-tapi-sulit-21dM5TZ7w0
3. Selvi Mayasari, "Porsi Pemberi Pinjaman Fintech Lending dari Kalangan Milenial Capai 65%", *kontan.co.id*, 8 July 2022, https://keuangan.kontan.co.id/news/porsi-pemberi-pinjaman-fintech-lending-dari-kalangan-milenial-capai-65

## References


Albert, Steven M., and John Duffy. 2012. "Differences in Risk Aversion between Young and Older Adults". *Neuroscience and Neuroeconomics* 1 (January): 3–9. http://doi.org/10.2147/NAN.S27184

Auer, Raphael, and David Tercero-Lucas. 2021. "Distrust or Speculation? The Socioeconomic Drivers of US Cryptocurrency Investments". July 2021. Working Paper No. 951, Bank for International Settlements (BIS). https://www.bis.org/publ/work951.pdf

Aydemir, Sibel Dinc, and Selim Aren. 2017. "Do the Effects of Individual Factors on Financial Risk-Taking Behavior Diversify with Financial Literacy?". *Kybernetes* 46, no. 10: 1706–34. https://www.emerald.com/insight/content/doi/10.1108/K-10-2016-0281/full/html?skipTracking=true

Badan Pusat Statistik (BPS). 2020. "Sensus Penduduk Indonesia Tahun 2020". https://sensus.bps.go.id/main/index/sp2020

Chen, Haiyang, and Ronald. P. Volpe. 2002. "Gender Differences in Personal Financial Literacy among College Students". *Financial Services Review* 11, no. 3: 289–307.

Chu, Zhong, Zhengwei Wang, Jing Jian Xiao, and Weiqiang Zhang. 2017. "Financial Literacy, Portfolio Choice, and Financial Well-Being". *Social Indicators Research* 132, no. 2: 799–820. https://doi.org/10.1007/s11205-016-1309-2

Cole, S.A., Thomas Andrew Sampson, and Bilal Husnain Zia. 2009. "Financial Literacy, Financial Decisions, and the Demand for Financial Services: Evidence from India and Indonesia", pp. 9–117. Cambridge, MA: Harvard Business School.

Fujiki, Hiroshi. 2020. "Who Adopts Crypto Assets in Japan? Evidence from the 2019 Financial Literacy Survey". *Journal of the Japanese and International Economies* 58 (December): 101107. https://doi.org/10.1016/j.jjie.2020.101107

Gudmunson, Clinton G., and Sharon. M. Danes. 2011. "Family Financial Socialization: Theory and Critical Review". *Journal of Family and Economic Issues* 32, no. 4: 644–67. https://doi.org/10.1007/s10834-011-9275-y

Henager, Robin, and Brenda. J. Cude. 2016. "Financial Literacy and Long- and Short-Term Financial Behavior in Different Age Groups". *Journal of Financial Counseling and Planning* 27, no. 1: 3–19. http://dx.doi.org/10.1891/1052-3073.27.1.3

Hermansson, Cecilia, and Sara Jonsson. 2021. "The Impact of Financial Literacy and Financial Interest on Risk Tolerance". *Journal of Behavioral and Experimental Finance* 29 (March): 100450. https://doi.org/10.1016/j.jbef.2020.100450

Huston, Sandra J. 2010. "Measuring Financial Literacy". *Journal of Consumer Affairs* 44, no. 2: 296–316. https://doi.org/10.1111/j.1745-6606.2010.01170.x

Kézdi, Gabor, and Robert. J. Willis. 2011. "Household Stock Market Beliefs and Learning". November 2011. Working Paper 17614, National Bureau of Economic Research. https://doi.org/ 10.3386/w17614

Kim, Hee Jin, Ji Sun Hong, Hyun Chan Hwang, Sun Mi Kim, and Doug Hyun Han. 2020. "Comparison of Psychological Status and Investment Style between Bitcoin Investors and Share Investors". *Frontiers in Psychology* 11 (November): 502295. https://doi.org/10.3389/fpsyg.2020.502295

Kim, Kyoung Tae, Sherman D. Hanna, and Sunwoo T Lee. 2022. "Investment Literacy, Overconfidence and Cryptocurrency Investment". *Financial Services Review* (accepted). Available at http://dx.doi.org/10.2139/ssrn.3953242

Kramer, Marc M. 2016. "Financial Literacy, Confidence and Financial Advice Seeking". *Journal of Economic Behavior & Organization* 131, Part A (November): 198–217. https://doi.org/10.1016/j.jebo.2016.08.016

Lestari, Diyan. 2019. "Measuring E-Commerce Adoption Behaviour among Gen-Z in Jakarta, Indonesia". *Economic Analysis and Policy* 64 (December): 103–15. https://doi.org/10.1016/j.eap.2019.08.004

Lusardi, Annamaria, and Olivia. S. Mitchell 2011. "Financial Literacy around the World: An Overview". *Journal of Pension Economics and Finance* 10, no. 4: 497–508. https://doi.org/10.1017/S1474747211000448

———, Olivia. S. Mitchell, and Vilsa Curto 2010. "Financial Literacy among the Young". *Journal of Consumer Affairs* 44, no. 2: 358–80. https://doi.org/10.1111/j.1745-6606.2010.01173.x

Nadhirrahman, F. 2022. "Intensi Masyarakat Milenial dalam Berinvestasi Reksa Dana Syariah di Era Pandemi COVID-19". Master's thesis, Universitas Indonesia, Jakarta.

Nidar, Sulaeman Rahman, and Sandi Bestari. 2012. "Personal Financial Literacy among University Students (Case Study at Padjadjaran University Students, Bandung, Indonesia)". *World Journal of Social Sciences* 2, no. 4: 162–71.

Nwosum, Oluebube. 2022. "Understanding the Interactions among Cryptocurrencies Adoption, Financial Inclusion and Income Growth Opportunities among Nigerian Youths". https://www.researchgate.net/publication/358725833_

Understanding_the_Interactions_among_Cryptocurrencies_adoption_Financial_Inclusion_and_Income_Growth_Opportunities_Among_Nigerian_Youths

OECD. 2014. "PISA 2012 Technical Background". In *PISA 2012 Results: Students and Money Volume VI Financial Literacy Skills for the 21st Century*. Paris: OECD Library. https://doi.org/10.1787/9789264208094-en

OECD-INFE. 2011. *Measuring Financial Literacy: Core Questionnaire in Measuring Financial Literacy: Questionnaire and Guidance Notes for Conducting an Internationally Comparable Survey of Financial Literacy*. 2011. Paris: OECD Publishing. https://www.oecd.org/finance/financial-education/49319977.pdf

Otoritas Jasa Keuangan (OJK). 2020. "Survei Nasional Literasi Dan Inklusi Keuangan 2019". Buku Statistik SNLIK 2019. https://sikapiuangmu.ojk.go.id/FrontEnd/CMS/DetailMateri/517

Pew Research Center. 2019. "Defining Generations: Where Millennials End and Generation Z Begins". https://www.pewresearch.org/fact-tank/2019/01/17/where-millennials-end-and-generation-z-begins/

Reimers, Stian, Elizabeth A. Maylor, Neil Stewart, and Nick Chater. 2009. "Associations between a One-Shot Delay Discounting Measure and Age, Income, Education and Real-World Impulsive Behavior". *Personality and Individual Differences* 47, no. 8: 973–78. https://doi.org/10.1016/j.paid.2009.07.026

Remund, David L. 2010. "Financial Literacy Explicated: The Case for a Clearer Definition in an Increasingly Complex Economy". *Journal of Consumer Affairs* 44, no. 2: 276–95. https://doi.org/10.1111/j.1745-6606.2010.01169.x

Sabarwal, Ishita. 2022. "Understanding the Attitude of Youth towards Cryptocurrency". University of Wollongong, Dubai.

Tanaka, Tomomi, Colin F. Camerer, and Quang Nguyen. 2010. "Risk and Time Preferences: Linking Experimental and Household Survey Data from Vietnam". *American Economic Review* 100, no. 1: 557–71. https://doi.org/10.1257/aer.100.1.557

Thapa and Nepal 2015 [Authors to supply bibliographic information]

Van Rooij, Maarten, Annamaria Lusardi, and Rob Alessie. 2011. "Financial Literacy and Stock Market Participation". *Journal of Financial Economics* 101, no. 2: 449–72. https://doi.org/10.1016/j.jfineco.2011.03.006

Worthington, Andrew. C. 2006. "Predicting Financial Literacy in Australia". Papers (Archives), Faculty of Commerce, University of Wollongong, Australia. https://ro.uow.edu.au/commpapers/116/

Želinský, Tomáš. 2021. "Intertemporal Choices of Children and Adults from Poor Roma Communities: A Case Study from Slovakia". *Eastern European Economics* 59, no. 4: 378–405. https://doi.org/10.1080/00128775.2021.1909424

Zhao, Haidong, and Lini Zhang. 2021. "Financial Literacy or Investment Experience: Which Is More Influential in Cryptocurrency Investment?". *International Journal of Bank Marketing* 39, no. 7: 1208–26. https://doi.org/10.1108/IJBM-11-2020-0552

# 5

# Digital Competencies of the Millennial Generation in Micro, Small, and Medium Enterprises in West Bandung District

Diana Sari and Caecilia Suprapti Dwi Takariani

**ABSTRACT**

*Digital technology opens up opportunities for small- and medium-sized enterprises (MSMEs) to penetrate the market and increase their access to middlemen and even to final consumers. This chapter is based on a quantitative study of MSME actors, including millennials from West Bandung District in West Java. The study used secondary data to examine the varying levels of digital competency among MSME actors from different generations. The results show a significant relationship between digital competence and the education levels of Generation X and millennial MSME actors: higher education levels among MSME actors from these two generations lead to higher digital competencies. This study also found that millennials with higher education have better digital competency levels in the areas of information management, collaboration, content and knowledge creation, and technical operation. Among MSME actors from Generation X, the tendency was for those with higher education levels to have better digital competency only in the area of information management. Due to the limited number of samples from baby boomers and Generation Z, this paper cannot make any conclusions about their digital competence.*

## INTRODUCTION

The rapid development of digital technology has increasingly driven interactions and transactions in the online space. The ability to use digital technology brings several essential benefits and conveniences, such as searching for information, communicating, transacting and accessing public services (Choi and Whinston 2000; Hanna, Rohm, and Crittenden 2011; Graham 2014). Digital technology has been adopted widely in various user environments. This tendency to use technology is closely related to motivation and skills (Gyr, Friedman, and Gyr 2010; Hanna et al. 2011; Deursen and Dijk 2011). Having physical access to devices like computers or laptops as well as other resources, such as software and an Internet subscription, is necessary to maintain connectivity and achieve adequate skills.

Various studies have indicated that despite the availability of infrastructure and access to digital technology, individual or organizational gaps in digital utilization are not solely attributed to physical access but also to skills and competencies (Livingstone 2003; Deursen and Dijk 2011; Dijk 2012). Users require adequate skills in utilizing digital technologies, particularly for productive purposes. The digital divide has shifted from inequality in the possession of information and communications technology (ICT) devices to skills and usage (Deursen and Dijk 2011; Dijk 2012).

Information technology has also transformed business processes, encouraging the growing adoption of digitalization. Such growth has also been experienced by micro, small and medium-sized enterprises (MSMEs) (Maguire, Koh, and Magrys 2007). Digital transformation has significantly transformed processes such as marketing, where direct access to consumers is now possible, cutting distribution channels and streamlining business costs (Tarutė and Gatautis 2014; Fan 2016). The adoption of e-commerce by MSMEs is limited by their lack of skilled employees (Maguire, Koh, and Magrys 2007; Vieru 2015). Other studies highlight different barriers, such as security and privacy concerns, the cost of implementing a digital business and the lack of a digital strategy and relevant resources (MacGregor et al. 2008; Maguire, Koh, and Magrys 2007).

In short, one of the critical determinants of digital adoption in MSMEs is digital skills. The widespread development of digital access and infrastructure does not necessarily encourage MSME players to adopt digitalization to optimize their business processes. Appropriate digital skills are required to participate and thrive in the digital age (Sarosa 20121999; Latour, 2005; Law, 1999; Ferrari 2013; Tarutė and Gatautis 2014; Vieru et al. 2015).

The development of MSMEs in the digital era opens up opportunities for people of all ages with digital competence. MSME actors come from various age groups with distinct characteristics. Millennials and later generations (Generations Z and Alpha) are known as the generations that are tech-savvy and frequently use social media and other forms of digital technology in their daily lives (Deal, Altman, and Rogelberg 2010; Cirilli and Nicolini 2019). Compared to previous generations (Generation X and baby boomers), millennials are more engaged with technology. The millennial generation in Indonesia, including MSME actors of the millennial generation, represents a productive population structure and plays an important part in supporting the Indonesian economy.

Recent research has established that age is a crucial factor in determining digital technology adoption and competency, with younger individuals demonstrating greater adaptability to digital technology compared to their older counterparts (Ifinedo 2011a; Ashurst et al. 2012; Kusumaningtyas and Suwarto 2015). The SUSENAS Survey (2020) reports that different age groups face distinct challenges, with Internet usage predominantly concentrated among young individuals: 77 per cent of individuals aged 10–29 years use the Internet, while the figure drops to only 21 per cent for those over 50 years of age. Furthermore, younger individuals demonstrate greater agility in adapting to changes and advancements in digital technology than their older counterparts. The main motivation for elderly people to use the Internet is maintaining social connections with their families and communities, as was particularly important during the pandemic when social interaction became increasingly challenging. However, it is imperative to ensure that they are equally equipped with the skills necessary for utilizing digital technology in support of MSMEs.

According to Eurostat (2020), an increasing number of older adults are utilizing the Internet in various Western countries. Unfortunately, older individuals remain one of the most susceptible groups to digital inequalities (Deursen and Dijk 2019). Despite the growing trend of Internet usage among older adults, many still struggle to acquire the necessary skills and confidence to fully participate in the digital world. However, it is important to note that portraying the elderly as a uniform group of technophobes and digital illiterates is a misrepresentation.

This leads to the question of whether the digital competence of MSME actors in Indonesia varies across different age groups, and, if so, how this affects their business performance. This study aims to provide a descriptive analysis of the differences in digital competency between millennial MSME actors and other generations of MSME actors. To achieve this, cross-tabulation analysis was conducted on variables such as generation, ICT device usage, Internet usage, gender, and education, using chi-square statistics.

Millennials are often referred to as "digital natives" due to their exposure to rapid technological development and adoption of digital technology during their formative years. They are known to rely heavily on social network applications (such as various social networking platforms and mobile applications) for their daily social interactions (Kim, Briley, and Ocepek 2015). It is assumed that millennials possess a high level of technology literacy and are expected to use social network applications in their professional lives, such as for communication, sharing and collaboration. Such usage can increase business productivity by enhancing knowledge sharing and open collaboration among employees (Kim, Briley, and Ocepek 2015).

Studies have consistently demonstrated that younger and more educated individuals are more likely to adopt innovative behaviours, including the use of ICT devices and services (Kim, Briley, and Ocepek 2015; Nuvriasari 2012; Oblinger and Oblinger 2005). The millennial generation is characterized by open communication, active engagement on social media, and openness to political and economic views (BPS and KPPA 2018). It is reasonable to assume that digital competency can be a valuable asset for this generation to thrive in the digital ecosystem (Cirilli and Nicolini 2019). The millennial generation is found to be the most likely to use ICT devices and services, consistent with demographic studies on innovative behaviour adoption.

Examining the digital competence of MSME actors across different generations can provide critical insights into the extent to which digital competency can enhance the utilization of digital technologies in business. These insights and associated policy implications can guide policymakers to improve the participation of all MSME generations in the digital economy.

This chapter offers an overview of the digital competencies of MSME actors, with a particular emphasis on comparing the millennial generation with other generations. Specifically, this study focuses on Generation Y, or millennials, who were born between 1981 and 1995. Investigating the digital competencies of millennial MSME actors and those of all other generations in the West Bandung District can serve as a reference point for narrowing the digital competence gap among MSME actors in the district.

## CONCEPTUAL FRAMEWORK

Digital competence refers to an individual's capacity to effectively use and combine knowledge, skills and attitudes from three interconnected areas of competency—technological, cognitive and social—and existing and newly acquired ICT skills to systematically analyse, select and evaluate information (Vieru et al. 2015). Several digital competency frameworks have been developed, including the European Union's Digital Competency Framework for Citizens as DigComp (Ferrari 2013). Digital skills can be seen as part of digital competence, focusing on an individual's practical skills in various dimensions. The DigComp framework divides digital skills into sub-skills (Ferrari 2013), with the skills domain encompassing information, communication, content creation, safety, and problem-solving skills (Ferrari 2013; Carretero, Vuorikari and Punie 2017). In general, the more digital skills an individual acquires, the greater their inclination to use digital technology for their needs and even experience the benefits of using this technology (Deursen, Helsper, and Eynon 2014).

### MSME Digital Competencies

Rapid technological developments in the business environment have created unique challenges for MSMEs, especially in their response to increasingly globalized markets (Deloitte 2015). To remain competitive, MSMEs must implement new strategies and business processes that incorporate the use of ICT. Internal efficiency, improved collaboration, the introduction of new products and services and investment in business digitalization are key drivers for MSMEs seeking to adapt to the digital economy. In short, MSMEs need digital competency to adapt to and successfully compete in the global marketplace (Deloitte 2015; Jensen et al. 2016).

However, success in the digital economy is not solely determined by investments in technology or direct technology adoption; it also requires the possession of appropriate expertise by individuals or teams within the organization to optimize resources in line with technological developments (Ifinedo 2011; Vieru et al. 2015). Therefore, MSMEs must focus on developing digital competency to support their development, growth and competitiveness.

The construct of digital competency is dynamic and constantly evolving, and is often adapted to fit specific contexts (Ala-Mutka 2011; Ferrari 2013; Vieru 2015). Digital competence is considered one of the essential competencies for organizations seeking sustainable competitiveness in achieving their goals (Selznick in Vieru et al. 2015). Individual capabilities in applying ICT are critical to developing this competency within the organization. Digital competency is most effectively analysed at the individual level, as most organizational competencies start with individuals. Digital competency within organizations is influenced by the interaction between IT skills, specific processes, and the norms and values of organizational culture (Pavlou and El Sawy 2006).

In the context of MSMEs, digital competency pertains to the ability to adapt and effectively use new or existing information technologies to solve work-related problems and develop collaborative knowledge within the organizational setting (Vieru 2015). The definition emphasizes the coexistence of several conceptual dimensions. This chapter uses a theoretical model developed by Vieru, based on a framework by Calvani, Fini, and Ranieri (2010) on organizational digital competence. Vieru's theoretical model was developed specifically to assess digital competence in the context of small and medium enterprises (Vieru et al. 2015) and is used in this study.

The proposed model is based on three intersecting and integrating dimensions:

(1) The technological dimension, which pertains to the effective and efficient use of existing and new ICT in the workplace;

(2) The cognitive dimension, which emphasizes the ability to read, select, interpret and evaluate the relevance and reliability of information for work in a specific organizational context;
(3) The social dimension, which emphasizes collaboration with other individuals using available ICT while adhering to existing organizational culture, i.e., work norms and values;
(4) Integration between the three dimensions, which describes the recognition of the benefits of ICT, such as facilitating the storage, transfer and sharing of information to collaboratively build a new knowledge base.

At the conceptual level, the definition of digital competency expands the integrative theoretical model of technology, cognitive skills and social skills into seven domains, as shown in Table 5.1 (Harison and Boonstra 2009; Vieru 2015).

## MILLENNIAL GENERATION

The definition of the term "millennial generation" varies among scholars. For instance, Tapscott (1998) in BPS and KPPA (2018) refers to the millennial generation as the digital generation born between 1976 and 2000. Zemke, Raines, and Filipczak (2000) refer to the millennial generation as the "Nexters", born between 1980 and 1999. Oblinger and Oblinger (2005) term the millennials "Generation Y", which refers to those born between 1981 and 1995. Meanwhile, Benesik, Csikos, and Juhes (2016) in BPS and KPPA (2018) identify the millennial generation as those born between 1980 and 1995. In general, many references identify the millennial generation as those born between 1981 and 1995. Hence, this chapter considers the millennial generation as those born between 1981 and 1995.

## METHOD

This study utilizes a quantitative approach to provide an overview of the digital competencies of millennials compared to other generations of MSMEs in the West Bandung District. The data is based on secondary data drawn from data originally collected in 2019 for a study on the digital competencies of MSMEs in West Bandung District conducted by the authors while working at the Centre for Human Resources Development and

**TABLE 5.1**
**Application Domains and Digital Competency Areas**

| *Domains* | *Digital Competency Areas* | *Description* |
|---|---|---|
| Information Management | Intersection of Technological and Cognitive | Identify, locate, access, retrieve, store and organize information. |
| Collaboration | Social | Link to others, participate in online networks and communities, and interact constructively and with a sense of responsibility. |
| Communication and Sharing | Intersection of Technological and Social | Communicate through online tools, taking into account privacy, safety and netiquette. |
| Content and Knowledge Creation | Cognitive | Construction of new knowledge through technology and media. Integrate previous knowledge; construct new knowledge. |
| Ethics and Responsibility | Intersection of Social and Cognitive | Behave ethically and responsibly, aware of the legal frame. |
| Evaluation and Problem-Solving | Integrated—Technological, Cognitive and Social | Identify digital needs, solve problems through digital means and assess the information retrieved. |
| Technical Operations | Technological | Use technology and media; perform tasks through digital tools. |

*Source:* Harison and Boonstra (2009); Vieru (2015).

Communication and Informatics Research—Bandung (BPSMDP Kominfo Bandung) at Indonesia's Ministry of Communication and Informatics (BPSDMP Kominfo Bandung 2019). The original data was collected through a questionnaire distributed to 11,090 MSME actors (people/representatives of MSMEs) spread over 16 subdistricts in West Bandung District, with a 10 per cent error margin. Sample size determination was performed using the Slovin method. The data used in this chapter is secondary data involving 101 MSME actors drawn from the wider pool in the original study. A proportionate random sampling technique was used to determine the proportion of MSME respondents in each subdistrict, while a random sampling technique was used to select respondents in each subdistrict. Because the sample of respondents in the research design is not stratified by generation, standard errors are given for analysis when using this breakdown. Generations are broken down into millennials, baby boomers, Gen X, and Gen Z.

The survey instrument used in this study (see Annex 5.1) has undergone a validity test and a reliability test through Cronbach's alpha test and therefore can be interpreted as a valid and reliable instrument. The self-assessment instrument was in the form of a Likert scale and was analysed using a percentage of the total score. Based on the percentage of the total score, digital competency levels are classified into three categories: basic level, intermediate level, and advanced level. Specifically, the basic level ranges from 0 per cent to 50 per cent, the intermediate level ranges from 51 per cent to 75 per cent, and the advanced level indicates scores above 75 per cent. This chapter focuses on the digital competency of the millennial generation in comparison with the other generations.

## RESULTS

### Respondent Profile

The study sampled MSME actors in West Bandung District aged 20–69 years, who were categorized into the baby boomer generation (aged above 54 years), Gen X (aged 38–54 years), millennials (aged 24–38 years), and Gen Z (below 24 years). The millennial generation constituted almost half of the total respondents (48.51 per cent), followed by Gen X (37.62 per cent), while Gen Z and baby boomers each represented less than 10 per cent. Table 5.2 shows that male MSME actors (56.4 per cent) outnumbered female MSME actors (43.6 per cent). Most of the MSME actors have a high school education.

Notably, the sample size for baby boomers and Gen Z was small (seven samples), which may limit the statistical significance of the analysis for these generations. However, given the focus of this chapter is on millennial MSME actors, the analysis is still informative in providing insights into their generation's digital competency and the factors that influence it. For further details on the sampling and categorization of respondents, refer to Table 5.2.

**TABLE 5.2**
**Profiles of Respondents**

| *Variable* | *Frequency* | *Percentage* | *Std. Error* | *95% Confidence Interval* | |
|---|---|---|---|---|---|
| | | | | *Lower (%)* | *Upper (%)* |
| *Generation* | | | | | |
| Baby boomer | 7 | 6.9 | .0 | 6.9 | 6.9 |
| Gen X | 38 | 37.6* | .0 | 37.6 | 37.6 |
| Millennial | 49 | 48.5* | .0 | 48.5 | 48.5 |
| Gen Z | 7 | 6.9 | .0 | 6.9 | 6.9 |
| Total | 101 | 100.0 | .0 | 100.0 | 100.0 |
| *Sex* | | | | | |
| Male | 57 | 56.4* | 5.4 | 47.1 | 69.7 |
| Female | 44 | 43.6 | 5.4 | 30.3 | 52.9 |
| Total | 101 | 100.0 | .0 | 100.0 | 100.0 |
| *Education* | | | | | |
| Elementary | 12 | 11.9 | 3.1 | 5.5 | 19.2 |
| Junior high | 13 | 12.9 | 3.2 | 6.5 | 19.2 |
| Senior high | 50 | 49.5* | 4.6 | 40.8 | 59.2 |
| Diploma | 11 | 10.9 | 3.0 | 4.0 | 16.8 |
| Bachelor | 15 | 14.9 | 3.5 | 6.5 | 21.2 |
| Total | 101 | 100.0 | .0 | 100.0 | 100.0 |

*Notes:* N=101; *The highest percentage.

## Usage of ICT Devices and the Internet, and Digital Competency Levels

The study reveals that ICT device usage among MSME actors in West Bandung District is almost universal (95 per cent), while Internet usage is reported by 89.1 per cent of the respondents. Analysis of digital competencies indicates that 17.8 per cent of MSMEs in the region exhibit a basic level of digital competency, 45.5 per cent show an intermediate level, and 36.6 per cent demonstrate an advanced level of digital competency (see Table 5.3).

**TABLE 5.3**
**Usage of ICT Devices and the Internet and Digital Competency Levels**

| *Variable* | *Frequency* | *Percentage* | *Std. Error* | *95% Confidence Interval* | |
|---|---|---|---|---|---|
| | | | | *Lower (%)* | *Upper (%)* |
| *Using ICT Devices* | | | | | |
| No | 5 | 5.0 | 1.8 | 1.0 | 8.3 |
| Yes | 96 | 95.0* | 1.8 | 91.7 | 99.0 |
| Total | 101 | 100.0 | 10.0 | 100.0 | 100.0 |
| *Using Internet* | | | | | |
| No | 11 | 10.9 | 3.0 | 5.0 | 16.2 |
| Yes | 90 | 89.1* | 3.0 | 83.8 | 95.0 |
| Total | 101 | 100.0 | .0 | 100.0 | 100.0 |
| *Digital Competencies* | | | | | |
| Basic | 18 | 17.8 | 3.4 | 10.5 | 24.2 |
| Intermediate | 46 | 45.5* | 4.7 | 37.2 | 56.7 |
| Advanced | 37 | 36.6 | 4.7 | 28.3 | 47.9 |
| Total | 101 | 100.0 | .0 | 100.0 | 100.0 |

*Notes:* N=101; *The highest percentage.

## Digital Competencies of Millennial and Other Generation MSME Actors

The cross-tabulation results for digital competency variables were analysed using the chi-square test, with each variable of gender, generation, education, use of ICT devices, and use of the Internet tested. The results indicate that digital competency has a significant relationship only with the variable of education (refer to Table 5.4 for details).

The chi-square test, stratified by a generation variable to provide an overview of digital competencies from an educational standpoint for each generation, reveals a significant positive relationship between digital competency and education (see Table 5.5). Notably, there is significant evidence in the Gen X and millennial generations ($p < 0.05$). The study indicates that millennials with a senior high school education background demonstrate diverse digital competency levels: 66.7 per cent at basic, 52.6 per cent at intermediate, and 37.5 per cent at advanced levels. Conversely, millennials with elementary and junior high school education exhibit basic and intermediate levels, while millennials with

**TABLE 5.4**
**The Relationship of Digital Competency with Social Aspects**

| *Variable* | | *Digital Competency Level* | | | | |
|---|---|---|---|---|---|---|
| | | *Basic* | *Intermediate* | *Advanced* | *Total* | *p-value* |
| Sex | Male | 1.0% | 2.0% | 2.0% | 5.0% | .432 |
| | Female | 16.8% | 43.5% | 34.7% | 95.0% | |
| | Total | 17.8% | 45.5% | 36.6% | 100.0% | |
| Education | Elementary | 5.9% | 3.0% | 3.0% | 11.9% | .001* |
| | Junior HS | 2.0% | 8.9% | 2.0% | 12.9% | |
| | Senior HS | 89% | 26.7% | 13.9% | 49.5% | |
| | Diploma | 1.0% | 4.0% | 5.9% | 10.9% | |
| | Bachelor | 0.0% | 3.0% | 11.9% | 14.9% | |
| | Total | 17.8% | 45.5% | 36.6% | 100.0% | |
| Generation | Baby boomer | 1.0% | 4.0% | 2.0% | 6.9% | .270 |
| | Gen X | 9.9% | 18.8% | 8.9% | 37.6% | |
| | Millennial | 5.9% | 18.8% | 23.8% | 48.5% | |
| | Gen Z | 1.0% | 4.0% | 2.0% | 6.9% | |
| | Total | 17.8% | 45.5% | 36.6% | 100.0% | |
| Using ICT Devices | No | 1.0% | 2.0% | 2.0% | 5.0% | .968 |
| | Yes | 16.8% | 43.5% | 34.6% | 95.0% | |
| | Total | 17.8% | 45.5% | 36.6% | 100.0% | |
| Using Internet | No | 1.9% | 5.0% | 4.0% | 10.9% | .782 |
| | Yes | 15.8% | 41.5% | 31.6% | 89.1% | |
| | Total | 17.8% | 45.5% | 36.6% | 100.0% | |

*Notes:* *$p < 0.05$; N=101.

diploma and undergraduate educational backgrounds are distributed at the intermediate and advanced levels of digital competency (see Table 5.5). This trend illustrates that higher education levels correspond to better digital competency.

Generation X individuals with elementary education backgrounds have the highest percentage at the basic level. Those with junior high school education are mostly distributed at the intermediate level. Gen X individuals with high school education have the highest percentage of digital competency at the intermediate level (63.2 per cent). Gen X individuals with a diploma education show an almost equal distribution of basic, intermediate and advanced level digital competencies. Meanwhile, those with undergraduate educational backgrounds have digital com-

**TABLE 5.5**
**The Relationship of Digital Competency with Educational Background and Generation**

| *Generation* | *Education* | *Digital Competencies* | | | *Total* |
|---|---|---|---|---|---|
| | | *Basic* | *Intermediate* | *Advanced* | |
| Baby boomer | Elementary | 100.0% | 25.0% | 50.0% | 42.9% |
| | Junior High | 0.0% | 25.0% | 50.0% | 28.6% |
| | Senior High | 0.0% | 50.0% | 0.0% | 28.6% |
| | Total | 100.0% | 100.0% | 100.0% | 100.0% |
| | | | | | *p*-value = 0.524 |
| Gen X | Elementary | 40.0% | 0.0% | 11.1% | 13.2% |
| | Junior High | 10.0% | 15.8% | 11.1% | 13.2% |
| | Senior High | 40.0% | 63.2% | 33.3% | 50.0% |
| | Diploma | 10.0% | 15.8% | 11.1% | 13.2% |
| | Bachelor | 0.0% | 5.3% | 33.3% | 10.5% |
| | Total | 100.0% | 100.0% | 100.0% | 100.0% |
| | | | | | *p*-value = 0.046* |
| Millennial | Elementary | 16.7% | 5.3% | 4.2% | 6.1% |
| | Junior High | 16.7% | 26.3% | 0.0% | 12.2% |
| | Senior High | 66.7% | 52.6% | 37.5% | 46.9% |
| | Diploma | 0.0% | 5.3% | 20.8% | 12.2% |
| | Bachelor | 0.0% | 10.5% | 37.5% | 22.4% |
| | | 100.0% | 100.0% | 100.0% | 100.0% |
| | | | | | *p*-value = 0.037* |
| Gen Z | Elementary | 0.0% | 25.0% | 0.0% | 14.3% |
| | Senior High | 100.0% | 75.0% | 100.0% | 85.7% |
| | | 100.0% | 100.0% | 100.0% | 100.0% |
| | | | | | *p*-value = 0.646 |
| Total | Elementary | 33.3% | 6.5% | 8.1% | 11.9% |
| | Junior High | 11.1% | 19.6% | 5.4% | 12.9% |
| | Senior High | 50.0% | 58.7% | 37.8% | 49.5% |
| | Diploma | 5.6% | 8.7% | 16.2% | 10.9% |
| | Bachelor | 0.0% | 6.5% | 32.4% | 14.9% |
| | | 100.0% | 100.0% | 100.0% | 100.0% |
| | | | | | *p*-value = 0.001* |

*Notes:* $^{*}p < 0.05$; N=101.

petencies distributed at the intermediate and advanced levels. The relationship between digital skills and education among Gen X is similar to that observed among millennials, where a higher level of education is associated with better digital competency.

The digital competence of MSME actors encompasses various dimensions, including information management, collaboration, communication and sharing, content and knowledge creation, ethics and responsibility, evaluation, problem-solving, and technical operations. These dimensions are the result of technological, social and cognitive competencies, which are integrated to form digital competency (Ferrari 2013; Vieru et al. 2015). To investigate the relationship between each element of digital competency and education for each generation, a chi-square test was conducted.

The results indicate that information management has a significant relationship with the education level of both Gen X and millennials, with the highest percentage at the senior high school education level for Gen X at the intermediate level (28.9 per cent) and for millennials at the advanced level (22.4 per cent) (see Table 5.6). They suggest that higher education is associated with a higher level of digital competency, particularly in information management. For example, Gen X and millennials with a diploma or bachelor's degree exhibit the highest percentage at the advanced digital competency level.

The results of the chi-square test reveal a significant relationship between the area of collaboration and the education level of millennials. The highest percentage of respondents in this area are those with senior high school education, with their collaboration skills being distributed at two competency levels: the intermediate level (20.4 per cent) and the advanced level (20.4 per cent) (see Table 5.7). Millennials with higher education tend to show a higher percentage of digital competency in this area. For instance, those educated to a diploma or bachelor's level constitute the highest percentage at the advanced digital competency level for collaboration.

Multiple studies have shown that millennials are inclined towards connecting and communicating with others (SMERU Research Institute 2022; Merchant 2012; Mansell 2002), and collaboration can provide them with various benefits such as developing and sharing creative projects and determining the quality and accuracy of online information (Cirilli and Nicolini 2019; Nyikes 2018). Collaboration has the potential to create new business opportunities, particularly for MSME actors who can benefit from marketing their products through various means. This can be achieved through strategy and/or routine collaboration activities with relevant networks that they are connected to or with consumers (Slamet et al. 2017; Hanna, Rohm, and Crittenden 2011).

**TABLE 5.6**
**The Relationship between Information Management and Educational Background by Generation**

| *Generation* | *Education* | *Digital Competency Area* | | | | *p*-value |
|---|---|---|---|---|---|---|
| | | *Information Management* | | | | |
| | | *Basic* | *Intermediate* | *Advanced* | *Total* | |
| Baby boomer | Elementary | 28.6% | 0.0% | 14.3% | 42.9% | .478 |
| | Junior High | 14.3% | 0.0% | 14.3% | 28.6% | |
| | Senior High | 14.3% | 14.3% | 0.0% | 28.6% | |
| | Diploma | 0.0% | 0.0% | 0.0% | 0.0% | |
| | Total | 57.1% | 14.3% | 28.6% | 100.0% | |
| Gen X | Elementary | 10.5% | 0.0% | 2.6% | 13.2% | .021* |
| | Junior High | 2.6% | 2.6% | 7.9% | 13.2% | |
| | Senior High | 5.3% | 28.9%** | 15.8% | 50.0% | |
| | Diploma | 2.6% | 2.6% | 7.9%** | 13.2% | |
| | Bachelor | 0.0% | 2.6% | 7.9%** | 10.5% | |
| | Total | 21.1% | 36.8% | 42.1% | 100.0% | |
| Millennial | Elementary | 4.1% | 0.0% | 2.0% | 6.1% | .018* |
| | Junior High | 2.0% | 8.2% | 2.0% | 12.2% | |
| | Senior High | 6.1% | 18.4% | 22.4%** | 46.9% | |
| | Diploma | 0.0% | 2.0% | 10.2%** | 12.2% | |
| | Bachelor | 0.0% | 4.1% | 18.4%** | 22.4% | |
| | Total | 12.2% | 32.7% | 55.1% | 100.0% | |
| Gen Z | Elementary | 0.0% | 14.3% | 0.0% | 14.3% | .459 |
| | Junior High | 0.0% | 0.0% | 0.0% | 0.0% | |
| | Senior High | 14.3% | 28.6% | 42.9% | 85.7% | |
| | Diploma | 0.0% | 0.0% | 0.0% | 0.0% | |
| | Total | 14.3% | 42.9% | 42.9% | 100.0% | |
| Total | Elementary | 7.9% | 1.0% | 3.0% | 11.9% | .000* |
| | Junior High | 3.0% | 5.0% | 5.0% | 12.9% | |
| | Senior High | 6.9% | 22.8% | 19.8% | 49.5% | |
| | Diploma | 1.0% | 2.0% | 7.9% | 10.9% | |
| | Bachelor | 0.0% | 3.0% | 11.9% | 14.9% | |
| | Total | 18.8% | 33.7% | 47.5% | 100.0% | |

*Notes:* *$p < 0.05$; **highest percentage; N=101.

In this study, a relationship between the content and knowledge creation area and the education of millennials was observed. The highest percentage of competency levels was found among those with senior high school education, distributed across two competency levels, with the

**TABLE 5.7**
**The Relationship between Collaboration and Educational Background by Generation**

| *Generation* | *Education* | *Digital Competency Area* | | | | *p*-value |
|---|---|---|---|---|---|---|
| | | *Collaboration* | | | | |
| | | *Basic* | *Intermediate* | *Advanced* | *Total* | |
| Baby boomer | Elementary | 14.3% | 14.3% | 14.3% | 42.9% | .370 |
| | Junior High | 14.3% | 0.0% | 14.3% | 28.6% | |
| | Senior High | 0.0% | 28.6% | 0.0% | 28.6% | |
| | Diploma | 0.0% | 0.0% | 0.0% | 0.0% | |
| | Total | 28.6% | 42.9% | 28.6% | 100.0% | |
| Gen X | Elementary | 5.3% | 5.3% | 2.6% | 13.2% | .640 |
| | Junior High | 2.6% | 7.9% | 2.6% | 13.2% | |
| | Senior High | 10.5% | 31.6% | 7.9% | 50.0% | |
| | Diploma | 5.3% | 2.6% | 5.3% | 13.2% | |
| | Bachelor | 0.0% | 5.3% | 5.3% | 10.5% | |
| | Total | 23.7% | 52.6% | 23.7% | 100.0% | |
| Millennial | Elementary | 4.1% | 0.0% | 2.0% | 6.1% | .026* |
| | Junior High | 0.0% | 10.2% | 2.0% | 12.2% | |
| | Senior High | 6.1% | 20.4%** | 20.4%** | 46.9% | |
| | Diploma | 0.0% | 4.1% | 8.2%** | 12.2% | |
| | Bachelor | 0.0% | 10.2% | 12.2%** | 22.4% | |
| | Total | 10.2% | 44.9% | 44.9% | 100.0% | |
| Gen Z | Elementary | 0.0% | 14.3% | 0.0% | 14.3% | .495 |
| | Junior High | 0.0% | 0.0% | 0.0% | 0.0% | |
| | Senior High | 0.0% | 57.1% | 28.6% | 85.7% | |
| | Diploma | 0.0% | 0.0% | 0.0% | 0.0% | |
| | Total | 0.0% | 71.4% | 28.6% | 100.0% | |
| Total | Elementary | 5.0% | 4.0% | 3.0% | 11.9% | .081 |
| | Junior High | 2.0% | 7.9% | 3.0% | 12.9% | |
| | Senior High | 6.9% | 27.7% | 14.9% | 49.5% | |
| | Diploma | 2.0% | 3.0% | 5.9% | 10.9% | |
| | Bachelor | 0.0% | 6.9% | 7.9% | 14.9% | |
| | Total | 15.8% | 49.5% | 34.7% | 100.0% | |

*Notes:* *$p < 0.05$; **highest percentage; N=101.

highest percentage at the intermediate level (22.4 per cent), followed by the basic level (20.4 per cent) (see Table 5.8). It was also noted that higher education was associated with higher levels of digital competency in this area. For example, millennials with diploma or bachelor's level education

**TABLE 5.8**
**The Relationship between Content and Knowledge Creation and Educational Background by Generation**

| *Generation* | *Education* | *Digital Competency Area* | | | | *p*-value |
|---|---|---|---|---|---|---|
| | | *Content & Knowledge Creation* | | | | |
| | | *Basic* | *Intermediate* | *Advanced* | *Total* | |
| Baby boomer | Elementary | 28.6% | 14.3% | 0.0% | 42.9% | .907 |
| | Junior High | 14.3% | 14.3% | 0.0% | 28.6% | |
| | Senior High | 14.3% | 14.3% | 0.0% | 28.6% | |
| | Diploma | 0.0% | 0.0% | 0.0% | 0.0% | |
| | Total | 57.1% | 42.9% | 0.0% | 100.0% | |
| Gen X | Elementary | 10.5% | 0.0% | 2.6% | 13.2% | .747 |
| | Junior High | 5.3% | 5.3% | 2.6% | 13.2% | |
| | Senior High | 31.6% | 13.2% | 5.3% | 50.0% | |
| | Diploma | 5.3% | 5.3% | 2.6% | 13.2% | |
| | Bachelor | 2.6% | 5.3% | 2.6% | 10.5% | |
| | Total | 55.3% | 28.9% | 15.8% | 100.0% | |
| Millennial | Elementary | 4.1% | 0.0% | 2.0% | 6.1% | .015* |
| | Junior High | 8.2% | 4.1% | 0.0% | 12.2% | |
| | Senior High | 20.4%** | 22.4%** | 4.1% | 46.9% | |
| | Diploma | 0.0% | 4.1% | 8.2%** | 12.2% | |
| | Bachelor | 2.0% | 12.2% | 8.2%** | 22.4% | |
| | Total | 34.7% | 42.9% | 22.4% | 100.0% | |
| Gen Z | Elementary | 0.0% | 14.3% | 0.0% | 14.3% | .659 |
| | Junior High | 0.0% | 0.0% | 0.0% | 0.0% | |
| | Senior High | 14.3% | 71.4% | 0.0% | 85.7% | |
| | Diploma | 0.0% | 0.0% | 0.0% | 0.0% | |
| | Total | 14.3% | 85.7% | 0.0% | 100.0% | |
| Total | Elementary | 7.9% | 2.0% | 2.0% | 11.9% | .010* |
| | Junior High | 6.9% | 5.0% | 1.0% | 12.9% | |
| | Senior High | 23.8% | 21.8% | 4.0% | 49.5% | |
| | Diploma | 2.0% | 4.0% | 5.0% | 10.9% | |
| | Bachelor | 2.0% | 7.9% | 5.0% | 14.9% | |
| | Total | 42.6% | 40.6% | 16.8% | 100.0% | |

*Notes:* $^{*}p < 0.05$; **highest percentage; N=101.

showed the highest percentage of advanced digital competency levels in content creation and knowledge compared to those with only a senior high school education.

A relationship was also evident between the digital competency area of technical operation and the educational level of millennials. Here, there is a tendency for those with higher education levels to show higher digital competency. For example, most millennials with a diploma or bachelor's

**TABLE 5.9**
**The Relationship between Technical Operation and Educational Background by Generation**

| *Generation* | *Education* | *Digital Competency Area* | | | | *p*-value |
|---|---|---|---|---|---|---|
| | | *Technical Operation* | | | | |
| | | *Basic* | *Intermediate* | *Advanced* | *Total* | |
| Baby boomer | Elementary | 28.6% | 14.3% | 0.0% | 42.9% | .327 |
| | Junior High | 0.0% | 28.6% | 0.0% | 28.6% | |
| | Senior High | 14.3% | 14.3% | 0.0% | 28.6% | |
| | Diploma | 0.0% | 0.0% | 0.0% | 0.0% | |
| | Total | 42.9% | 57.1% | 0.0% | 100.0% | |
| Gen X | Elementary | 10.5% | 0.0% | 2.6% | 13.2% | .294 |
| | Junior High | 7.9% | 5.3% | 0.0% | 13.2% | |
| | Senior High | 18.4% | 26.3% | 5.3% | 50.0% | |
| | Diploma | 2.6% | 7.9% | 2.6% | 13.2% | |
| | Bachelor | 0.0% | 7.9% | 2.6% | 10.5% | |
| | Total | 39.5% | 47.4% | 13.2% | 100.0% | |
| Millennial | Elementary | 2.0% | 2.0% | 6.1% | | .036* |
| | Junior High | 6.1% | 6.1% | 0.0% | 12.2% | |
| | Senior High | 16.3%** | 20.4%** | 10.2% | 46.9% | |
| | Diploma | 0.0% | 2.0% | 10.2%** | 12.2% | |
| | Bachelor | 0.0% | 10.2% | 12.2%** | 22.4% | |
| | Total | 24.5% | 40.8% | 34.7% | 100.0% | |
| Gen Z | Elementary | 14.3% | 0.0% | 0.0% | 14.3% | .233 |
| | Junior High | 0.0% | 0.0% | 0.0% | 0.0% | |
| | Senior High | 14.3% | 57.1% | 14.3% | 85.7% | |
| | Diploma | 0.0% | 0.0% | 0.0% | 0.0% | |
| | Total | 28.6% | 57.1% | 14.3% | 100.0% | |
| Total | Elementary | 7.9% | 2.0% | 2.0% | 11.9% | .000* |
| | Junior High | 5.9% | 6.9% | 0.0% | 12.9% | |
| | Senior High | 16.8% | 24.8% | 7.9% | 49.5% | |
| | Diploma | 1.0% | 4.0% | 5.9% | 10.9% | |
| | Bachelor | 0.0% | 7.9% | 6.9% | 14.9% | |
| | Total | 31.7% | 45.5% | 22.8% | 100.0% | |

*Notes:* *$p < 0.05$; **highest percentage; N=101.

degree have advanced digital competency in this area, compared with those with only a senior high school education.

Several significant findings have emerged from the study:

1. The digital competency variable for MSMEs has a significant relationship with the education variable for Gen X and millennial MSME actors. The higher the education of people from Gen X and the millennial generation, the higher the digital competencies of MSMEs in these two generations. This finding is consistent with previous research conducted by the SMERU Research Institute, which shows that higher education is associated with higher levels of digital literacy (Bachtiar et al. 2020). However, the study's ability to assess the relationship between digital competency and education levels of Gen Z and baby boomers was limited due to the small sample size for these two generations.
2. There is a significant relationship between the millennial generation's education level and their digital competency in the areas of information management, collaboration, content creation and knowledge, and technical operation. The higher their education level, the higher their level of digital competency in these four areas. However, there is no significant relationship between the millennial generation's education level and their digital competency in the areas of communication and sharing, ethics and responsibility, and evaluation and problem-solving (Annex 5.1).
3. Information management is the only area of digital competency significantly correlated with the education level of Gen X. The higher the education level of Gen X, the higher their level of digital competency in information management.

## DISCUSSION

According to the results of this study, there is a significant relationship between various digital competencies and the education of millennial MSME actors. Specifically, higher education levels among millennials are associated with higher digital competencies in areas such as information management area, collaboration, content creation and knowledge, and technical operation. Additionally, the study found that Gen X individuals with higher education exhibit higher levels of collaboration competency.

However, due to the limited number of samples from the baby boomer and Gen Z generations, the findings related to these two generations are inconclusive.

Digitalization has opened boundless opportunities in various sectors. Consequently, one of the key national agendas for digital transformation should be to enhance and cultivate digital competencies. As human resources play a crucial role in the digital ecosystem, individuals must be motivated to become adaptable and competitive in the face of technological changes and various economic challenges.

Stakeholders in MSMEs should prioritize strengthening their business actors' digital skills in various aspects of business management. One way to promote greater digital competencies among MSME actors is through training programmes that focus on improving their digital competency in multiple dimensions. To effectively encourage digital competency, various parties, including MSME actors themselves, the government, and other stakeholders involved in facilitating MSME actors, must work together to prepare MSMEs to seize the opportunities in the digital economy era.

The analysis presented in this chapter relies solely on secondary data obtained from MSMEs located in the West Bandung District. A more comprehensive understanding of the digital competencies of cross-generational MSME actors in Indonesia can be achieved through comparative studies conducted in other regions of the country. Therefore, further research is needed to obtain more conclusive and generalizable findings.

## ANNEX 5.1
## Questionnaire of Digital Competence of MSME Actors

**Digital Competence of MSME Actors**
Instructions: From each of the following statements, circle the answer that best fits you.

SS/SL: Strongly Agree/Always
TS/JR: Disagree/rarely agree
S/SR: Agree/frequently
STS/TP: Strongly Disagree/Never

| *Digital Competency Areas* | *Statement* | *Answer* | | | |
|---|---|---|---|---|---|
| Information Management | I'm looking for information online | SS | S | TS | STS |
| | I get information online from trusted sources | SS | S | TS | STS |
| | I browse information via the Internet and can access and find the information I need | SS | S | TS | STS |
| | I use search engines to get information (e.g., Google, Yahoo Search, Bing) | SS | S | TS | STS |
| | I know how to download information from the Internet | SS | S | TS | STS |
| | I know how to save files, content, and/or information (e.g., text, images, music, videos, web pages) | SS | S | TS | STS |
| | I retrieve files, content, and/or information that I have stored | SS | S | TS | STS |
| | I organize and manage information and content stored in an organized manner | SS | S | TS | STS |
| | | | | | |
| Collaboration | I am using a social network account | SS | S | TS | STS |
| | I participate in social networking sites and/or online community groups or forums | SS | S | TS | STS |
| | I discuss online | SS | S | TS | STS |
| | I actively share knowledge, content, and/or information with others through online communities, social networks, and/or other collaborative media | SS | S | TS | STS |
| | I collaborate or work with others online | SS | S | TS | STS |
| | I collaborate digitally responsibly | SS | S | TS | STS |

| *Digital Competency Areas* | *Statement* | *Answer* | | | |
|---|---|---|---|---|---|
| Communication and Sharing | I interact with other people using communication devices and/or online media (smartphones, social messaging, etc.) | SS | S | TS | STS |
| | I use e-mail to communicate | SS | S | TS | STS |
| | I understand privacy and can protect my privacy and that of others when communicating online | SS | S | TS | STS |
| | I know what information is okay to share online | SS | S | TS | STS |
| | I protect the communication and digital devices used (using passwords, antivirus software, etc.) | SS | S | TS | STS |
| | I communicate online in an ethical manner | SS | S | TS | STS |
| | I am aware of inappropriate behaviour when communicating online | SS | S | TS | STS |
| | I share content and information (text, images, photos, and videos) via digital devices | SS | S | TS | STS |
| | | | | | |
| Content and Knowledge Creation | I can create digital content in various formats (e.g., text, images, music, videos, web pages) and/or use several tools (digital devices) to create digital content | SS | S | TS | STS |
| | I can edit, correct, and change back (modify) digital content that has been created | SS | S | TS | STS |
| | I can create new digital content by combining multiple digital contents | SS | S | TS | STS |
| | I am applying basic programming to make changes to software or applications | SS | S | TS | STS |
| | I can create, modify, or write source code and do programming in a programming language | SS | S | TS | STS |
| | I can innovate and create with my previous knowledge | SS | S | TS | STS |

*continued on next page*

**ANNEX 5.1 — *cont'd***

| *Digital Competency Areas* | *Statement* | *Answer* | | | |
|---|---|---|---|---|---|
| Ethics and Responsibility | I know the ethics of interacting online and apply them responsibly | SS | S | TS | STS |
| | I know the negative and positive aspects of using technology (digital devices) and the Internet | SS | S | TS | STS |
| | I am aware of some of the differences between digital licences and intellectual property rights (e.g., copyright, copyleft, creative commons) | SS | S | TS | STS |
| | I know about the laws and regulations that apply to interacting online | SS | S | TS | STS |
| | | | | | |
| Evaluation and Problem-solving | I can choose what applications I need to market my MSME products or services | SS | S | TS | STS |
| | I know which digital devices I must use in my business | SS | S | TS | STS |
| | I can choose information based on my requirements | SS | S | TS | STS |
| | I can assess, validate and/or re-evaluate information obtained online or via digital devices | SS | S | TS | STS |
| | I learnt to do something new through technology | SS | S | TS | STS |
| | I can improve my knowledge and skills related to technology and digital | SS | S | TS | STS |
| | I can put my ICT knowledge and skills to use in business | SS | S | TS | STS |
| | I can use technology to solve a problem | SS | S | TS | STS |
| | | | | | |

| *Digital Competency Areas* | *Statement* | *Answer* | | | |
|---|---|---|---|---|---|
| Technical Operation | I know the hardware specifications of the ICT devices | SS | S | TS | STS |
| | I understand how to install software on ICT devices | SS | S | TS | STS |
| | I know how to install applications on mobile devices | SS | S | TS | STS |
| | I can use technology and media devices in my business (computer, laptop) | SS | S | TS | STS |
| | In my business, I can use technology and mobile media (smartphone, tablet, etc.) | SS | S | TS | STS |
| | I can use office applications for my business | SS | S | TS | STS |
| | I can use an e-commerce application | SS | S | TS | STS |

## ANNEX 5.2
## Chi-square Test

**Table A5.2.1: The Relationship between Communication and Sharing and Educational Background by Generation**

| *Generation* | *Education* | *Digital Competency Area* | | | | *p*-value |
|---|---|---|---|---|---|---|
| | | *Communication and Sharing* | | | | |
| | | *Basic* | *Intermediate* | *Advanced* | *Total* | |
| Baby boomer | Elementary<br>Junior High<br>Senior High<br>Diploma | | 28.6%<br>0.0%<br>28.6% | 14.3%<br>28.6%<br>0.0% | 42.9%<br>28.6%<br>28.6% | .118 |
| | Total | | 57.1% | 42.9% | 100.0% | |
| Gen X | Elementary<br>Junior High<br>Senior High<br>Diploma<br>Bachelor | 2.6%<br>2.6%<br>7.9%<br>2.6%<br>0.0% | 7.9%<br>5.3%<br>26.3%<br>7.9%<br>5.3% | 2.6%<br>5.3%<br>15.8%<br>2.6%<br>5.3% | 13.2%<br>13.2%<br>50.0%<br>13.2%<br>10.5% | .980 |
| | Total | 15.8% | 52.6% | 31.6% | 100.0% | |
| Millennial | Elementary<br>Junior High<br>Senior High<br>Diploma<br>Bachelor | 2.0%<br>2.0%<br>4.1%<br>0.0%<br>0.0% | 2.0%<br>8.2%<br>26.5%<br>4.1%<br>4.1% | 2.0%<br>2.0%<br>16.3%<br>8.2%<br>18.4% | 6.1%<br>12.2%<br>46.9%<br>12.2%<br>22.4% | .113 |
| | Total | 8.2% | 44.9% | 46.9% | 100.0% | |
| Gen Z | Elementary<br>Junior High<br>Senior High<br>Diploma | 0.0%<br><br>14.3% | 14.3%<br><br>28.6% | 0.0%<br><br>42.9% | 14.3%<br><br>85.7% | .459 |
| | Total | 14.3% | 42.9% | 42.9% | 100.0% | |
| Total | Elementary<br>Junior High<br>Senior High<br>Diploma<br>Bachelor | 2.0%<br>2.0%<br>5.9%<br>1.0%<br>0.0% | 6.9%<br>5.9%<br>26.7%<br>5.0%<br>4.0% | 3.0%<br>5.0%<br>16.8%<br>5.0%<br>10.9% | 11.9%<br>12.9%<br>49.5%<br>10.9%<br>14.9% | .288 |
| | Total | 10.9% | 48.5% | 40.6% | 100.0% | |

*Notes:* $^*p < 0.05$; N=101.
*Source:* Processed by the authors.

**Table A5.2.2: The Relationship between Ethics and Responsibility and Educational Background by Generation**

| *Generation* | *Education* | *Digital Competency Area* | | | | *p*-value |
|---|---|---|---|---|---|---|
| | | *Ethics and Responsibility* | | | | |
| | | *Basic* | *Intermediate* | *Advanced* | *Total* | |
| Baby boomer | Elementary | 14.3% | 0.0% | 28.6% | 42.9% | .524 |
| | Junior High | 0.0% | 0.0% | 28.6% | 28.6% | |
| | Senior High | 0.0% | 28.6% | 0.0% | 28.6% | |
| | Diploma | | | | | |
| | Total | 14.3% | 28.6% | 57.1% | 100.0% | |
| Gen X | Elementary | 10.5% | 0.0% | 2.6% | 13.2% | .649 |
| | Junior High | 2.6% | 7.9% | 2.6% | 13.2% | |
| | Senior High | 10.5% | 23.7% | 15.8% | 50.0% | |
| | Diploma | 5.3% | 2.6% | 5.3% | 13.2% | |
| | Bachelor | 0.0% | 5.3% | 5.3% | 10.5% | |
| | Total | 28.9% | 39.5% | 31.6% | 100.0% | |
| Millennial | Elementary | 2.0% | 2.0% | 2.0% | 6.1% | .175 |
| | Junior High | 2.0% | 8.2% | 2.0% | 12.2% | |
| | Senior High | 6.1% | 22.4% | 18.4% | 46.9% | |
| | Diploma | 0.0% | 4.1% | 8.2% | 12.2% | |
| | Bachelor | 0.0% | 6.1% | 16.3% | 22.4% | |
| | Total | 10.2% | 42.9% | 46.9% | 100.0% | |
| Gen Z | Elementary | | 14.3% | 0.0% | 14.3% | .659 |
| | Junior High | | | | | |
| | Senior High | | 71.4% | 14.3% | 85.7% | |
| | Diploma | | | | | |
| | Total | | 85.7% | 14.3% | 100.0% | |
| Total | Elementary | 5.9% | 2.0% | 4.0% | 11.9% | .112 |
| | Junior High | 2.0% | 6.9% | 4.0% | 12.9% | |
| | Senior High | 6.9% | 26.7% | 15.8% | 49.5% | |
| | Diploma | 2.0% | 3.0% | 5.9% | 10.9% | |
| | Bachelor | 0.0% | 5.0% | 9.9% | 14.9% | |
| | Total | 16.8% | 43.6% | 39.6% | 100.0% | |

*Note:* N=101
*Source:* Processed by the authors.

**Table A5.2.3: The Relationship between Evaluation and Problem-Solving and Educational Background by Generation**

| *Generation* | *Education* | *Digital Competency Area* | | | | *p*-value |
|---|---|---|---|---|---|---|
| | | *Evaluation & Problem Solving* | | | | |
| | | *Basic* | *Intermediate* | *Advanced* | *Total* | |
| Baby boomer | Elementary | 14.3% | 0.0% | 28.6% | 42.9% | .086 |
| | Junior High | 0.0% | 0.0% | 28.6% | 28.6% | |
| | Senior High | 0.0% | 28.6% | 0.0% | 28.6% | |
| | Diploma | | | | | |
| | Total | 14.3% | 28.6% | 57.1% | 100.0% | |
| Gen X | Elementary | 10.5% | 0.0% | 2.6% | 13.2% | .214 |
| | Junior High | 2.6% | 7.9% | 2.6% | 13.2% | |
| | Senior High | 10.5% | 23.7% | 15.8% | 50.0% | |
| | Diploma | 5.3% | 2.6% | 5.3% | 13.2% | |
| | Bachelor | 0.0% | 5.3% | 5.3% | 10.5% | |
| | Total | 28.9% | 39.5% | 31.6% | 100.0% | |
| Millennial | Elementary | 2.0% | 2.0% | 2.0% | 6.1% | .332 |
| | Junior High | 2.0% | 8.2% | 2.0% | 12.2% | |
| | Senior High | 6.1% | 22.4% | 18.4% | 46.9% | |
| | Diploma | 0.0% | 4.1% | 8.2% | 12.2% | |
| | Bachelor | 0.0% | 6.1% | 16.3% | 22.4% | |
| | Total | 10.2% | 42.9% | 46.9% | 100.0% | |
| Gen Z | Elementary | | 14.3% | 0.0% | 14.3% | .659 |
| | Junior High | | | | | |
| | Senior High | | 71.4% | 14.3% | 85.7% | |
| | Diploma | | | | | |
| | Total | | 85.7% | 14.3% | 100.0% | |
| Total | Elementary | 5.9% | 2.0% | 4.0% | 11.9% | .011* |
| | Junior High | 2.0% | 6.9% | 4.0% | 12.9% | |
| | Senior High | 6.9% | 26.7% | 15.8% | 49.5% | |
| | Diploma | 2.0% | 3.0% | 5.9% | 10.9% | |
| | Bachelor | 0.0% | 5.0% | 9.9% | 14.9% | |
| | Total | 16.8% | 43.6% | 39.6% | 100.0% | |

*Notes:* *$p < 0.05$; N=101

*Source:* Processed by the authors.

## References

Ala-Mutka, Kirsti. 2011. *Mapping Digital Competence: Towards a Conceptual Understanding.* Technical Note JRC 67075, 2011. Joint Research Centre (JRC). Seville: Institute for Prospective Technological Studies. https://www.academia.edu/42521335/Mapping_Digital_Competence_Towards_a_Conceptual_Understanding

Ashurst, Colin, Paul Cragg, and Pauline Herring. 2012. "The Role of IT Competences in Gaining Value from E-Business: An SME Case Study". *International Small Business Journal* 30, no. 6: 64058. https://doi.org/10.1177/0266242610375703

Bachtiar, Palmira Permata, Rendy Adriyan Diningrat, Ahmad Zuhdi Dwi Kusuma, Ridho Al Izzati, and Abella Diandra. 2020. *Who Is Digital Economy for? Toward an Inclusive Digital Economy in Indonesia.* Report, December 2020. SMERU Research Institute. https://smeru.or.id/id/publication-id/ekonomi-digital-untuk-siapa-menuju-ekonomi-digital-yang-inklusif-di-indonesia

Badan Pusat Statistik (BPS). 2017. *Keadaan Angkatan Kerja di Indonesia.* August 2017. Catalog Number: 2303004, 30 November 2017. https://www.bps.go.id/publication/2017/11/30/0daa04d8d9e8e30e43a55d1a/keadaan-angkatan-kerja-di-indonesia-agustus-2017.html

———, and Kementerian Pemberdayaan Perempuan dan Perlindungan Anak (KPPA). 2018. *Profil Generasi Milenial Indonesia.* https://www.kemenpppa.go.id/lib/uploads/list/9acde-buku-profil-generasi-milenia.pdf

BPSDMP Kominfo Bandung. 2019. "Penelitian Aspirasi Daerah: Kompetensi Digital Pelaku Usaha Mikro Kecil Menengah Kabupaten Bandung Barat". Bandung.

Calvani, Antonio, Antonio Fini, and Maria Ranieri. 2010. "Digital Competence in K-12. Theoretical Models, Assessment Tools and Empirical Research". *Anàlisi: quaderns de comunicació i cultura* 40, (November): 157–71. https://ddd.uab.cat/pub/analisi/02112175n40/02112175n40p157.pdf

Carretero, Stephanie, Riina Vuorikari, and Yves Punie. 2017. "DigComp 2.1: The Digital Competence Framework for Citizens with Eight Proficiency Levels and Examples of Use". Joint Research Centre, 3 May 2017. https://apo.org.au/node/221736

Choi, Soon-Yong, and Andrew B. Whinston. 2000. "The Future of the Digital Economy". In *Handbook on Electronic Commerce,* edited by Michael Shaw, Robert Blanning, Troy Strader, and Andrew Whinston, pp. 25–52. Heidelberg: Springer Berlin Heidelberg. https://doi.org/10.1007/978-3-642-58327-8_2

Cirilli, Elisa, and Paola Nicolini. 2019. "Digital Skills and Profile of Each Generation: A Review". *International Journal of Developmental and Educational Psychology* 3, no. 1:487–96. https://doi.org/10.17060/ijodaep.2019.n1.v3.1525

Deal, J.J., D.G. Altman, and S.G. Rogelberg. 2010. "Millennials at Work: What

We Know and What We Need to Do (If Anything)". *J Bus Psychol* 25: 191–99. https://doi.org/10.1007/s10869-010-9177-2

Deloitte. 2015. "SMEs Powering Indonesia's Success: The Connected Archipelago's Growth Engine". Sydney: Deloitte Access Economics.

Deursen, Alexander J.A.M. van, and Jan van Dijk. 2011. "Internet Skills and the Digital Divide". *New Media and Society* 13, no. 6: 893–911. https://doi.org/10.1177/1461444810386774

———, and Jan van Dijk. 2019. "The First-Level Digital Divide Shifts from Inequalities in Physical Access to Inequalities in Material Access". *New Media and Society* 21, no. 2: 354–75. https://doi.org/10.1177/1461444818797082

———, Ellen J. Helsper, and Rebecca Eynon. 2014. *Measuring Digital Skills: From Digital Skills to Tangible Outcomes*. Project Report 2014. London School of Economics and Political Science, University of Twente, Oxford Internet Institute, University of Oxford. https://www.lse.ac.uk/media-and-communications/assets/documents/research/projects/disto/Measuring-Digital-Skills.pdf

Dijk, Johannes A.G.M van. 2012. "The Evolution of the Digital Divide: The Digital Divide Turns to Inequality of Skills and Usage". In *Digital Enlightenment Yearbook 2012*, edited by Jacques Bus, Malcolm Crompton, Mireille Hildebrandt, and George Metakides, pp. 57–75. IOS Press.

Eurostat. 2020. "Do Young People in the EU Have Digital Skills?". https://ec.europa.eu/eurostat/en/web/products-eurostat-news/-/edn-20200715-1

Fan, Qiuyan. 2016. "Factors Affecting Adoption of Digital Business: Evidence from Australia". *Global Journal of Business Research* 10, no. 3: 79–84.

Ferrari, Anusca. 2013. "DIGCOMP: A Framework for Developing and Understanding Digital Competence in Europe". Report EUR 26035 EN and JRC83167. Publications Office of the European Union, Luxembourg.

Graham, Melissa. W. 2014. "Government Communication in the Digital Age: Social Media's Effect on Local Government Public Relations". *Public Relations Inquiry* 3, no. 3: 361–76. https://doi.org/10.1177/2046147X14545371

Gyr, Alex, Lisa Friedman, and Herman Gyr. 2010. "The Changing Audience in the Digital Era". Enterprise Development Group, p. 112.

Hanna, Richard, Andrew Rohm, and Victoria L. Crittenden. 2011. "We're All Connected: The Power of the Social Media Ecosystem". *Business Horizons* 54, no. 3: 265–73. https://doi.org/10.1016/j.bushor.2011.01.007

Harison, Elad, and Albert Boonstra. 2009. "Essential Competencies for Technochange Management: Towards an Assessment Model". *International Journal of Information Management* 29, no. 4: 28394. https://doi.org/10.1016/j.ijinfomgt.2008.11.003

Ifinedo, Princely. 2011. "Internet/E-business Technologies Acceptance in Canada's SMEs: An Exploratory Investigation". *Internet Research* 21, no. 3: 255–81. https://doi.org/10.1108/10662241111139309

Jensen, Henrik Valentin, Sebastiano Tofalleti, Clare Thornley, and Sinéad Murnane.

2016. *Digital Skills for SMEs: Get Inspired Now!* Project Report, 4 October 2016. European Commission, Brussels. http://ec.europa.eu/newsroom/dae/document.cfm?action=display&doc_id=15027

Kim, Yeolib, Daniel A. Briley, and Melissa G. Ocepek. 2015. "Differential Innovation of Smartphone and Application Use by Sociodemographics and Personality". *Computers in Human Behavior* 44 (March): 141–47. https://doi.org/10.1016/j.chb.2014.11.059

Kusumaningtyas, Nurhidayati, and Dyna Herlina Suwarto. 2015. "ICT Adoption, Skill and Use Differences among Small and Medium Enterprises Managers Based on Demographic Factors". *Procedia - Social and Behavioral Sciences* 169 (August 2014): 296302. https://doi.org/10.1016/j.sbspro.2015.01.313

Livingstone, Sonia. 2003. "The Changing Nature and Uses of Media Literacy". MEDIA @ LSE Electronic Working Papers, no. 4. http://eprints.lse.ac.uk/13476/1/The_changing_nature_and_uses_of_media_literacy.pdf

MacGregor, Rob, and Lejla Vrazalic. 2008. "A Profile of Australian Regional SME Non-Adopters of E-Commerce". *Small Enterprise Research* 16, no. 1: 27–46. https://doi.org/10.5172/ser.16.1.27

Maguire, S., Lenny S.C. Koh, and A. Magrys. 2007. "The Adoption of E-business and Knowledge Management in SMEs". *Benchmarking: An International Journal* 14, no. 1: 37–58. https://doi.org/10.1108/14635770710730928

Mansell, Robin. 2002. "From Digital Divides to Digital Entitlements in Knowledge Societies". *Current Sociology* 50, no. 3: 407–26. https://doi.org/10.1177/0011392102050003007

Merchant, Guy. 2012. "Unravelling the Social Network: Theory and Research". *Learning, Media and Technology* 37, no. 1: 419.

Nuvriasari, Audita. 2012. "Peran Dukungan Organisasional, Kompetensi Teknologi dan Lingkungan Eksternal dalam Rangka Mendorong Pengadopsian E-Commerce pada Usaha Kecil Menengah". *Jurnal Siasat Bisnis* 16, no. 2 (2012): 205–17. https://journal.uii.ac.id/JSB/article/view/3302

Nyikes, Zoltán. 2018. "Digital Competence and the Safety Awareness Base on the Assessments Results of the Middle East-European Generations". *Procedia Manufacturing* 22: 916–22. https://doi.org/10.1016/j.promfg.2018.03.130

Oblinger, Diana G., and James L. Oblinger, eds. 2005. *Educating the Net Generation*. https://www.educause.edu/ir/library/PDF/pub7101.PDF

Pavlou, Paul A., and Omar A. El Sawy. 2006. "From IT Leveraging Competence to Competitive Advantage in Turbulent Environments: The Case of New Product Development". *Information Systems Research* 17, no. 3: 198–227. https://doi.org/10.1287/isre.1060.0094

Sarosa, Samiaji. 2012. "Adoption of Social Media Networks by Indonesian SME: A Case Study". *Procedia Economics and Finance* 4, 2012: 244–54. https://doi.org/10.1016/s2212-5671(12)00339-5

Slamet, Rachmat, Bilpen Nainggolan, Roessobiyatno Roessobiyatno, Heru Ramdani, Agung Hendriyanto, and Luk Lu'ul Ilma. 2017. "Strategi Pengembangan Ukm Digital Dalam Menghadapi Era Pasar Bebas". *Jurnal Manajemen Indonesia* 16, no. 2: 136. https://doi.org/10.25124/jmi.v16i2.319

SMERU Research Institute, The. 2022. "Digital Skills Landscape in Indonesia". *Digital Skills Landscape in Indonesia* (April): 15.

Tarutė, Asta, and Rimantas Gatautis. 2014. "ICT Impact on SMEs Performance". *Procedia—Social and Behavioral Sciences* 110 (24 January 2014): 1218–25. https://doi.org/10.1016/j.sbspro.2013.12.968

Vieru, Dragos. 2015. "Towards a Multi-Dimensional Model of Digital Competence in Small- and Medium-Sized Enterprises". In *Encyclopedia of Information Science and Technology*. 3rd ed., pp. 6715–25. USA: IGI Global. https://doi.org/10.4018/978-1-4666-5888-2.ch660

———, Simon Bourdeau, Amelie Bernier, and Severin Yapo. 2015. "Digital Competence: A Multi-Dimensional Conceptualization and a Typology in an SME Context". In *Proceedings of the Annual Hawaii International Conference on System Sciences 2015* (March): 4681–90. https://doi.org/10.1109/HICSS.2015.557

Vrontis, Demetris, Gianpaolo Basile, M. Simona Andreano, Andrea Mazzitelli, and Ioanna Papasolomou. 2020. "The Profile of Innovation Driven Italian SMEs and the Relationship Between the Firms' Networking Abilities and Dynamic Capabilities". *Journal of Business Research* 114 (June): 313–24. https://doi.org/10.1016/j.jbusres.2020.04.009

Zemke, R., C. Raines, and B. Filipczak. 2000. *Generations at Work: Managing the Clash of Veterans, Boomers, Xers and Nexters in Your Workplace*. New York: AMACOM Books.

# 6

# Millennial Muslims and "Haram Fatwas" on Cryptocurrency in Contemporary Indonesia

Endi Aulia Garadian and Harun Arrasyid

## ABSTRACT

*This chapter explores how Muslim millennials construe the "haram fatwas" on cryptocurrencies, especially Bitcoin. The term "haram fatwas" in this context refers to the legal opinions (fatwas) issued by Indonesia's religious authorities that deem cryptocurrencies to be impermissible under Islamic law (haram). Muslim millennials are presented with a dilemma in which their religious ideals clash with their interest in trading for financial gain. On the one hand, religious authorities forbid them to profit from trading in cryptocurrency, while, on the other hand, they believe that trading in cryptocurrencies may increase their asset values multiple times. This chapter demonstrates that when confronted with a delicate interaction between religion and economics, millennials tend to be secular and simply think about the profit margin. Furthermore, some of them compensate for having compromised their faith by donating the bulk of their cryptocurrency trading profits. For them, this is a means to atone for their sins after partaking in religiously forbidden activities. Data for this chapter was derived from statements made by millennials in open Telegram groups. The data helped to provide a comprehensive understanding of Indonesian millennials' perceptions of the fatwas forbidding cryptocurrencies and the cryptocurrency trading context in general.*

## INTRODUCTION

Cryptocurrency fever has afflicted the Indonesian millennial generation, that is, anyone born between the 1980s and 1996 (Irawanto 2019). Aside from an increase in searches for the word "crypto" on Google Trends Indonesia from 2020 to 2022, conversations about this asset are becoming more common on YouTube and Telegram. Millennials produce almost all the content on cryptocurrencies (Allcot 2021). Notable channels include those run by millennials like Kevin Sailly,[1] Andy Senjaya,[2] Ngomongin Uang (Glenn Ardi),[3] Felicia Putri Tjiasaka,[4] and Kasisolusi (Deryansha).[5] Since the outbreak of the COVID-19 pandemic, the millennial generation has become one of the most important agents in the growth of cryptocurrencies in Indonesia. This trend is similar to that in the United States, where 49 per cent of millennials feel comfortable with cryptocurrencies (Royal 2021). One possible explanation is that millennials are regarded as the generation that fully utilizes the Internet (Vogels 2019). Use of the Internet involves everyday tasks like interacting with others, shopping, working and earning money.

Despite millennials' enthusiasm for cryptocurrencies, the Indonesian authorities have been prohibiting cryptocurrencies since 2015. This is particularly the case with Bitcoin, the first and most popular cryptocurrency. One of the reasons is that cryptocurrency assets are highly volatile, making them riskier than any other investment asset, such as stocks and bonds. Several regulations worth mentioning are Law no. 7 of 2011 regarding Currency, and Bank Indonesia Regulation no. 17 of 2015 regarding the Obligation to Use Rupiah in the Territory of the Republic of Indonesia. In line with the government's rulings, formal legal opinions forbidding cryptocurrencies and Bitcoin were also issued by religious authorities from Majelis Ulama Indonesia, Indonesian's apex body of Islamic scholars, and the country's two largest Islamic mass organizations, Muhammadiyah and Nahdlatul Ulama. These legal opinions are collectively termed the "haram fatwas". The major reasons cryptocurrencies, particularly Bitcoin, are prohibited by religious authorities are their uncertainty (*gharar*), gambling (*qimar*) and harmful (*dharar*) natures.

Fatwas issued by religious authorities are typically given broader publicity by the media. Multiple sources state that the fatwas, despite their lack of legal weight, may discourage Muslims from investing in cryptocurrencies and cause local financial institutions to reconsider their own investments in cryptocurrency assets. We collected 1,263 comments carrying the words "crypto", "fatwa", "halal," and "haram" from YouTube (Figure 6.1). The data shows that the word "haram" was frequently used from 29 October 2021 to 14 April 2022. It also indicates rising awareness among YouTube users of the haram fatwas.

However, it appears that those fatwas have had no influence on supporters of cryptocurrencies. After the fatwas were issued in late 2021, the number of cryptocurrency investors increased significantly (Primadhyta

**FIGURE 6.1**
**Frequency of Terms in YouTube Comments Regarding the Haram Fatwas**

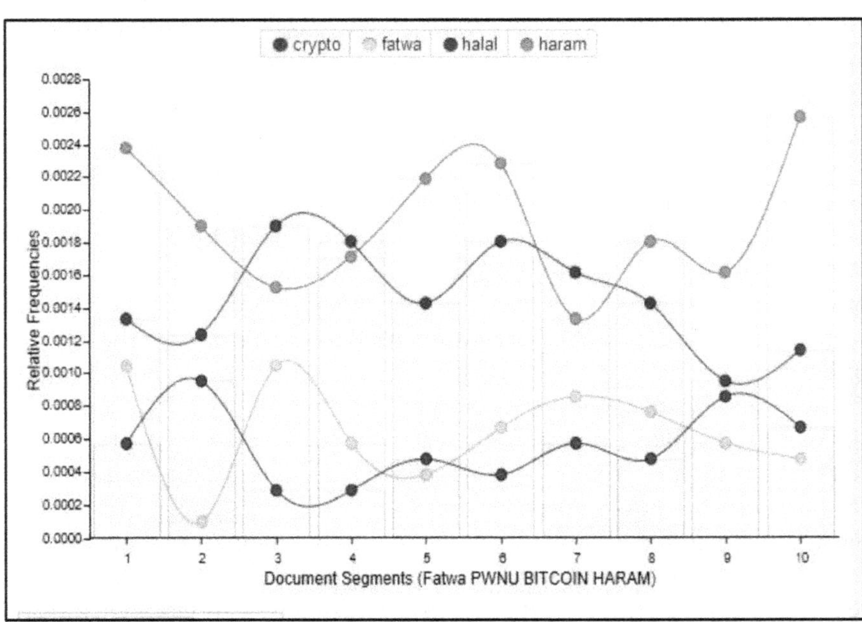


*Source:* Data derived from a YouTube channel named "Cryptoiz research", 2022.

2021), from 7 million in 2021 to 15.1 million as of June 2022 (Putri 2022). Among those numbers, the majority were millennial and Generation Z investors (Purwanti 2022). Considering that more than 80 per cent of Indonesia's population are Muslims, it is reasonable to assume that the majority of Indonesia's cryptocurrency investors are Muslims.

Numerous celebrity preachers, such as Gus Miftah, Abdul Somad and Yusuf Mansur, have refrained from forbidding the use of cryptocurrencies. They suggest that cryptocurrencies may become broadly acceptable assets or currencies in the future. In February 2022, Wirda Mansur, a 22-year-old Muslim millennial crypto influencer (Putsanra 2023) and the eldest daughter of Ustaz Yusuf Mansur, even launched a cryptocurrency coin called "I-COIN". It was founded to capitalize on the enthusiasm of Indonesia's young Muslim investors. Wirda promised that the coin would bring huge profits for those who joined its pre-sale (Primadhyta 2022).

This chapter explores how Muslim millennials construe the haram fatwas on cryptocurrencies, particularly Bitcoin. It asks whether the fatwas have any influence on the crypto-investing practices of millennial Muslims. If they have no effect, then why is it so? What is the most plausible explanation for the fatwas having no weight? To answer this question, we conducted a qualitative and quantitative analysis of open group discussions on the instant messaging platform Telegram between 7 January 2021 and 20 July 2022. First, we identified various crypto-focused open Telegram groups. Telegram was chosen because it is the most effective platform for easily mobilizing cryptocurrency investors, especially for attracting investors to "pump-and-dump" schemes.[6] Moreover, in the Indonesian context, cryptocurrency discussions are more active on Telegram rather than Twitter. The discussions and active members of the Telegram groups were important aspects for describing the dialectics between millennials. We then collected the data from Telegram's "Export Chat History" feature. Second, we filtered the data and keywords such as "halal" (permissible) and "haram". This was done using Microsoft Excel. We got 5,165 comments on discussions relating to haram and halal in the context of cryptocurrencies.

## CRYPTOCURRENCY: INVESTMENT, TRADING AND GAMBLING

A cryptocurrency is a digital currency that is designed to function as a means of exchange via a computer network and is not heavily reliant on any central authority, such as a government or bank, to support or maintain it. It is based on what is known as blockchain technology, which is a form of distributed ledger that can identify and prove the existence and ownership of digital assets. Simply put, cryptocurrency is a form of currency that speeds up transactions by utilizing computers. However, cryptocurrencies have served not only as a means of exchange but also as investment assets. Some have hit the jackpot by purchasing various cryptocurrencies such as Bitcoin (BTC), Ethereum (ETH), Binance coin (BNB) and Cardano (ADA).

New young millionaires emerge one after another on social media platforms such as Twitter and TikTok. Furthermore, the COVID-19 pandemic has swiftly contributed to the changing nature of cryptocurrencies from being merely digital breakthrough currencies to investment assets. The social distancing policy induced people of various generations, not just millennials, to earn money from home by buying and selling cryptocurrencies (Sifat 2021). In addition to being an investment asset, cryptocurrencies are also traded between investors and traders, who take advantage of the pricing disparity.

But what precisely are cryptocurrencies? Why do some people regard them as an investment asset and a tradeable commodity, while others regard them as tantamount to Ponzi schemes and a form of gambling? This chapter will first explain cryptocurrencies as investment assets. The essence of investing is purchasing something in the present with the expectation that its value will increase over time. From the perspective of investors, land, commodities (gold and silver), property, stocks and cryptocurrencies all have the same mechanism: "buy low, sell high".[7]

Every cryptocurrency exchanger has access to "spot" (spot market) as an asset. Spot is a "virtual market" in which investors can purchase as well as sell crypto assets and then wait for their value to climb. Generally, investors or traders will purchase cryptocurrencies at a low price and hold them until their value rises before selling them. Because of the nature of spot trading, this kind of investing or trading allows you to hold your crypto token or coin for an extended period. For example, if an investor purchases Bitcoin for $10,000, he or she would want to sell it only when the price of Bitcoin rises above $10,000. The investor or trader can wait for an indefinite period until the price hits the ideal target. In addition, you can only purchase the asset with your own money on the spot market. This means that you can buy only as much as you can afford. However, it must be kept in mind that earnings are realized only when you trade your cryptocurrency for fiat currency such as the US dollar.

At first look, cryptocurrency transactions on the spot market are similar to buying and selling stocks on the stock market. Indeed, cryptocurrencies are not entirely risk-free financial instruments. Many nations have still not made lawful the status of cryptocurrencies as an asset. As a result, cryptocurrencies are not typically seen as a viable investment option compared with other financial products such as stocks and bonds. This then makes cryptocurrency transactions a gamble rather than an investment. Whether or not the purchase of crypto assets constitutes gambling or not is determined by each investor's behaviour. It is common for people to purchase an asset without doing due diligence or sufficient research. Many investors are influenced by exaggerated narratives of an asset's future valuation (Shiller 2019). People buy something in the hope of winning the lottery simply because of the narrative that circulates in the public space. This then makes the purchase of cryptocurrencies a form of gambling (Delfabbro et al. 2021).

Aside from that, the fact that Bitcoin has leverage facilities makes it unsuitable as an investment instrument. Several cryptocurrency trading exchanges, including Binance, BingX and FTX, provide this leverage function. As in the stock market, leverage in cryptocurrency transactions entails borrowing a portion of the funds required to purchase a cryptocurrency. Typically, the funds are borrowed from an exchange site. Trading with high leverage provides people with huge profits but at significant risk. Leverage, often known as "margin trading", is the use of a smaller amount of capital to gain exposure to greater trading positions.

In the financial market, the term "margin" refers to the collateral that an investor must deposit with their broker or exchange to cover the credit risk that the holder offers to the broker or exchange. Credit risk is created when an investor borrows money from a broker to buy financial products, borrows money to sell them short, or enters into a derivative transaction. Assume you have $20 in cash to deposit into your account and spend on cryptocurrency trading. If your leverage is 5:1, your broker adds 5 times the original value of your cash, allowing you to make a trade valued at $100. If you were given 10:1 leverage or 10 per cent margin, you could trade $200 because each dollar represents 10 per cent of the whole deal, which amounts to $10 with the leverage. If the leverage was 20:1, or a 5 per cent margin, you could trade $400 for a $20 investment.

Even though leverage appears to make it easier for investors with low capital to enter the cryptocurrency market, many religious authorities still forbid the use of the practice by Muslims when trading or investing in financial assets. The use of leverage is complicated by the fact that it employs instruments such as options and futures, which violate the essence of a sound, Sharia-compliant contract (Usmani 2015).

Moreover, margin trading entails entering into an interest-bearing contract with the broker. A *hadith* prohibiting interest says, "The Messenger of Allah, Allah bless him and give him peace, cursed the one who takes interest, the one who gives it, the one who writes [the contract], and those who witness it" (cited in Qadri 2019).

The collapse of cryptocurrencies in 2022 (La Monic 2022), combined with several global economic crises, pushed their status in society closer to a Ponzi scheme or gambling asset. Anyone who bought cryptocurrencies during the late 2021 peak may today feel as though they had been dealt a dud hand. The combination of a falling valuation, numerous horror stories of life savings being frozen in the accounts of crypto companies (such as the now-bankrupt crypto-lending companies Celsius Network and FTX [Wells 2022]), governmental intervention such as China's ban on crypto mining, and the general volatile and unpredictable nature of the crypto beast makes investment in cryptocurrencies less than appealing (Smith 2022).

## CRYPTOCURRENCIES IN THE ISLAMICATE WORLD: PROS AND CONS

Having grasped the nature of cryptocurrencies as investment and trading assets, currencies, and digital gambling machines, it is critical to understand how state and religious authorities in various parts of the Islamic world regard this commodity. This chapter notes that there are numerous restrictions involving cryptocurrencies, both from the state and religious authorities. As it is, all Islamic countries have various viewpoints on cryptocurrencies. Some states reject them, while many others accept them with conditions.

According to the Library of Congress (2018), the Central Bank of the United Arab Emirates (UAE) does not recognize cryptocurrencies as a form of payment yet. However, the central bank is working on a new regulation for retail payment services to introduce the concept of tokens that could be used for payment purposes (Library of Congress 2018).

Moreover, in November 2020, the UAE's Securities and Commodities Authority published the Chairman of the Authority's Board of Directors' Decision No. (23/Chairman) of 2020 Concerning Crypto Assets Activities Regulation. The decision establishes a regulatory framework for the offering, issuance, listing and trading of crypto assets and requires that crypto asset providers must be incorporated onshore (Securities and Commodities Authority, UAE).

In Egypt, Grand Mufti Shawki Allam ushered in the year 2018 with a harsh fatwa declaring that Bitcoin transactions lead to "fraud, betrayal and ignorance". Allam further stated that terrorist and criminal organizations can utilize cryptocurrencies to fund illegal activities such as the transportation of drugs and weapons (BBC 2018).

In Turkey, the Central Bank of the Republic of Turkey issued a regulation on 16 April 2021 prohibiting, as of 30 April 2021, the use of cryptocurrencies, including Bitcoin and other digital assets based on distributed ledger technology, to pay for goods and services, directly or indirectly. It cited potential "irreparable" damage and transaction risks (Library of Congress 2021).

Cryptocurrencies, including Bitcoin, are not formally regulated in Pakistan. However, they are not illegal or prohibited. Nevertheless, the State Bank of Pakistan has not permitted any individual or organization to sell, buy, exchange or invest in virtual currencies, coins or tokens as of 16 January 2021. The Cyber Crime Wing of the country's Federal Investigation Agency has made several arrests in connection with Bitcoin and other cryptocurrency mining. These arrests were conducted on suspicion of money laundering (Farooq 2021b).

In Indonesia, the Central Bank of Indonesia announced a policy on 7 December 2017 prohibiting the use of cryptocurrencies, including Bitcoin, as payment methods (*Jakarta Post*, 11 December 2021; Sianipar 2017). Subsequently, on 11 November 2021, Majelis Ulama Indonesia (MUI), that is the Indonesian Ulama Council, issued a haram fatwa prohibiting the use of cryptocurrencies, including Bitcoin, as currency (MUI Fatwa Decision on Cryptocurrency, 11 November 2021 [*Nahdlatul Ulama Online*, 21 June 2021; MUI 2021]). The fatwa also prohibits cryptocurrency trading and holding unless the cryptocurrencies meet the Islamic norms of tradeable and own-able items, which include having physical form, clear worth, a known number, being truly owned, transferrable and not wholly speculative (Lewis 2021).

Following MUI, the two largest Muslim organizations in Indonesia, Muhammadiyah and Nahdlatul Ulama, also issued their own haram fatwas against cryptocurrency. As can be seen from Table 6.1, Muhammadiyah's fatwa (Fatwa Tarjih Muhammadiyah in *Suara Muhammadiyah* no. 1 of 2022) holds that there are two different aspects of cryptocurrency, as investment assets and payment tools *Muhammadiyah Online* 2022). According to Muhammadiyah, these two instruments are illegal. Muhammadiyah also believes that Bitcoin is just a number without any tangible asset; unlike gold and stocks, Bitcoin is only an asset that exists on the Internet and is stored in an electronic wallet, so its value cannot be determined clearly

**TABLE 6.1**
**MUI Haram Fatwa on Cryptocurrency and Bitcoin**

| *No.* | *Fatwa* |
|---|---|
| 1 | Using cryptocurrency as legal currency is illegal because it involves *gharar* (gambling), *dharar* (harmful nature) and is contrary to Law no. 7 of 2011 and Bank Indonesia Regulation no. 17 of 2015.<br><br>(Menggunakan cryptocurrency sebagai mata uang hukumnya haram, karena mengandung gharar, dharar dan bertentangan dengan Undang-Undang nomor 7 tahun 2011 dan Peraturan Bank Indonesia nomor 17 tahun 2015) |
| 2 | Cryptocurrency as a digital commodity/asset is illegal to be traded because it involves *gharar*, *qimar* (gambling), and *dharar* and does not fulfil the Sharia requirements of *sil'ah* (commodity), namely, that there is a physical form, has value, the amount is known with certainty, there are property rights and they can be handed over to the buyer.<br><br>(Cryptocurrency sebagai komoditi/aset digital tidak sah diperjualbelikan karena mengandung gharar, dharar, qimar dan tidak memenuhi syarat sil'ah (komoditas) secara syar'i, yaitu: ada wujud fisik, memiliki nilai, diketahui jumlahnya secara pasti, hak milik dan bisa diserahkan ke pembeli.) |
| 3 | Cryptocurrency is a commodity/asset that fulfils the requirements as a *sil'ah* and has underlying and clear legal benefits to be traded.<br><br>(Cryptocurrency sebagai komoditi/aset yang memenuhi syarat sebagai sil'ah (komoditas) dan memiliki underlying serta memiliki manfaat yang jelas hukumnya sah untuk diperjualbelikan.) |

*Source:* Majelis Ulama Indonesia, "Keputusan Fatwa Hukum Uang Kripto atau Cryptocurrency", 12 November 2021, https://mui.or.id/berita/32209/keputusan-fatwa-hukum-uang-kripto-atau-cryptocurrency/

(CNN Indonesia 2021). Meanwhile, Nahdlatul Ulama prohibited the use of cryptocurrencies because digital currencies have the potential to eliminate the legality of transactions (Decision of Bahtsul Masail Regional Executive Nahdlatul Ulama [PWNU] East Java of 10–11 February 2018 in Tuban regarding Bitcoin [Nugraha 2021; *Nahdlatul Ulama Online* 2023]). Nahdlatul Ulama concluded that cryptocurrencies are haram because they involve too much speculation and thus cannot be considered legitimate investments. Another reason for the haram status of cryptocurrencies is that they could be used to commit fraud. According to some Muslim scholars, investing in cryptocurrencies is similar to gambling, which is prohibited under Islamic law (*Jakarta Post*, 11 December 2021).

According to the numerous explanations provided above, there are several reasons why governmental and religious authorities restrict cryptocurrencies in general, and Bitcoin in particular. First, these assets are frequently used for illegal purposes such as money laundering or as transaction tools for the mafia. Second, from a religious standpoint, several scholars claim that these assets do not fit the asset norms that have been agreed upon by many Islamic law experts. An entity can be considered an asset if it can be traded and owned.

However, different points of view strive to challenge religious authority. Despite the myriad controversies surrounding cryptocurrencies, prominent Pakistani bloggers and social media influencers openly trade in Bitcoin and frequently promote social media articles in support of cryptocurrency regulation. The government of Khyber Pakhtunkhwa was the first in Pakistan to adopt a resolution legalizing cryptocurrencies in December 2020 (Farooq 2021b). Atef Al Khateeb, a Cairo-based Bitcoin trader, has created a Facebook group to discuss the intricacies of cryptocurrency and help new traders understand how to invest their money. He said "It's all commerce in the end; you win some, you lose some. Even the Prophet Muhammad was a trader" (Farid 2018).

Similar views have been expressed by Indonesian investors and traders. Some believe that the MUI's haram fatwa simply specifies that Bitcoin is illegal when used as a means of payment, but it is legal when used as an investment asset:

> What is forbidden by the MUI fatwa is that if crypto becomes a means of payment, and indeed this has been regulated by law in Indonesia, the legal means of payment in Indonesia is only rupiah … Cryptocurrency

> is also not permissible to become an investment asset. It is not the same problem as gold. Gold is also prohibited in Indonesia as a means of payment, but as an asset, it's okay (Pertiwi 2021).

Cryptocurrency supporters in the Muslim world do not necessarily respect the authorities, both state and religious. Some investors and traders in Indonesia regard fatwas issued by religious authorities as opinions that can be contested.

## FOMO INVESTMENTS AMONG MILLENNIALS

Demographic profiles show that younger people are more interested in cryptocurrency. Millennial investors, along with Gen Z investors, easily outnumber investors of other generations. According to one study, only 12 per cent of Gen X are interested in becoming cryptocurrency investors. Meanwhile, millennial crypto investors account for 56 per cent of total crypto investors, with Gen Z accounting for 32 per cent (Iman 2022). Another study shows that people who use social media heavily tend to trade online more often (Bizzi and Labban 2019). It is a striking fact if we consider that millennials are active monthly users of social media (Halimatusa'diyah et al. 2023). Moreover, millennials' cryptocurrency trading decisions are highly influenced by influencers and social media networks, particularly the news as well as rumours circulated through social media (ibid.).

Given the above trend, it will be extremely beneficial if social media becomes the primary venue for cryptocurrency investors in Indonesia. Telegram is the main media platform capable of connecting many Bitcoin communities in Indonesia. There are numerous communities on the site, including some of the largest, such as Binance Indonesian, Indonesian Crypto Forum, and Tokocrypto Official, as shown in Table 6.2.

According to one study, Telegram is also one of the elements that drive people to purchase cryptocurrencies (Nizzoli et al. 2020). Telegram ranks third as a driver of crypto transactions ahead of news and analysis published by crypto influencers. The data in the study shows that millennials have a strong tendency to be influenced by the FOMO phenomenon—that is, the fear of missing out—when they get involved in trading activities and investing in cryptocurrencies.

FOMO is a feeling of anxiety often felt when others are having a good time (or talking about having a good time) (Przybylski et al. 2013). In the

**TABLE 6.2**
**Indonesian Crypto Discussion Groups on Telegram**

| *Creation Date* | *Telegram Group* | *Members* |
|---|---|---|
| 26 April 2021 | Binance Indonesian | 33,904 |
| 1 October 2021 | Buff Doge Coin | 23,418 |
| 27 April 2020 | Crypto Addict Forum | 1,949 |
| 03 May 2020 | INDODAX | 75,299 |
| 14 December 2021 | Indonesian Crypto Forum | 12,939 |
| Unknown | Jackcryptodiscussion | 24,012 |
| Unknown | PintuOfficial | 126,001 |
| Unknown | Crypto Discussion Group Room | 1,032 |
| 23 January 2022 | Tokocrypto Official | 142,433 |
| 07 October 2019 | Zipmex Indonesia | 15,739 |

*Source:* Statistics obtained from Telegram open groups, 2022.

cryptocurrency industry, plenty of investors were afflicted by FOMO in 2020 and 2021, when the prices of many cryptocurrencies were soaring (Scharfman 2022). These emotions were amplified by frequent social media posts from people touting their incredible life-changing investment returns from buying the right cryptocurrency or digital asset (such as non-fungible tokens or NFTs) at the right time (Frank 2021) (see Figure 6.2).

In such circumstances, there is likely to be widespread FOMO in the community. As a result, many people tend to enter the market and acquire assets at the wrong time, suffering losses as their assets undergo big corrections. FOMO can affect anyone, but it is most common among new investors who are searching for the holy grail to gain instant wealth while ignoring the potential future pitfalls of the technology on offer.

Bitcoin's tremendous volatility was on full show on 14 April 2021, when it reached an all-time high of just under US$65,000. This record-breaking gain sparked FOMO among day traders and hedge fund managers alike, resulting in increased interest in retail investing in the crypto market.

This *de facto* gold rush was also spurred by comments from institutional investors like Tesla. Elon Musk, the owner of the electric vehicles company, said in February 2021 that Tesla had invested US$1.5 billion in Bitcoin (Lahiff 2021).

**FIGURE 6.2**
**Various Tools That Are Used to Make Cryptocurrency Trading Decisions**

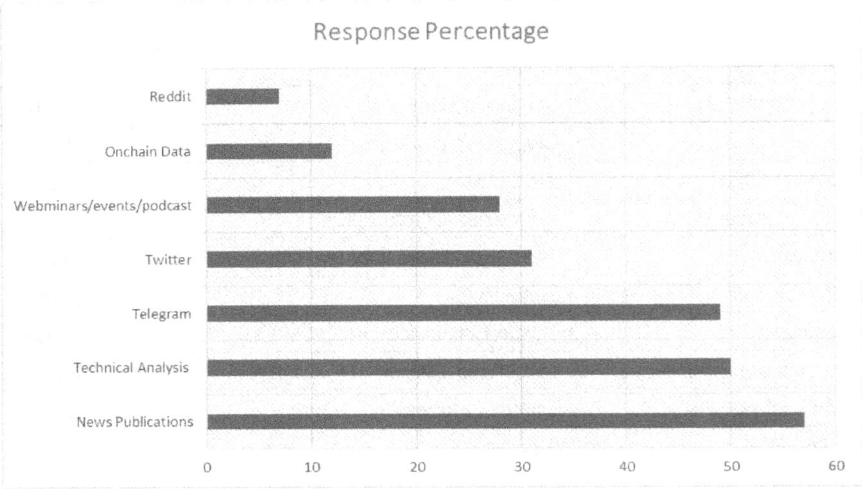

*Source:* Tennant (2021).

Many cryptocurrency investors are well aware of the enormous opportunities that cryptocurrencies offer, and no one wants to lose out on the next big gain. This means that as soon as enough people believe that a specific cryptocurrency has the potential to go on a major run, a large number of people will begin purchasing that currency because of their FOMO propensity.

FOMO plays a far larger role in the Bitcoin market than it does in many other sectors. This is because blockchain technology and cryptocurrencies are still in their early stages, and many individuals believe there is huge potential for exponential growth in the sector. The investors who make the most money on an asset are often the ones who get in first. This has historically been true for many stocks and for industries where titans such as Facebook (Meta), Amazon, Apple, Netflix, Google (Alphabet), Microsoft and Tesla have had first mover advantage. The same is true for cryptocurrencies. Anyone who purchased US$50 or US$100 worth of Bitcoin in 2010 would have seen their assets rise to millions of dollars today. As a result, the massive profits gained by some of the leading cryptocurrencies fuel investment in other cryptocurrencies. This is partly driven by FOMO.

The temptation of attractive and promising financial returns drives the FOMO tendency. This trend has also occurred in Indonesia, where it has been successful in drawing young people and millennials as new investors in cryptocurrencies. Young Muslims, no doubt, are also inextricably linked to this phenomenon.

What exactly are millennial Muslims? They are an age category of Muslims who use social media extensively, particularly for information-seeking. They also use social media information as a source of political (Andersen et al. 2020) and religious knowledge (Slama 2018; Lengauer 2018). Muslim millennials have even coalesced into politically informed groups that greatly influenced the outcome of the 2014 presidential election (Jati 2016).

Some millennial Muslim figures have even gone to the extent of promoting cryptocurrencies like Bitcoin. Wirda Mansur, a young entrepreneur and the daughter of the popular Muslim preacher Ustaz Yusuf Mansur, frequently asks her followers to invest in cryptocurrencies (Primadhyta 2022). As Muslim millennial influencers who are expected to adhere to the narrative that cryptocurrency is haram, Wirda and her father instead support digital assets like cryptocurrencies. They say that the millennial generation of Indonesian Muslims must support cryptocurrency as an attractive digital asset (Okezone 2022).

In February 2022, Wirda launched a cryptocurrency called "I-COIN". It was founded to capitalize on the enthusiasm of Indonesia's young Muslim investors. Wirda promised that the coin would bring huge profits for those who joined its pre-sale. She claimed that her cryptocurrency project had over 3 million social media followers and 400,000 members who were willing to promote the use of I-COIN. Interestingly, one of the functions of this cryptocurrency is I-GACHA. According to the White Paper on I-COIN, I-GACHA is a feature used to purchase a box containing random things and characters. Fundamentally, this function is closely tied to slot machines, which Islamic law vehemently opposes.

In addition to Wirda Mansur, the Muslim millennial investor identified as having a huge effect is the 22-year-old Sultan Gustaf Al Ghozali, whose images have gone viral (CNBC TV18 2022). Ghozali enthralled Indonesian social media followers by utilizing NFTs, that is, blockchain-based tokens that represent a unique digital asset like a piece of art, image or video.

Ghozali's NFTs are based on the Ethereum blockchain's smart contracts (Wang et al. 2021). Using his everyday selfies, Ghozali has created NFTs that he sells on OpenSea, a cryptocurrency marketplace where users can buy and sell various items and games. The high number of enthusiasts who support Ghozali in NFT trading demonstrates that cryptocurrency has piqued the curiosity of new investors interested in the digital economy. Indeed, cryptocurrencies and NFTs have emerged as two of the most important types of digital assets in Indonesia (Ramadhan 2022).

There are also indicators of strong support for Wirda among the Indonesian Muslim grassroots. For example, Wirda's supporters claimed that I-COIN has elements of halal utilities, long-term investment prospects (Telegram 2022), peer-to-peer (P2P) trading facilities, and the approval of MUI's National Sharia Council (Zaki 2022). Wirda's supporters also emphasize that they have developer experts to support the I-COIN ecosystem with blockchain technology.[8] The project entails a low fee and claims to have a Sharia-compliant NFT marketplace where users can upload and sell their NFT projects using I-COIN as currency (see Figure 6.3). Several millennial Muslims were seen supporting Wirda's campaign in a Telegram group chat, as shown below:[9]

> I-COIN is an exception, coins with religious aspects should not be insulted. It is illegal to insult it.[10]
>
> Haram, huh? Just buy a halal crypto I-COIN, c'mon![11]
>
> I-COIN in 2030 will become the official US dollar currency; buy now before it becomes a stable coin.[12]

However, not all millennial Muslims are FOMOers, as evidenced by supporters of Wirda's I-COIN. Sceptics have questioned Wirda's approach since it is considered to be "selling religion" (TV One News 2022):

> What matters is profit. The apple doesn't fall far from the tree, but unfortunately it always carries the name of Allah (Telegram chat).[13]
>
> Father [Yusuf Mansur] and daughter [Wirda Mansur] have said, Inshallah to the moon [the I-Coin]. The father said [the coin will be going] to the heavens [the price will skyrocket]; I said to hell [price will hit the bottom] (TV One News 2022).

Some argue that Wirda and her father are unable to tell the difference between what is halal and what is haram. Furthermore, they say the I-COIN that the father and daughter promote should be considered a scam.

**FIGURE 6.3**
**I-Coin NFT Marketplace**

*Source:* I-Coin (@_icoin). "I-Market Is COMING SOON!!!". Twitter, 12 April 2022, https://twitter.com/_icoin/status/1513827420729602052/photo/1

> He doesn't use the terms *ghirar, qimar* or *dharar;* even for halal and haram, he doesn't care. The strange thing is the government permit doesn't even exist yet, but it's already very profitable. In the past, Paytren [a payment app] was like that too. In the end, people are disappointed. Now he launches again I-COIN. Does anyone still believe and buy it? ... I swear you're cool Cup [Yusuf Mansur].[14]

Several points should be highlighted. FOMO is one of the primary motivators for millennials to invest in and trade in Bitcoin. Many millennials neglect the risks that could await them in the future because they are afraid of being left behind by others. Furthermore, some millennial Muslim crypto influencers amplify the FOMO drive for those who have yet to invest in the cryptocurrency industry. However, not all investors accept an invitation from an influencer. Some conduct research and are sceptical of the narrative advanced by millennial Muslim crypto influencers.

## HARAM FATWAS AND MUSLIM MILLENNIALS: SEVERAL TYPOLOGIES

This section presents several typologies of millennial Muslim investors or traders based on their perceptions of the various haram fatwas. We undertook an in-depth analysis of millennial Muslim interactions on open Telegram groups, including those who support and those who oppose the existence of the haram fatwas. There are at least five major categories in our typology that illustrate the attitudes of millennial Muslims regarding cryptocurrency as well as the fatwas against them.

We analysed ten Telegram open groups on cryptocurrencies whose members are Indonesian millennials. The names of the open Telegram groups are: Binance Indonesian, Buff Doge Coin, Bitcoin Trading Discussion, INDODAX—Indonesia Bitcoin & Crypto Exchange Official Group, Indonesian Crypto Forum, Jackcrypto Discussion, PintuOfficial, Crypto Discussion Group Room, Tokocrypto Official and Zipmex Indonesia. From these groups, we obtained at least 5,165 chats or comments for analysis (see Figure 6.4).

First, as shown in Figure 6.4, we separated Muslim millennial reactions to and perspectives on cryptocurrency into four broad classifications (circles):

- "economy": these are comments related to the economy, such as how to get benefits from cryptocurrencies and those characterizing Bitcoin as a "new field" for making money amid the pandemic;
- "support for fatwas": these are comments that agree with the haram fatwas;
- "against haram fatwas": these are comments that reject the haram fatwas; and
- "utilitarian": these are comments that exemplify a prioritization or maximization of overall utility in the context of trading cryptocurrencies, supported by reasoned arguments that navigate the complexities of the haram fatwas.

The second step was to examine the replies that cut across two classifications (circles). We then came up with the following categories:

**FIGURE 6.4**
**Muslim Millennial Reactions Towards Haram Fatwas on Cryptocurrency**

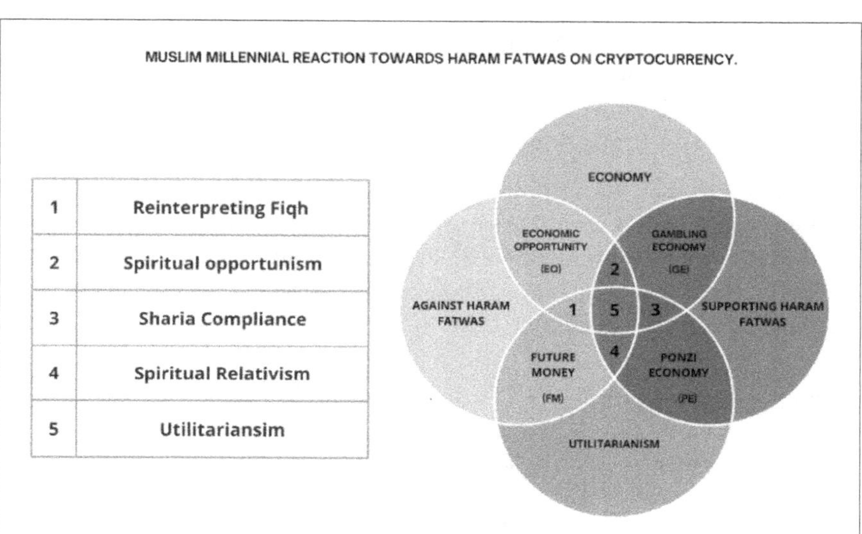


*Source:* Data derived from Telegram groups, 23 July 2022.

- "Gambling Economy" (GE), involving the intersection of "economy" and "supporting haram fatwas". This refers to responses that believe Bitcoin has economic potential, but because it has been prohibited by religious authorities, the nature of cryptocurrencies is believed to have been changed to gambling.
- "Economic Opportunity" (EO), involving the intersection of "economy" and "against haram fatwas". This refers to comments accepting that there are economic prospects in cryptocurrency while ignoring fatwas issued by religious authorities.
- "Future Money" (FM), involving the intersection of "utilitarian" and "against haram fatwas". This refers to comments that perceive cryptocurrencies as a future digital asset that adheres to religious precepts.
- "Ponzi Economy" (PE), involving the intersection of "utilitarian" and "supporting haram fatwas". This includes reactions that highlight features of Ponzi scams in cryptocurrencies, allowing them to be categorized as non-halal assets.

The third division examined the intersection of three classifications (circles), namely:

- economy—against haram fatwas—supporting haram fatwas;
- economy—against haram fatwas—utilitarian;
- utilitarian—against haram fatwas—supporting haram fatwas; and
- utilitarian—against haram fatwas—economy.

This gave birth to the following categories: reinterpreting *fiqh*, spiritual opportunism, Sharia compliance, and spiritual relativism.

Finally, we examined when the four overlapping classes merged into one, which we refer to as the classification "between religion, economics, and utilitarianism". See Table 6.3.

## 1. Reinterpreting Fiqh

The haram fatwas, which emphasize the existence of elements such as uncertainty (*gharar*), harmful nature (*dharar*) and gambling (*qimar*), have evoked various reactions from Indonesia's millennial Muslims. Furthermore, these reactions create unique patterns, one of which we have termed "Reinterpreting *Fiqh*". *Fiqh* refers to Islamic jurisprudence or the body of juristic interpretations of Islamic law. Reinterpreting *fiqh*, in our classification system, refers to situations where millennials take a new approach to the Islamic laws relevant to cryptocurrency to suit their views. Millennial Muslims have the ability to pick and choose fragments of *fiqh*; each person creates his or her own narrative, forming an intersectional spirituality that includes multiple viewpoints and reactions. Whether cryptocurrencies are indeed permissible, however, is a matter of debate. Hence, the haram fatwas on cryptocurrencies are just one of many interpretations by religious authorities.

For example, those who believe that cryptocurrencies are halal argue that *fiqh* can accommodate cryptocurrencies. One example of the justification for this statement is: that cryptocurrencies are similar to any other type of commodity; we can buy or sell this asset; we can also save cryptocurrencies as investment instruments and wait for their values to increase in the future; the prices of cryptocurrencies are transparent for all to see. One of the comments was:

> Halal, because it does not contain elements of *riba'* [usury] ... and trading like this was recommended by Rasulullah [the Prophet], because there is

**TABLE 6.3**
**Classification of Muslim Millennial Reactions Towards Haram Fatwas on Cryptocurrency**

| *No.* | *Classification* |
|---|---|
| 1. | *Reinterpreting Fiqh*<br>This term refers to the reactions of millennial Muslims who believe the haram fatwas on cryptocurrencies are a matter of reinterpretation. For them, Islamic jurisprudence (*fiqh*) is a field of interpretation that cannot be dominated by any single narrative by religious authorities. |
| 2. | *Spiritual Opportunism*<br>This term refers to the reactions of millennial Muslims who believe that the haram fatwas on cryptocurrencies must be followed as long as the logic is reasonable and acceptable; but, if the logic is inappropriate, there is no responsibility to follow the fatwas. Especially if there are still prospects for profits in the cryptocurrency industry. |
| 3. | *Sharia Compliance*<br>This term refers to the reactions of millennial Muslims who believe that the haram fatwa on cryptocurrencies must be followed because the nature of cryptocurrencies contradicts religious teachings and cryptocurrency investment and trading tend to result in economic losses. |
| 4. | *Spiritual Relativism*<br>This term refers to the reactions of millennial Muslims who believe the haram fatwas on cryptocurrency constitute advice that is highly relative and does not have to be followed, especially because the fatwas are also issued by humans. |
| 5. | *Between Faith, Economics and Utilitarianism*<br>This term refers to the reactions of millennial Muslims who believe the haram fatwas on cryptocurrency to be an arena for discussion. Faith can be moderated by the principles of utilitarianism, to the extent that cryptocurrencies can generate profits for millennial Muslims. Therefore, the haram fatwas on cryptocurrency are not seen as an obstacle, but rather as a product of religious authority that is not binding on millennial Muslim activities. |

no element of *gharar* or manipulation, because [market] prices are clear, peer-to-peer, between *bai'* [seller] and *mustari* [buyer], or in the *fiqh* term it is *yaddan bi yaddin* [must be paid in cash]; this is what makes mutual agreement between the two parties ... back to the subject of Islamic economics, in terms of *muamalah* [transactions], there are two conditions of *adamul gharar* [no manipulation] and *antaradin* [mutual agreement

> between the two parties]; crypto is different from the traditional market, which has many middlemen [brokers] intervening or manipulating the market prices.[15]

Some argue that the haram fatwas issued by the religious authorities are problematic because they contradict Qur'anic teachings and the Hadith. For these persons, everything is considered halal unless the Qur'an explicitly defines it as haram. For example:

> Bro, if you say it's haram, you have to be able to prove it by looking at the verses in Al-Qur'an and Hadith. Because all things are lawful, unless they are forbidden in Al-Qur'an. So, it is those who say it's illegal who have to prove it, not those who say it's halal.[16]

Several points should be highlighted. The reinterpretation of *fiqh* is one of the primary narratives to support millennials investing and trading in cryptocurrency. Some millennials believe that the haram fatwas are just recommendations that may or may not be followed.

## 2. Spiritual Opportunism

Those whose views are included in this category tend to argue under the third point of the MUI fatwa. They believe there is still the opportunity to invest and trade in cryptocurrencies. For some millennial Muslims, the fatwa allows them to trade in cryptocurrencies for profit based on Islamic jurisprudence, even though the other two points of the MUI fatwa explicitly forbid Muslims to trade and invest in cryptocurrency. Aside from that, the fatwa states that for cryptocurrencies to be considered a type of commodity, they must have underlying assets to sustain them. While this is true in the case of some cryptocurrency initiatives, it is a rare occurrence. We consider such millennials to be engaged in "Spiritual Opportunism". If millennials consider cryptocurrency as a source of economic opportunity, yet acknowledge that it is only partly acceptable in Islamic law, their behaviours or statements can be categorized as opportunistic. In this instance, a millennial Muslim who appreciates economic value more than spiritual value considers the haram fatwas to be a breach of logic. Thus, they can use it to their advantage, as explained below:

> In my opinion, "trading" comes from English, which, if translated into Indonesian, means *berdagang*. In trading, the main goal is to make a profit from what we trade. So, if there is a question of whether it is haram or

> not, let's return to each other's point of view. Is seeking profits in trading illegal or not?[17]

In addition, some comments include a comparison between cryptocurrencies and stocks, arguing that stocks actually have aspects of usury because they are subjected to a bank's influence. Some comments on Telegram even carry the argument that cryptocurrencies do not have a usury element as they are not related to banks. For example:

> If you want to forbid stock assets, why not just ban all Indonesian index shares? What is clear is that every company is related to banks, which are all usurious. In fact, crypto is an asset that is non-usurious and not related to banks.[18]

Some of the comments held that there was a similarity in context between cryptocurrencies and assets. They construed cryptocurrencies as a form of asset with economic value that an individual or a group of individuals expect will yield a profit. Statements that typify this view include:

> It's like trading alcohol. Alcohol, according to Islam, is haram because it's often abused. But if it's used medicinally, it's *mubah* [permitted]. So trading is like that.[19]

The important thing about millennial Muslims who engage in spiritual opportunism is that they see cryptocurrencies as an asset that can only be traded by looking at the context of the benefits. Furthermore, not only are millennial Muslims more focused on the substantive principles and procedures of trading in cryptocurrencies, but they also seek references in Islamic jurisprudence to back up their arguments.

## 3. Sharia Compliance

When the religious authorities declared that Bitcoin and other cryptocurrencies were haram, many millennial Muslims adhered to their fatwas. Most of them argued that religious authorities have religious explanations for not recommending cryptocurrencies for investment. Millennial Muslims who express such statements could be classified in the "Sharia Compliance" category. The term "Sharia compliance" refers to something that is in line with the Sharia. For some millennial Muslims, religious authorities are decision-makers or evaluators in many aspects of life. Compared with Bitcoin or cryptocurrencies in general, stocks are more acceptable for them because stocks have a physical form and are regulated by the state and subjected to the procedures that are in place in financial institutions. Examples of comments from this category of millennial Muslims include:

> Stocks have physical form and a hedge fund is real ... It's not haram. Meanwhile, Bitcoin is illegal because it doesn't have a physical form. Do you really believe that [Bitcoin or cryptocurrencies] are intangible assets?[20]

> Why do you invest in assets that are illegal? An investment that doesn't have a physical form is illegitimate ... when you [i.e., those who have invested in such an instrument] die, you will go to hell.[21]

Many millennial Muslims in this category immediately sold their cryptocurrencies when the religious authorities issued their haram fatwas. They also emphasized that human beings in general are greedy by nature and sinners. Although not binding, the haram fatwas can be a source of significant influence for devout Muslims who are often looking for the guidance of religious authorities.

## 4. Spiritual Relativism

Millennial Muslims whose opinions fall into this classification tend to see the haram fatwas as mere suggestions. They think the advice provided by religious authorities is relative: it could be right; it could be wrong. Relativism plays an important role in this classification; thus, we call it "Spiritual Relativism". Millennial Muslims of this category believe that the truth is always bound to its own social and cultural context. For example, when religious authorities declared cryptocurrencies to be haram, some millennials believed that the context for the word haram was the scams related to cryptocurrencies. This view is understandable because cryptocurrencies are virtually like the Wild West. Some cryptocurrency projects are worth investing in, while the bulk of them are merely Ponzi scheme—like scams. This view is exemplified by the following:

> I read the details [of the fatwas] yesterday. In conclusion, what is forbidden is cryptocurrency projects that are bad and rigged; the term [haram] refers to [crypto] coins that have a high possibility of being scams.[22]

Furthermore, within the context of this classification, millennials perceive cryptocurrencies as haram when they are portrayed as a form of fiat currency. Whether considered halal or haram, the issue lies not in the benefits or drawbacks one may experience from cryptocurrency trading activities, but rather in the subjective nature of such experiences, which may vary for individuals. This perspective holds true from a legal standpoint, as many countries express scepticism towards most cryptocurrency projects. See, for instance, the statement below:

> What is meant by haram if crypto becomes a currency? Because it is against the law in Indonesia. If it's seen as an asset, crypto is still permissible and halal because there are underlying assets. So crypto is not haram [as an asset], but if it's used as currency for new transactions that's illegal.[23]

Several points need to be underlined here. First, when it comes to defining what the haram fatwas mean, millennials tend to use relativist arguments. There are no universal criteria for adjudicating what is haram, at least for those who fall into this category. Some of them argue that the existence of cryptocurrencies based on Ponzi schemes and similar scams is the main reason for forbidding cryptocurrencies. Others argue that the legal status of cryptocurrencies is the main reason why it is illegal to invest or trade in them.

## 5. Between Faith, Economics and Utilitarianism

This classification refers to the freedom of millennial Muslims to make their own decisions despite the authorities having forbidden cryptocurrencies. For these Muslim millennials, the haram fatwas are a matter for negotiation within the notion of "rational self-interest" in cases where cryptocurrencies can give them economic benefits. The status of cryptocurrencies, either halal or haram, always depends on their trading or investment positions. The following statements are illustrative of this view:

> Haram if you lose, halal if it brings profits.[24]

> If profit, it says halal, if liquid [loss of an investment or loss in trading], it says gambling.[25]

> Take the lesson and don't easily believe what people say! Remember, people forget that when they see money; they don't see whatever to be halal or haram; money has no religion.[26]

One close friend, a 30-year-old employee of a state-owned corporation who is also an active crypto trader, is a devoted Muslim. We have known him since 2007, and it feels like he has only been very pious in the last five years. He began growing a beard, prayed and fasted regularly, following the lifestyle and teachings of the Prophet, and was quite rigid about following the fatwas issued by religious leaders. He even dreamt of constructing a mosque in his village. However, what is different is that when the fatwas on cryptocurrency and Bitcoin trading were issued, he disputed them.

Trading cryptocurrencies is similar to any kind of buying and selling activity, he said. The Prophet Muhammad traded to make ends meet, he added. He went on to say that when MUI issued the fatwas, they did not appear to be based on real trading experiences. Incidentally, this friend is currently a relatively successful crypto trader, having earned at least US$10,000 in one month.

Several Muslims who are still unsure about their stance regarding the permissibility of cryptocurrencies will try to redeem themselves by doing some good deeds, as prescribed by religion. This is meant to atone for their sins for trading in cryptocurrencies, which they know is haram. For them, doing good deeds is the way to receive forgiveness from God. Such deeds include giving alms (*zakat*) or engaging in other religious-based charity activities (e.g., *sadaqah* or voluntary charity, and *infaq* or donations). Another example is to help orphans and the poor. Here are several examples of statements that exemplify these views:

> Playing crypto also has an element of *gharar* [uncertainty]. But if you donate at least 10–20 per cent of the profits, God willing, it will be halal.[27]

> Crypto is really haram, bro [because whenever] you get profits, you will use it to open BO [hire prostitutes]. So that's why you should give about 2.5 per cent of your profits to charity.[28]

> Crypto is illegal, bro. Seriously. I'm not lying, but yes, we are degenerate humans. So equalize it with *infaq* so that the virtue and sins are balanced.[29]

Indonesia's millennial Muslims, at least as shown in our study, believe that giving donations or engaging in charitable activities is the way to salvation. They are aware that trading in cryptocurrencies is haram. However, they believe that whatever money they get in unlawful ways should be cleansed and that those who fail to cleanse their wealth will get punishment from God. The following statement exemplifies this view:

> There's already a fatwa that clearly says it's haram, so there's no need to argue. Just accept that crypto is unlawful, O human beings who are

> greedy and covered in sin. Don't forget to give donations and do good deeds so that the sins are balanced with virtue. Remember, because you guys have committed a sin, and it is called *istidraj* [omission].[30]

Departing from the above explanations, the question is: what is the position of the majority of millennial Muslims regarding the haram fatwas? According to the 5,165 chats that we collected from various Telegram groups, we found that the majority of millennials can be classed within the fifth typology, "Between faith, economics and utilitarianism". The second largest number of millennials falls within the third typology, Sharia compliance. The other typologies are not significantly observable from the discourse of millennial Muslim investors and traders on Telegram (see Figure 6.5).

In short, the results show that there are two dominant reactions among millennial Muslims: (1) those who believe the haram fatwas do not prevent them from getting involved in the cryptocurrency industry; and (2) those who are extraordinarily compliant with the haram fatwas. These two types of millennials are opposites.

Several studies on millennial Muslims in Indonesia show that this generation is not religious but the most conservative (PPIM 2021). In other words, they rarely observe religious rituals, but when it comes to

**FIGURE 6.5**
**Muslim Millennial Comments on Haram Fatwas on Cryptocurrency**

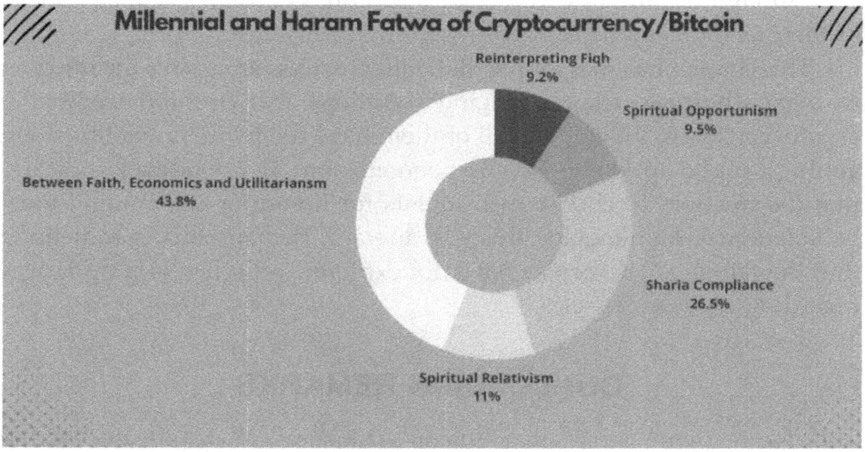

*Source:* Data derived from Telegram groups, 23 July 2022.

defending religious values, they can become extremely militant. The results of the Alvara Institute survey (2021) show that the majority of millennial Muslims believe that religion plays an important role in their lives. This means that religion provides guidance and is a way of life for Indonesian millennials. This finding is no different from previous research findings, which surveyed Muslim communities broadly without a breakdown along generational lines (IDN Research Institute 2019).

This chapter, however, departs from those surveys. The number of millennial Muslims who obey religious fatwas is indeed quite large, but not as large as those who consider the fatwas as merely religious opinions (that is, views that are not legally binding). Some do adhere to the haram fatwas, but they outsmart the fatwas by doing various good deeds to erase their sins, knowing that they have done something unlawful in dealing with cryptocurrencies. The most frequent action is to carry out religious charity activities (*zakat, infaq* and *sadaqah*). For them, such activities are a means to atone for their sins after partaking in activities considered "religiously forbidden".

The findings of our study indicate that, in general, when confronted with a delicate interaction between religion and economics—where religious authorities prohibit Muslims from gaining profits through trading in cryptocurrencies but such trading is perceived as a means to potentially multiply one's asset values—millennials tend to be secular. Their utilitarian character makes them simply focus on the profit margin even though trading in cryptocurrencies runs contrary to the advisories of their religious authorities.

This chapter has also shown that millennial Muslims have the freedom to make choices—despite religious opinions that prohibit trading in cryptocurrencies. Indeed, not all of them have the temperament to avoid getting caught up in the FOMO phenomenon. This tendency indicates that the freedom to choose instruments for investing and trading must be balanced with adequate financial literacy. Perhaps this is something that the religious authorities have not explored yet when issuing fatwas regarding cryptocurrencies.

## CONCLUDING REMARKS

This chapter demonstrates that millennial Muslims can dispute the validity of the haram fatwas on cryptocurrencies and Bitcoin when it comes to opportunity cost. Even if they do not overtly reject the fatwas, they will attempt to negotiate around them by offering arguments that they believe are adequate. The reason for ignoring the fatwas is simple: rationality at times involves negotiating one's faith.

Some millennial Muslims may identify themselves as not religious but also hold conservative beliefs or values. Moreover, being religious and conservative are not necessarily tied together. Millennial Muslims who are not religious may still hold conservative beliefs on financial matters.

It is also important to note that the haram fatwas can be subjected to a wide range of interpretations, based on one's beliefs and values, and can mean different things to different people. Some people may consider the haram fatwas to be absolute because they prioritize tradition and stability, while others may define them by their views on financial matters.

Furthermore, the questionable and sometimes half-baked Islamic reasoning used by some religious authorities in the process of issuing fatwas is one reason why not all millennial Muslims adhere to their fatwas. The views of the *ulama* (religious scholars) expressed in the form of fatwas cannot prevent millennial Muslims from investing and trading in high-risk products such as cryptocurrencies. These Muslims believe they are allowed to express their investment preferences, even if they are outlawed by the religious authorities or not legalized by state authorities.

## Notes

1. Indonesian cryptocurrency influencer on Instagram with a following of 17,900 followers.
2. Indonesian trader and YouTuber with 539,000 subscribers.
3. A YouTube channel targeted at Indonesian viewers and aimed at building financial literacy.
4. A content creator and entrepreneur in the financial and investment industry in Indonesia.
5. A content creator whose avowed aim is to build financial literacy among the Muslim community.
6. According to Investopedia, pump-and-dump is a manipulative scheme that attempts to boost the price of a stock or security through fake recommendations. These recommendations are based on false, misleading or greatly exaggerated statements. The perpetrators of a pump-and-dump scheme already have an established position in a company's stock and will sell their positions after the hype has led to a higher share price. This practice is illegal based on securities

law and can lead to heavy fines. The burgeoning popularity of cryptocurrencies has resulted in the proliferation of pump-and-dump schemes within the industry. Source: Investopedia, https://www.investopedia.com/terms/p/pumpanddump.asp

7. According to Investopedia, buy low, sell high is a strategy where one buys stocks or securities at a low price and sells them at a higher price. This strategy can be difficult as prices reflect human emotions and are difficult to predict. Source: https://www.investopedia.com/articles/investing/081415/look-buy-low-sell-high-strategy.asp
8. Data from Telegram Groups.
9. Ibid.
10. Ibid.
11. Ibid.
12. Ibid.
13. Ibid.
14. Ibid.
15. Ibid.
16. Ibid.
17. Ibid.
18. Ibid.
19. Ibid.
20. Ibid.
21. Ibid.
22. Ibid.
23. Ibid.
24. Ibid.
25. Ibid.
26. Ibid.
27. Ibid.
28. Ibid.
29. Ibid.
30. Ibid.

## References

Allcot, Dawn. 2021. "Millennials Own More Crypto Than Any Other Generation". GoBankingRates, 30 May 2021. https://www.gobankingrates.com/investing/crypto/millennials-own-more-crypto-any-other-generation

Alvara Strategic. 2021. *Potret Umat Beragama 2021*. 9 January 2021. https://alvara-strategic.com/potret-umat-beragama-2021/, https://alvara-strategic.com/potret-umat-beragama-2021

Andersen, Kim, Jakob Ohme, Camilla Bjarnøe, Mats Joe Bordacconi, Erik Albæk, and Claes H. De Vreese. 2020. *Generational Gaps in Political Media Use and Civic Engagement: From Baby Boomers to Generation Z*. London: Routledge. https://doi.org/10.4324/9781003111498

BBC News. "Egypt's Grand Mufti Endorses Bitcoin Trading Ban". *BBC News Middle East*, 2 January 2018. https://www.bbc.com/news/world-middle-east-42541270

Bizzi, Lorenzo, and Alice Labban. 2019. "The Double-Edged Impact of Social Media on Online Trading: Opportunities, Threats, and Recommendations for Organizations". *Business Horizons* 62, no. 4 (1 July 2019): 509–19. https://doi.org/10.1016/j.bushor.2019.03.003

*CNBCTV18.com*. 2022. "This NFT Collection Sells for Millions; and It's Just a Bunch of Selfies". 14 January 2022. https://www.cnbctv18.com/business/this-nft-collection-sells-for-millions-and-its-just-a-bunch-of-selfies-12127192.htm

CNN Indonesia. 2021. "Haramkan Kripto, Tarjih Muhammadiyah Soroti Spekulasi-Nihil Jaminan". 19 January 2021. https://www.cnnindonesia.com/nasional/20220118181629-20-748246/haramkan-kripto-tarjih-muhammadiyah-soroti-spekulasi-nihil-jaminan

Data from Telegram Groups, 27 July 2022.

Delfabbro, Paul, Daniel King, Jennifer Williams, and Neophytos Georgiou. 2021. "Cryptocurrency Trading, Gambling and Problem Gambling". *Addictive Behaviors* 122 (November): 107021. https://doi.org/10.1016/j.addbeh.2021.107021

Farid, Farid. Y. 2018. "Egypt's Top Islamic Cleric Has Issued a Fatwa against Bitcoin". *Quartz*, 4 January 2018. https://qz.com/africa/1171431/egypts-bitcoin-fatwa-cleric-bans-bitcoin-trading

Farooq, Umar. 2021a. "Pakistani Province Plans to Build Pilot Crypto Currency Mining Farms". Reuters, 18 March 2021. https://www.reuters.com/article/us-crypto-currency-pakistan-idUSKBN2BA0KW

———. 2021b. "Pakistan Moves to Bring Cryptocurrency Boom out of the Dark". Reuters, 16 July 2021. https://www.reuters.com/technology/pakistan-moves-bring-cryptocurrency-boom-out-dark-2021-07-16

Frank, Robert. 2021. "Millennial Millionaires Plan to Add More Crypto in 2022, CNBC Millionaire Survey Finds". CNBC, 16 December 2021. https://www.cnbc.com/2021/12/16/millennial-millionaires-plan-to-add-more-crypto-in-2022.html

Halimatusa'diyah, Iim, Afrimadona, Aptiani Nur Jannah, Endi Aulia Garadian, Fahmi Imam Fauzy, and Haula Noor. 2023. *Media dan Paham Keagamaan: Efek Media Sosial, Televisi, Radio, dan Podcast Terhadap Paham Keagamaan di Indonesia*. Jakarta: Prenada Media, 2023. https://prenadamedia.com/product/media-dan-paham-keagamaan-efek-media-sosial-televisi-radio-dan-podcast-terhadap-paham-keagamaan-di-indonesia/.

IDN Research Institute. 2019. *Indonesia Millennial Report 2019*. 17–18 January 2019. Indonesia Millennial Summit 2020. https://ims.idntimes.com/report

Iman, Aldi Khusmufa Nur. 2022. "Perilaku Investor Muslim Millennial Dalam Industri Crypto Asset Di Jawa Timur Perspektif Ekonomi Islam". PhD dissertation, UIN Sunan Ampel Surabaya.

Irawanto, Budi. 2019. "Young and Faithless: Wooing Millennials in Indonesia's 2019 Presidential Election". *ISEAS Perspective*, no. 2019/1, 4 January 2019. https://www.iseas.edu.sg/images/pdf/ISEAS_Perspective_2019_1.pdf

*Jakarta Post*. 2018. "Bank Indonesia, Police Prevent Bitcoin Transactions in Bali". 15 January 2018. https://www.thejakartapost.com/news/2018/01/15/bank-indonesia-police-prevent-bitcoin-transactions-in-bali.html

———. 2021. "Indonesia Ulema Council Forbids Cryptocurrency Trading". 11 December 2021. https://www.thejakartapost.com/indonesia/2021/11/12/indonesia-ulema-council-forbids-cryptocurrency-trading-.html

Jati, Wasisto Raharjo. 2014. "Aktivisme Kelas Menengah Berbasis Media Sosial: Munculnya Relawan Dalam Pemilu 2014". *Jurnal Ilmu Sosial Dan Ilmu Politik* 20, no. 2: 147–62. https://doi.org/10.22146/jsp.24795

La Monic, Paul R. 2022. "Crypto Crash and Gold Sell-off Show There's No Place for Investors to Hide". CNN Business, 11 October 2022. https://edition.cnn.com/2022/11/10/investing/bitcoin-crypto-ftx-gold/index.html

Lahiff, Keris. 2021. "Tesla Purchases $1.5 Billion in Bitcoin—Here's What Could Happen Next". CNBC, 8 February 2021. https://www.cnbc.com/2021/02/08/tesla-purchases-1point5-billion-in-bitcoin-what-could-happen-next-.html.

Lengauer, Dayana. 2018. "Sharing Semangat Taqwa: Social Media and Digital Islamic Socialites in Bandung". *Indonesia and the Malay World* 46, no. 134: 5–23. https://doi.org/10.1080/13639811.2018.1415276

Lewis, Lauren. 2021. "Cryptocurrency Is Forbidden for Muslims, Indonesia's Religious Council Declares". *Daily Mail Australia*, 11 November 2021. https://www.dailymail.co.uk/news/article-10191723/Cryptocurrency-forbidden-Muslims-Indonesias-religious-council-declares.html

Library of Congress (Law Library). 2018. "Regulation of Cryptocurrency around the World". Library of Congress, USA, June 2018.

———. 2021. "Regulation of Cryptocurrency around the World". Library of Congress, USA.

Majelis Ulama Indonesia (MUI). 2021. "Keputusan Fatwa Hukum Uang Kripto atau Cryptocurrency". 12 November 2021. https://mui.or.id/berita/32209/keputusan-fatwa-hukum-uang-kripto-atau-cryptocurrency

Mansur, Wirda. 2022. "All About I-Coin!!!". YouTube Livestreaming, 2022. https://www.youtube.com/watch?v=qMoPV8tbzvo

*Muhammadiyah Online*. 2022. "Pandangan Majelis Tarjih Terkait Mata Uang Kripto." *Majelis Tarjih*, 19 January 2022. https://muhammadiyah.or.id/pandangan-majelis-tarjih-terkait-mata-uang-kripto/

Nizzoli, Leonardo, Serena Tardelli, Marco Avvenuti, Stefano Cresci, Maurizio Tesconi, and Emilio Ferrara. 2020. "Charting the Landscape of Online

Cryptocurrency Manipulation". *IEEE Access* 8: 113230–45. https://doi.org/10.1109/ACCESS.2020.3003370

Nugraha, Ricky Mohammad. 2021. "Cryptocurrency Considered 'Haram' By East Java Nahdlatul Ulama". *Tempo*, 28 October 2021. https://en.tempo.co/read/1522026/cryptocurrency-considered-haram-by-east-java-nahdlatul-ulama

*Nahdlatul Ulama Online*. 2021. "Hasil Bahtsul Masail tentang Halal dan Haram Transaksi Kripto". 21 June 2021. https://www.nu.or.id/nasional/hasil-bahtsul-masail-tentang-halal-dan-haram-transaksi-kripto-IhUDC (accessed 9 January 2023).

Okezone, Feby Novalius. 2022. "Promosikan Token I-COIN Wirda Mansur, Yusuf Mansur Ingin RI Jadi Pusat Kripto: Okezone Economy". *Okefinance*, 22 February 2022. https://economy.okezone.com/read/2022/02/22/320/2550940/promosikan-token-i-coin-wirda-mansur-yusuf-mansur-ingin-ri-jadi-pusat-kripto

Pertiwi, Wahyunanda Kusuma. 2021. "Kripto Halal Sebagai Aset, Haram Jika Dipakai Untuk Alat Pembayaran". *Kompas*, 12 November 2021. https://tekno.kompas.com/read/2021/11/12/11250257/kripto-halal-sebagai-aset-haram-jika-dipakai-untuk-alat-pembayaran?page=all

PPIM. 2021. "Launching Hasil Penelitian PPIM UIN Jakarta Beragama Ala Anak Muda: Ritual No, Konservatif Yes". PPIM UIN Jakarta, 9 December 2021. https://ppim.uinjkt.ac.id/2021/12/09/launching-hasil-penelitian-ppim-uin-jakarta-beragama-ala-anak-muda-ritual-no-konservatif-yes

Primadhyta, Safyra. 2021. "Kripto, Instrumen Investasi Yang Naik Daun di Tengah Fatwa Haram". CNN Indonesia, 30 December 2021. https://www.cnnindonesia.com/ekonomi/20211228131428-92-739610/kripto-instrumen-investasi-yang-naik-daun-di-tengah-fatwa-haram

———. 2022. "Token Kripto Anak Yusuf Mansur I-COIN Presale Hari Ini". CNN Indonesia, 16 February 2022. https://www.cnnindonesia.com/ekonomi/20220216143509-92-759970/token-kripto-anak-yusuf-mansur-i-coin-presale-hari-ini.

Przybylski, Andrew K., Kou Murayama, Cody R. DeHaan, and Valerie Gladwell. 2013. "Motivational, Emotional, and Behavioral Correlates of Fear of Missing Out". *Computers in Human Behavior* 29, no. 4: 1841–48. https://doi.org/10.1016/j.chb.2013.02.014

Purwanti, Teti. 2022. "Trader Kripto Di RI Ada 7 Juta, Dominasi Gen Z Dan Milenial". CNBC Indonesia, 16 June 2022. https://www.cnbcindonesia.com/market/20220616141918-17-347680/trader-kripto-di-ri-ada-7-juta-dominasi-gen-z-dan-milenial

Putri, Cantika Adinda. 2022. "Magic! Investor Kripto RI Capai 15 Juta, Kalahkan Pasar Modal". CNBC Indonesia, 19 August 2022. https://www.cnbcindonesia.com/tech/20220819122418-37-365028/magic-investor-kripto-ri-capai-15-juta-kalahkan-pasar-modal

Putsanra, Dipna Videlia. 2023. "Profil Wirda Mansur: Kuliah Dimana, LinkedIn, dan Crypto I-COIN". *Tirto.id,* 24 February 2023. https://tirto.id/profil-wirda-mansur-kuliah-dimana-linkedin-dan-crypto-i-coin-gpnq

Qadri, Hussain Mohi-ud-Din. 2019. *Business Ethics in Islam*. London: Routledge. https://doi.org/10.4324/9780429326189

Ramadhan, Fitra Moerat. 2022. "Fakta-Fakta Populernya NFT Ghozali Everyday, Termasuk Takut Kecewakan Orang Tua". *Tempo,* 17 January 2022. https://grafis.tempo.co/read/2915/fakta-fakta-populernya-nft-ghozali-everyday-termasuk-takut-kecewakan-orang-tua

Royal, James. 2021. "Survey: Nearly Half of Millennials Comfortable Owning Cryptocurrencies". *Bankrate,* 11 January 2021. https://www.bankrate.com/investing/survey-millennials-cryptocurrency-investing-2021

Scharfman, Jason. 2022. "Cryptocurrency Compliance and Operations Case Studies". In *Cryptocurrency Compliance and Operations,* pp. 155–170. London: Palgrave Macmillan. https://doi.org/10.1007/978-3-030-88000-2_8

Securities and Commodities Authority, UAE. 2020. "Concerning the Regulation of Crypto Assets". https://www.sca.gov.ae/Content/Userfiles/Assets/Documents/f79fbf6.pdf

Shiller, Robert J. 2019. *Narrative Economics: How Stories Go Viral and Drive Major Economic Events.* Princeton: Princeton University Press. https://doi.org/10.2307/j.ctvdf0jm5

Sianipar, Tito. 2017. "Bitcoin dilarang otoritas keuangan Indonesia, ini fakta-faktanya". BBC Indonesia, 7 December 2017. https://www.bbc.com/indonesia/indonesia-42265038

Sifat, Imtiaz. 2021. "On Cryptocurrencies as an Independent Asset Class: Long-Horizon and COVID-19 Pandemic Era Decoupling from Global Sentiments". *Finance Research Letters* 43 (November): 102013. https://doi.org/10.1016/j.frl.2021.102013

Slama, Martin. 2018. "Practising Islam through Social Media in Indonesia". *Indonesia and the Malay World* 46, no. 134: 1–4. https://doi.org/10.1080/13639811.2018.1416798

Smith, Hannah. 2022. "Bitcoin Crash: What's behind Crypto Collapse?". *The Times,* 14 November 2022.

Tennant, Jake. 2021. "Indonesia Cryptocurrency Investor Report Part 1: The Growth in Adoption of Crypto Assets in Indonesia". *Tokenomy,* 18 March 2021, via Medium.com. https://tokenomy.medium.com/2021-indodax-cryptocurrency-investor-report-part-1-the-growth-of-crypto-assets-in-indonesia-127c93da3975

*TV One News*. "Ikuti Anang Hermansyah, Putri Ustaz Yusuf Mansur Luncurkan Token Kripto I-COIN". 2022. https://www.youtube.com/watch?v=MugD9o8zMzk.

Usmani, Mufti Muhammad Taqi. 2015. *Fiqh al-Buyu 2 Volume Set by Mufti Taqi Usmani.* Karachi: Maktaba Ma'ariful Quran.

Vogels, Emily A. 2019. "Millennials Stand Out for Their Technology Use, but Older

Generations Also Embrace Digital Life". Pew Research Center, 9 September 2019. https://www.pewresearch.org/fact-tank/2019/09/09/us-generations-technology-use

Wang, Qin, Rujia Li, Qi Wang, and Shiping Chen. 2021. "Non-Fungible Token (NFT): Overview, Evaluation, Opportunities and Challenges". *ArXiv* (Cornell University): 2105.07447. https://doi.org/10.48550/arXiv.2105.07447

Wells, Charles. 2022. "Bloomberg Wealth: Where Does Crypto Go from Here?". Bloomberg, 17 November 2022. https://www.bloomberg.com/news/newsletters/2022-11-17/ftx-collapse-why-the-fall-of-sam-bankman-fried-will-change-the-future-of-crypto

Zaki, Faiz. 2022. "Yusuf Mansur Tanggapi Kripto I-COIN Halal: Insya Allah, Udah Perhatiin Rambu". *Tempo,* 24 February 2022. https://bisnis.tempo.co/read/1564216/yusuf-mansur-tanggapi-kripto-i-coin-halal-insya-allah-udah-perhatiin-rambu

# 7

# Youth and Religious Disaffiliation
## A Study of Indonesian Millennials Learning Buddhism during Spiritual Disruption

Fuji Riang Prastowo


### ABSTRACT

*From the positive youth development perspective, Indonesian millennials are in a transitional phase to adulthood, vulnerable to identity crises. Pressures from social and cultural constructs present various challenges to their well-being during this transitional phase. This chapter explores the religious identity of millennials drawing upon several concepts from youth studies. Data was collected at Karangdjati Monastery in the student city of Yogyakarta from 2020 to 2022 amid the pandemic. The data collection method involved participatory observation of a purposive sample of ten informants. A narrative model was used to analyse their life histories. The main finding was that the informants were interested in Buddhism because of its universal appeal and inclusive nature regardless of one's faith, the absence of formal conversion orders, and its Ehipassiko principle of critical thinking. The main argument in this paper is that Indonesia's state power, which requires that every citizen should have a religion that should be stated on their national identity card and that they should practise its teachings, causes a sense of exclusion for Indonesian millennials who practise religious teachings flexibly. To overcome the spiritual disruption they experience, some millennials negotiate their identity by converting or reconstructing a hybrid identity as a process of self-discovery.*

## BACKGROUND

> During the very long spiritual journey of the *visudhi*,[1] I cried when I heard Venerable Pannavaro say, "There is no conversion order in the *Tipitaka*."[2] So, *visudhi* is interpreted as a lifestyle conversion from behaviour that was tainted with defilements (*Kilesa*) to behaviour that is in tune with the Buddhist lifestyle in coping with suffering and being happy. (Carini [female, b. 1996], May 2022).

Carini, the Buddhist name given by Venerable Sri Pannavaro Mahathera of the Vihara Mendut on Saturday, 7 May 2022, was one of twenty-seven youths at a formal Buddhist procession that day at the *vihara* (monastery). The *vihara* in Magelang, Central Java, was founded in 1977 and is one of the pioneers of the Indonesian Theravada movement. The majority at the procession that day were millennials and Generation Zs from Karangdjati Vihara, Yogyakarta. Throughout the procession, Carini burst into tears. She had endured long-term bullying from her friends of the Abrahamic faiths, who threatened her for her conversion after she had graduated from her master's studies in the United Kingdom. In addition, her parents were bullied in her neighbourhood for allowing their children to convert from Islam to Buddhism. This chapter's short story is about religious disaffiliation and spiritual disruption.

The scene at the procession was fascinating. Carini's mother, who wears a hijab, joined the procession under the guidance of Ven. Pannavaro at Mendut Vihara. Carini was lucky enough to have supportive parents, who gave her spiritual freedom. Ven. Pannavaro said in his opening remarks, as quoted above, that "there is no conversion order in the *Tipitaka*"; the teachings of Buddhism are universal and inclusive for all humankind. Of the twenty-seven people at the procession, only three were born Buddhists and listed in the administrative records of the population's identities as Buddhists. Most were born Christian, Catholic, Muslim or adherents of folk beliefs like Kejawen. In Indonesia, the Buddhist baptismal name is

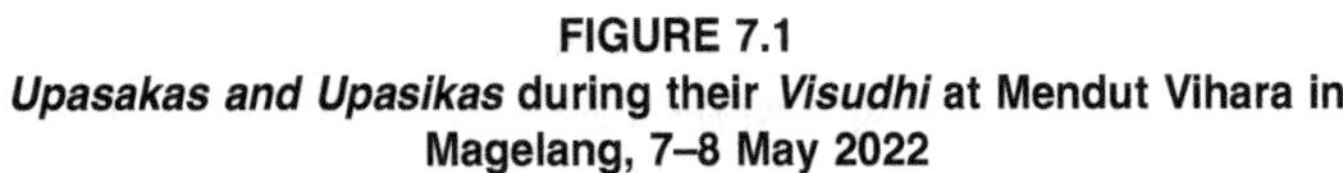

**FIGURE 7.1**
***Upasakas and Upasikas* during their *Visudhi* at Mendut Vihara in Magelang, 7–8 May 2022**

*Source:* Fuji Prastowo, 2022.

one of the unique features of the Theravada tradition, inspired by the Catholic tradition.

One of the followers of the Karangdjati Vihara bearing the pseudonym Mes shocked the virtual world because a tattoo of the Virgin Mary was evident on his shoulder as he wore the robes of a *samanera* (renunciate) at the *Tipitaka* chanting event in Borobudur Temple on 8 July 2022. He did not participate in the *visudhi* like his peers did but instead participated in the highest ritual of *pabajja samanera*, a two-week programme of practising celibacy as a Theravada monk, at Mendut Vihara. Mes has a unique background. He is a millennial youth who openly claims to be "non-binary" in terms of gender. His photo gained attention on the Twitter and Instagram accounts known as "Catholic *Garis Lucu*" (literally, Catholic funny lines). Netizens created these two social media accounts for light-hearted discussions of sensitive religious issues experienced by minorities.

**FIGURE 7.2**
**The Virgin Mary Tattoo on the Shoulder of *Samanera* Mes**

*Source:* Katolik Garis Lucu Instagram account, 9 July 2022, with permission for publication.

The presence of Buddhist millennials who were not born as Buddhists and whose official religious identity is also not Buddhist illustrates the existence of spiritual disruption among them. Lectures on Buddhism and meditation sessions became more easily accessible to the general public during the COVID-19 pandemic because they were delivered largely through social media (Ichwayudi and Sayfullah 2021; Schedneck 2021). The use of social media led to the emergence of terms such as "digital *dhamma*" and "simulated *sangha*" as the Internet had become a bridge to popularize meditation in secular spaces (Gooren 2010). Social media and the Internet have become intermediaries for spreading the *dhamma* (or *dharma*), intermediaries that are easily accessible by people of all religions without having to go to a monastery.

In addition, a critical leadership factor is essential for creating a sense of inclusion for millennial Buddhist learners. One of these figures is Ven. Pannavaro, whose interfaith lectures often go viral on YouTube or other social media. He is known as a Buddhist preacher who can contextualize his teachings on everyday issues, especially mental health issues. Indeed, Ven. Pannavaro himself has a background similar to the millennials and Generation Zs who go through the *visudhi*. His background is similar not in the sense of being of the same generational category but in having had a similar life journey: Pannavaro was not born a Buddhist. He converted to Buddhism while attending lectures at the Psychology Faculty of the University of Gadjah Mada at a young age. The conversion was part of his spiritual journey. Since his ordination as a Theravada monk in Thailand in 1977, he has been a pioneer monk in Indonesia's revival of Buddhism in the modern era. He had studied Buddhism through his junior high school history teacher, Mr Suprapto. His junior high school days coincided with what is known as the 1965 incident in Indonesia, which involved genocide against those who adhered to communist ideology and culminated in the state demanding that all citizens adhere to one of the government's officially recognized religions. Buddhist missionaries from Thailand began appearing in the country subsequently. Ven. Pannavaro was one of the Theravada monks who were ordained on 21 February 1977 at Wat Bovoranives, Bangkok, by His Holiness Somdeth Phra Nyanasamvara, Sangharaja (Great Monk of the Kingdom of Thailand).

By way of socio-political context, more than 500 years after the collapse of the Hindu-Buddhist civilization in Indonesia in the fifteenth century, Buddhism had been incubating in Jakarta and other cities since the sixteenth century through Chinese temples that practised Buddhism with a mix of Chinese traditional beliefs. The preservation of Buddhism was facilitated largely by an inclusive theosophy group from the Dutch colonial period and the indigenous aristocratic group professing Kejawen. The arrival in 1934 of a Theravada monk from Sri Lanka, namely Bhikkhu Narada Maha Thera, at the invitation of Ong Soe An's theosophical community of Khong Kauw Hwee, who were connected to Peranakan Chinese Buddhist transnational networks, lay the historical foundation of modern Buddhism in Indonesia. In 1953, Bhikkhu Ashin Jinarakkhita or Bhante Ashin became the first Indonesian to be ordained as a monk, after undergoing education at Sasana Yeiktha in Yangon, Myanmar, under the tutelage of Mahasi Sayadaw. One of the biggest challenges for reconstructing Buddhism in Indonesia in the modern era was having to adapt to the concept of God after the 1965 incident. This was in line with one of the precepts of Pancasila, the foundational philosophy of Indonesia (Setiawan 2020).

Many existing studies have highlighted the phenomenon of urban middle-class youth experiencing a quarter-life crisis, leading to spiritual disruption and "the death of God". Secularization, atheism and agnosticism are widespread in the Western world, which prioritizes rationality (Bellour 2016; McGrath 2004; Williams-Oerberg 2021). In the United Kingdom, young agnostics are interested in studying Buddhism because of the positive view of Buddhism, that is, as a religion of peace that is also good for one's mental health (Page and Yip 2021). In Australia, atheist youths say they are interested in studying Buddhism because of the principle of focusing on life in the "here and now", which is in line with the principles of atheism and New Age practices, which are based on rationality—that is, life is what it is (Hughes, Suwanbubbha, and Janran 2008). The Buddhist community in the United States is positive about the religion because of its inclusive nature regarding gender expression and its view that one's life choices are not based on divine judgement (Gleig 2019; Page and Yip 2021). Gordon-Finlayson and Daniels (2008) put forward a similar conclusion in their grounded study showing that Westerners convert to Buddhism because of the cognitive foundation of new religious movements. Alternatively, James Coleman (1999) analyses "new Buddhism" as a counter-narrative of the life of the industrialized nations of the West.

The stories of urban middle-class youths are in line with Max Weber's concept of the "calling", which talks about the urban middle class changing their outlooks on life to live in a new spirit based on religious morality

(Suprijanto and Rudyansjah 2021). This new spirit was the product of mental health problems, one of which was about feeling empty and lonely. Spencer (2018) says that "calling" is not always related to conversion because calling can also be related to increasing a person's spiritual level. Tweed (1999) analyses Buddhism in Western circles, where some whom he calls "night-stand Buddhists", understand Buddhism, accept Buddhist practices, beliefs and lifestyles, and see the religion only as a way of life, as opposed to "convert Buddhists", who undertake conversion and are fully committed to the religion. This approach to Buddhism is not only evident in Western countries; even in Buddhist countries such as Korea and Japan, the return to spiritualism movement reflects a post-developmentalism stage that encourages people to reconstruct identities and lifestyles (Beck 1994). The trend of "engaged Buddhism", exemplified by the late Thich Nhat Hanh and the Dalai Lama, has also contributed to the modernization of Buddhist movements, such as the Jungto Society in South Korea, which has been able to attract young people in the digital era.

To sum up, in some understandings, religious conversion is still seen as a social pathology. Travisano (1970) calls conversion the "complete disruption" in the context of human identity. In Indonesia, religious disruption is a long process of contested religious identity due to state intervention in regulating religion (Jubba 2019).

At the legal level, religious conversion in Indonesia is a human right protected by the 1945 State Constitution of the Republic of Indonesia.[3] Paragraph 1 of Article 28E states that "every person shall be free to embrace a religion and to worship according to his/her religion, choose education and teaching, to choose work, to choose citizenship, to choose a place to reside in the territory of the state and leave it, as well as to be entitled to return", while paragraph 2 states that "every person shall be entitled to freedom to be convinced of a belief, to express thought and attitude in accordance with his/her conscience". Nevertheless, in practice, converting to another religion is a challenging endeavour in Indonesia. One of the complexities of religious conversion is represented by the policy laid down by a January 2023 ruling by the Constitutional Court, which rejects interfaith marriages in Indonesia, instead requiring conversion on the part of one party to a marriage so that both parties adhere to one religion in line with Law No. 1 of 1974 concerning Marriage (Argawati 2023). Indonesian citizens are used to getting around interfaith marriages by registering a formal change of religion in their *kartu tanda penduduk*

(KTP) or national identity (ID) card. However, many continue to worship according to their respective beliefs before marriage (Hidayat 2022; Sinaga 2015). Religious conversion is a negotiation around state regulations. In this case, religion is seen as a public issue that the state can regulate. In practice, the administrative requirements for religious conversion entail obtaining a statement from the subdistrict (*kelurahan*) that includes a letter from the individual's previous religious institution permitting religious conversion for a specific reason. Culturally, this administrative process becomes more complicated if the applicant submits a conversion from Islam to another religion because it requires a letter of approval from family, village officers and religious institutions.

Reflecting on these observations, the central questions in this study are: How do Indonesian millennials interpret the importance of their spiritual identity in the transitional phase? What causes them to experience religious disaffiliation and motivates their interest in learning Buddhism as an alternative to managing their mental health? Moreover, how do they negotiate their spiritual values and practices with their families and social environment?

## METHODOLOGY AND THEORETICAL DISCUSSION

### Methodology

Using the phenomenology-based ethnography method, this study was conducted during the pandemic period from February 2020 to July 2022 at Karangdjati Vihara in the student city of Yogyakarta. It was intended to capture what motivates millennials to study Buddhism. According to data from Yogyakarta Province, there are twenty-two *viharas* and two *cetiya* (smaller monasteries) in the province (BPS Statistics of D.I.Yogyakarta, 2022).

Data was collected using participatory observation, and a narrative model within the framework of a life biography was utilized to analyse the data collected from ten informants purposively selected. The Nvivo R1 technique was used in the narrative. The informants, millennials born between 1981 and 1996 and living in Yogyakarta, generally had not been raised as Buddhists and used reflexive strategies to navigate their transition to adulthood. Millennials are the generation born after 1980 (Barnard, Cosgrove, and Welsh 1998; Ng, Schweitzer, and Lyons 2010) and are also

**TABLE 7.1**
**Informant Snapshots**

<table>
<tr><td>Participation Observation Area</td><td colspan="4">• Main Area: Karangdjati Vihara, Yogyakarta. Karangdjati Vihara, located close to major universities in the student city of Yogyakarta, was chosen as the research location because it is a melting pot of students throughout Indonesia and is open to the public across religions, especially for meditation programmes.<br>• Secondary Areas: areas related to the Karangdjati Vihara, namely Mendut Vihara and Borobudur Great Temple, Magelang.</td></tr>
<tr><td>Period of Study</td><td colspan="4">• February 2020 to July 2022</td></tr>
<tr><td colspan="5">Informants</td></tr>
<tr><td>No.</td><td>Pseudonym</td><td>Gender</td><td>Year of Birth</td><td>Spiritual/Religious Affiliation Before Becoming Buddhist</td></tr>
<tr><td>1</td><td>Nandini</td><td>Female</td><td>1987</td><td>Agnostic</td></tr>
<tr><td>2</td><td>Sarano</td><td>Female</td><td>1996</td><td>Muslim</td></tr>
<tr><td>3</td><td>Acca</td><td>Male</td><td>1994</td><td>Folk Belief/Kejawen</td></tr>
<tr><td>4</td><td>Kusalo</td><td>Non-binary</td><td>1995</td><td>Taoist/Confucianist</td></tr>
<tr><td>5</td><td>Mangalo</td><td>Male</td><td>1996</td><td>Taoist/Confucianist</td></tr>
<tr><td>6</td><td>Kalyani</td><td>Female</td><td>1989</td><td>Atheist</td></tr>
<tr><td>7</td><td>Carini</td><td>Female</td><td>1996</td><td>Muslim</td></tr>
<tr><td>8</td><td>Mes</td><td>Non-binary</td><td>1994</td><td>Catholic</td></tr>
<tr><td>9</td><td>Siri</td><td>Female</td><td>1982</td><td>Muslim</td></tr>
<tr><td>10</td><td>Gata</td><td>Non-binary</td><td>1983</td><td>Agnostic</td></tr>
</table>

known as the Nexus Generation (Zemke, Raines, and Filipczak 2000). The Pew Research Center defines millennials as those born between 1981 and 1996 or those aged 26 to 41 in 2022 (Lazzi et al. 2019; Zachara 2020). The researchers collected data by actively participating in religious activities, namely, small-scale talks. Buddhist baptismal names or pseudonyms have been used for all the informants named in Table 7.1 to maintain their privacy.

## Youth and Buddhism

Millennials, who are still identified as "youth" in many studies, are classified as the generation at the level of "social being" or "social becoming". This means that the youth experience changes as youths negotiate the construction of social values and cultural norms by constructing counter-positions to prevailing norms (Christiansen, Mats, and Vigh 2006). Youth are also referred to as "social shifters", a term that represents changes in the level of life that they continue to experience (Durham 2000). While searching for identity, not only young people but also some adults have spiritual concerns, seeking the meaning and purpose of life through spiritual means (Tirri and Quinn 2010). In other words, spiritual quests are common across all ages and are not restricted to young people, who are the focus of this study (Bagnall 2005; Bennett and Robards 2014; Furlong 2013; Thomson 2009).

The process of social becoming is related to the production of intersubjectivity, which is phenomenologically related to the problem of (other) minds (Pagis 2010). Therefore, studies of a person's subjective experience with religion are always related to the "anthropology of mind", which contains different subjective interpretations of a person that contribute to various patterns of thinking about life and anything that affects life (Luhrmann and Fortier 2017).

In the context of spirituality in Buddhism, several studies have explained that many young people are interested in studying Buddhism as a way of life because its doctrines are organically based on secular culture and rationality (Turner 2011). Williams-Oerberg's study (2021) specifically uses the term "Youth Buddhism" to show that by studying how young people engage with Buddhism one gets "a more complex and compelling picture of the intersections of Buddhism and modernity". One of the Buddhist practices—meditation—is favoured as a healthy lifestyle and then reconstructed as high culture so that it can serve as a tool for self-realization in reducing mental health problems (Prasi 2017). This experience is also in line with what was put forward by Schulze (2008), who introduced the concept of "experience society", which emphasizes the individual tastes and preferences experienced by late modern society and their commodification.

## *Youth and Spirituality*

The transformation in the way spirituality is viewed and experienced is part of the self-discovery process experienced by youth. Spirituality and religion are two related concepts but are not the same. Reich (1998) reveals four possible relationships between religion and spirituality: identical, subdomain of the other, separate, or overlapping. The spiritual dimension includes the spiritual quest, namely the ability to answer life's questions, compassion, and inner peace. In contrast, the religious dimension includes commitment and obedience to rituals (Shek 2012). Spirituality in youth studies, especially in positive youth development, is also related to the capacity for positive cognitive appraisal to face life's challenges (Davis, Keer, and Kurpius 2003). Furthermore, Suprijanto and Rudyansjah (2021) call this rational process a "second conversion" phenomenon in which individuals do not need to change religions to interpret new beliefs and understand the dimension of spirituality.

Benson and Roehlkepartin (2008) state that there are at least three intrinsic processes in adolescent spirituality, namely (1) the process of experiencing awareness or awakening that contributes to spiritual development, (2) the process of interconnecting or belonging to relationships with others, especially divine beings, and (3) the final process in which spiritual identity has been established with daily activities and becomes a way of life. Furthermore, Hay and Nye (1998) note that there are at least three categories of spiritual sensitivity, namely (1) awareness sensing, which indicates a deeper understanding of life, (2) mystery sensing, which is connected with imagination in our daily lives, and (3) value sensing, which is related to the emphasis on the importance of belief as a measure of what people value. It is important here to highlight these notions of spirituality to better understand the stages of the spiritual search that millennials undergo.

## Analysis

### *Karangdjati Vihara: Urban Sanctuary for Spiritual Seekers*

Karangdjati Vihara was established in 1965, or the year 2505 in the Buddhist era. It was a dairy cow pen during the Dutch occupation, with the surrounding area being a sugarcane plantation. Its location near higher education centres such as Gadjah Mada University and Yogyakarta State University makes the *vihara* an urban sanctuary for interfaith students. Karangdjati Vihara has long been a cultural space open to people of all faiths and has never posed a problem for the local residents, the majority of whom are practitioners of Kejawen, which has some elements of Buddhism. Its location close to a mosque is also not a problem because

Muslims often attend the *vihara* to study meditation. The founder of the Karangdjati Vihara was Rama Among Pradjarto, a Buddhist missionary in the Temanggung area of Central Java. Transforming a cowshed into a place of worship occurred in 1958 when Bhante Jinaputa performed the *vassa* (the three-month annual retreat during the rainy season for Theravada Buddhist monks to study Buddha's *dharma*) in Yogyakarta. During that *vassa*, a discussion about Buddhism was held, which was attended by the majority of the Kejawen community, who were affiliated with the aristocratic class.[4] Since then, Karangdjati Vihara has been crowded with visitors for *bakti pujas* (devotional worship) every Wednesday night and public meditation on Friday nights. In the 1960s and 1970s, the Karangdjati Vihara became the forerunner in sending missionaries to Central Java villages such as Kaloran, Kandangan, Parakan, Candiroto, and the Menoreh mountain area in Kulonprogo.

> I believe this *vihara* has the energy vibration of the late Rama Among, its founder. Of all the monasteries in Indonesia, I believe Karangdjati Vihara is the most outstanding. Apart from the fact that the people here are from various faiths, it is also unique because the people who attend are like outpatients [because of their mental health]. So, yes, this is about how this *vihara* can be a home for people of all faiths. That's why I believe that if this monastery is renovated and made magnificent, not many people will come. It's better to keep it simple, like a home. (Pandita Muda Totok Tejamano, Head of Karangdjati Vihara, on Vesak Day, 16 May 2022)

In examining Buddhist youth in Seoul, Kim (2016) notes that most South Korean temples were previously located exclusively in the mountains. This made Buddhism inaccessible to the urban middle class, who were then pulled towards Christianity, which was popular in urban areas. Korean Buddhism was traditionally referred to as Mountain Buddhism because of its adherents' seclusion in the mountains and its ascetic, individualistic nature. But as awareness grew of the benefits of meditation for one's mental health, Buddhism spread to the cities and soon became an interfaith cultural space. In the 2000s, Buddhist-related meditation centres emerged in Seoul as a healing place for young urbanites who were seeking spirituality in response to the anxieties induced by materialism and identity crises.

What took place in South Korea was also seen at Karangdjati Vihara. The striking difference is that the city location of Karangdjati Vihara made it easy to accommodate the quest for spirituality among young urbanites

**FIGURE 7.3**
**Meditation Session Attended by People of Various Faiths**

*Source:* Fuji Prastowo, 2022.

and fostered the engaged Buddhism movement. Jiang, Ryan, and Zhang (2018) note the commodification of Zen meditation camps in China in the form of meditation tourism or wellness tourism. Such commodification, which is common in Western countries, has not occurred at Karangdjati Vihara, which organizes meditation for free because of a stipulation from the Indonesian Theravada Sangha, the patron of the *vihara*, not to sell *dhamma* commercially.

Karangdjati Vihara can be regarded as a new attraction for urbanites because it includes interfaith groups and cross-gender groups marginalized in Muslim-majority countries such as Indonesia. The following statement by one of the informants explains the attraction of the *vihara*:

> As a lesbian who has come out in public, I feel comfortable in this monastery, as my spiritual home. (Gata, non-binary, b. 1983)

Gilbert and Parkes (2011) define meditation locations in urban centres as the front door for Western society to understand Eastern philosophies, especially Buddhism, which is characterized by its spiritual dimension rather than any religious doctrine. Eastern spirituality has become a post-industrial lifestyle represented by the boom in Buddhist lifestyles such as meditation and vegetarianism (Bell 1992; Lynch 2007). Although the commodification of meditation has been widely criticized, for example, by Zizek (2001), who talks about spiritual fetishes, the growing interest of urbanites in the Buddhist lifestyle remains high.

The popularity of Karangdjati Vihara among young people experiencing spiritual disruption has been reinforced by the pandemic, which has made Buddha *dhamma* lectures easily accessible to the general public via the Internet. Taylor (2004) describes this trend as the birth of "cyber monastic communities". The average non-Buddhist millennial knows the Buddha *dhamma* through meditation. Meditation classes are held every Friday night for people of various faiths. Those who feel comfortable with the spiritual sanctuary at Karangdjati Vihara then move on to increase their spiritual activity through Buddhist religious rituals such as *bakti pujas* and *dhamma yatra* (pilgrimage to Buddhist temples to raise awareness) and even become renunciates.

## *Spiritual Disruption: Intrapersonal Dialogue in Becoming a Buddhist*

The findings from the field showed that there are three conversion typologies, namely, complete committed conversion, partial conversion, and verbal conversion. Verbal conversions are limited to claims that someone is interested in pursuing a religion other than the official religion listed on the national identity card; partial conversions involve undergoing *visuddhi* or proclamation as a Buddhist but do not entail changing the religion on the national IDs, while committed conversions involve a formal change of religion on the ID card, as well as internalizing the values of Buddhism in daily life by completely replacing the teachings of the previous religion with the teachings of Buddhism.

The informants cited several reasons for embracing Buddhism. The first reason is the inclusiveness of Buddhism, which offers a safe space for all youth identities, free from the stigmas that some encounter in the rest of society. Youths with non-binary gender identities and those who are not heterosexual feel that Buddhism is a safe place for them to grow (Page and Yip 2021). Inclusiveness can also mean those who are not born as Buddhists still have a place in the Buddhist community because of the doctrine of reincarnation, which includes the belief that in a previous birth, these people would have studied Buddhism. Hay and Nye (1998) note that the inclusive side of religious teachings manifests spiritual sensitivity.

The second reason cited is the rationalism of Buddhism, which is based on the Buddha's *Kalama Sutta* discourse, which depicts Buddhism not as a religion of revelation by a divine being but as the fruit of Gautama Buddha's inquiry to understand the roots of human suffering and how to eliminate that suffering. Critical thinking is the spirit of Buddhism. In addition, Buddhism's principle of *Ehipassiko*—come and see for yourself—gives Buddhism a rational quality. The emphasis in Buddhism is not so much on judgement after death as on the ethos of being a good person in the present. The doctrine of judgement after death is one of the reasons people become agnostics or atheists because this doctrine causes religious alienation and a sense of crisis in a person (Bellour 2016). The following statement by one of the informants confirms the appeal of *Ehipassiko*:

> As a researcher, *Ehipassiko* is an ethos that is in line with systematic thinking in philosophy, namely, the importance of investigating all the suffering we experience because the source of suffering is in our minds and hearts. (Siri, female, b. 1982)

The third reason cited is that the teachings are centred on the management of mental health. The *Abhidhamma*, the ancient Buddhist text, teaches that the self-concept consists of *raga* (character afflictions), *citta* (consciousness) and *cetasika* (mental factors). Every Buddhist should constantly develop self-awareness to understand the concepts of *anicca* (all is impermanent), *dukkha* (suffering) and *anatta* (non-self or substanceless). According to Mariano and Damon (2008), spirituality and religious beliefs will help adolescents organize their life goals, namely, by first arranging what they want and what they can contribute, and then what meaning they can derive from a life journey.

> Consciousness is like the flow of a river; it looks the same from the outside, but actually the water droplets are changing every second. That's *anicca's* concept of life—when we believe that everything changes, we have nothing to worry about, even about facing death later. In Javanese belief, it is called with *suwung* or emptiness. (Acca, male, b. 1994)

The fourth reason cited is the nostalgia for Hindu-Buddhism as an ancestral religion that once triumphed before Islam became the majority religion of Indonesia. From the beginning of the common era to the end of the fifteenth century (after the collapse of the Hindu-Buddhist kingdom of Majapahit in 1478), Buddhism was the majority religion in Indonesia, along with Hindu *dhamma*. For some people who have a nostalgic yearning for their past lives before their current rebirth, studying Buddhism is part of filial piety. Several informants claimed to pursue Buddhism by worshipping at the Hindu temples in Yogyakarta as a way of remembering the Hindu-Buddhist civilization.

### *Religious Disaffiliation: The Middle Way in Reconciling Interpersonal Conflict*

Almost all the informants—perhaps most people who convert—are branded as social pathologists. Like the journey of Prince Sudhana, whose image is carved in the Gandvayuha panel at Borobudur Temple, their journey to seek spirituality has undoubtedly been full of obstacles. People's encounter with Buddhism is highly complex when it takes place in a country where the majority are Muslims or people of other Abrahamic faiths, which strictly forbid conversion as the most significant human sin. Usually, the decision to convert to another religion arouses fear owing to the stigma attached to conversions. After going through the stage of inner conflict, millennials who wish to convert usually experience conflict with conservative families. This stage is called "value sensing" because the conflict occurs due to the clash of old and new values between family members. The stage is also commonly called "anomie" because of alienation in the mind and by other people.

> My mother chatted with my friends so that I could be returned to the right path in Islam; [She thought] I might be in *ruqyah* [possession by a spirit] [and that she needed] to expel the jinn that led me to this path. (Acca, male, b. 1994)

> I have been bullied by my high school friends for a long time. Then my neighbours found out when my mother sent me to convert. Now, the problem is that my dogs are considered a nuisance to them. (Carini, female, b. 1996)

The experiences of the two informants quoted above show that the stigma of being a *murtad,* or apostate in the Abrahamic religions, especially Islam, is the biggest obstacle for young people studying Buddhism. Both were ostracized by their peers during their spiritual disruption. After going through and overcoming the stages of conflict within the social environment, they engage in what is called a conversion expression, where the individual can show their new religious identity (Umam and Syafiq 2014). Some of these expressions are expressed through actions or at the administrative level by changing the religious status in the national IDs. One of the informants, Genia (b. 1990), explained the faith development model as involving a five-stage process: the egocentric faith stage, the dogmatic faith stage, the transitional faith stage, the reconstructed internalized faith stage, and the transcendent faith stage. Rambo (1993) describes the process of religious conversion through a systematic seven-stage model: context, crisis, quest, interaction, encounter, commitment, and consequences.

During the process of reconciliation to find a middle way in the interpersonal phase, Benson and Roehlkepartin (2008), as cited earlier, explained that there are at least three intrinsic processes in adolescent spirituality, namely, the process of awakening or growing awareness, the process of interconnecting or being in relationship with others, and the final phase of making this spiritual identity a way of life. This view is in line with that of Hay and Nye (1998), who saw three main categories in spiritual sensitivity, namely, awareness sensing, mystery sensing, and value sensing. In Buddhist doctrine, becoming a human being is about bringing out good moral values, such as *metta* or loving-kindness, which is one of the elements of the Buddhist ethos. Followers of Buddhism nurture the *metta* experience, an intrinsic process of spirituality in the phase of spiritual identity as a way of life or value sensing. This can be done through three learning processes in Buddhism: cognitive learning or *pariyatti,* practice-based learning or *patipatti,* and meditation-based learning to gain first-hand knowledge of each individual's reflective capacity or *pativedha. Pariyatti* and *patipatti* are phases that are called awareness sensing. At the same time, the process of inner development understands things beyond reasoning that result from human cognitive abilities; it is obtained by practising meditation to gain value sensing. In sum, the Buddhist lifestyle can be described in terms of three elements, as captured in Figure 7.4.

In dealing with conflicts due to their choice of spiritual journey, millennials prefer the path of moderation to deal with clashes of different

**FIGURE 7.4**
**Buddhist Way of Life**

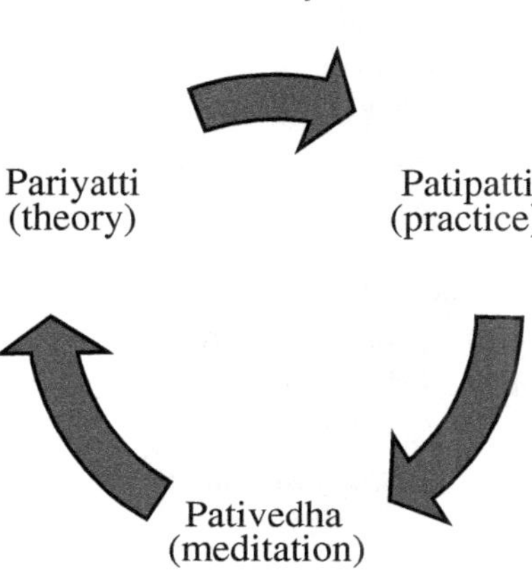


*Source:* Vijjananda (2019), p. 217.

life values. As stated by Binh (2017), the ultimate goal of Buddhism is to realize emptiness or *anatta* (the non-self). Self-identity is considered something that is not absolute, according to the Buddhist concept of *anatta,* so one must avoid egocentrism that serves to protect one's identity. After overcoming egocentrism, people will attain the state of *Boddhisatva,* that is, community sensing to think about their life goals for social purposes (Tirri and Quinn 2010).

Shek (2012) revealed that in positive youth development, there are at least three elements of spirituality. The first is the horizontal and vertical elements in human existence. The second element is the beliefs and values needed to answer spiritual questions about the nature of life and death. The third element is the meaning of life. Worthington et al. (2010) state that there are at least four types of spirituality, namely, religious spirituality, which is related to religion; humanistic spirituality, which is related to the connection to humanity; nature spirituality, which is close to nature; and cosmos spirituality, which is close to the whole of creation. This is in line with the three phases of the Buddhist way of life mentioned above, which states that self-balance can be achieved through a process of learning, practice and meditation in which the three stages form a humanistic spiritual self.

### *Ehipassiko: Building a New Identity*

As noted earlier, Worthington et al. (2010) state that there are at least four types of spirituality: religious, humanistic, nature, and cosmos. The majority of informants in this study felt that Buddhism was more compatible with them because of their humanistic spirituality based on the five precepts of the Buddhist Pancasila as follows:

1. *Pāṇātipātā veramaṇī sikkhāpadaṁ samādiyāmi* (I am determined to train myself to avoid killing sentient beings);
2. *Adinnādānā veramaṇī sikkhāpadaṁ samādiyāmi* (I am determined to train myself not to take things that are not given);
3. *Kāmesu micchācārā veramaṇī sikkhāpadaṁ samādiyāmi* (I am determined to train myself not to commit immoral acts);
4. *Musāvāda veramaṇī sikkhāpadaṁ samādiyāmi* (I resolve to train myself to avoid untrue speech);
5. *Surā-meraya-majja-pamādaṭṭhānā veramaṇī sikkhāpadaṁ samādiyāmi* (I resolve to train myself to abstain from all drink and food which can cause weakness of consciousness and alertness).

> Since observing the Buddhist precepts, I have been able to control myself to reach renunciation of all attachments. (Nandini, female, b. 1987)

> Of all the precepts, it is my urge to drink alcohol that I cannot control. Fortunately, Buddhism is not a set of teachings with many prohibitions but more the determination to change. If it is not possible, we can moderate it. (Siri, female, b. 1983; and Mes, non-binary, b. 1994)

The views of the informants quoted above are in line with the research conducted by Kim (2016) on Buddhist youth in Seoul, that is, some of the main reasons why Buddhism is just starting to emerge. The rebirth of Buddhism in Korea is based on the transformational changes in Buddhism, known initially as the teaching of self-exile as the "religion of the mountain", which then began to evolve with changes in the cities following the emergence and development of the Abrahamic religions in the capital. Several secular Buddhist communities have developed humanistic spirituality to instil in the people some fundamental Korean Buddhist values such as *gong* (emptiness), *mu-a* (non-self), *yeongi gwan* (self-reflection on the law of cause and effect) and *jari ita* (improving oneself and bringing benefit to others).

In line with developments in South Korea, Buddhism in Indonesia's large cities is developing in an inclusive manner, with meditation being taught to people of all faiths to improve their well-being. One example is in Yogyakarta as the centre of Javanese civilization, which is dominant in the inner teachings or *roso* in Kejawen folk belief. By believing in the power of karma, which is based on cause and effect, some informants develop *hiri* (shame arising from making mistakes) and *ottapa* (fear of the consequences of wrongdoing). *Hiri* comes from within oneself in the form of shame.

> The law of karma is a universal law; you don't need to be a Buddhist to believe in the law of karma. That's why I always take care of *hiri* and *ottapa* to avoid the seeds of bad karma. (Sarano, female, b. 1996).

Buddhism teaches belief in the law of karma, that is, in the existence of rebirth, or *punarbhava*. Buddhists are taught to accept that there is a strong connection between past and present lives. Several informants, who emphasize religious spirituality, strongly believe in doctrines such as rebirth. Some of them are highly disciplined in carrying out morning prayers, which they perform in accordance with the rituals practised by various Buddhist sects such as Theravada, Mahayana and Buddhayana. In addition to Karangdjati Vihara, he is very active in several *viharas* in Yogyakarta. He believes that he was related to the Chinese temple of Klenteng in Yogyakarta City in his past life.

> I like rituals and perseverance, so that the mind does not think about all kinds of things. In one week, I can participate in several worship services (Mangalo, male, b. 1996).

> After being in the *visudhi* led by Bhante Pannavaro, head of the Indonesian Theravada Sangha, I am determined to repay all my karmic debts with kindness. (Gata, non-binary, b. 1983).

Some of the informants were vegetarians before they became acquainted with Buddhism, namely, Siri (female, b. 1982), Acca (male, b. 1994) and Kalyani (female, b. 1989). After getting to know about Buddhism, they became more diligent in reconstructing their good relationship with nature. They developed nature spirituality through regular *abhaya dana* (acting in a way that other beings do not have cause to fear oneself), namely, *fangsheng*, or releasing captive animals such as fish and birds, to show compassion for all beings in the universe.

> The thing that calmed me the most was seeing the birds being able to fly freely without having to live in a cage. (Kusalo, non-binary, b. 1995)

One informant continued to perform a Kejawen rite, a habit his parents had inculcated in him during his childhood. So apart from practising Buddhism, he also combines several Kejawen rites, such as fasting in the Javanese tradition to control oneself. After successfully controlling oneself through several fasting rites, the purpose of Javanese human life is to be in harmony with the universe according to the Javanese philosophy known as Golong Gilig, which regulates the harmonization between the macro cosmos (universe) and micro cosmos (self). The form of this harmonious relationship is to love animals and plants. In this context, fasting can be related to cosmos spirituality with its ascetic properties. Of all the types of spirituality, the goal of the informants is to get rid of all the attachments that disturb their minds so that they too can become Buddhas, meaning, they too can be enlightened (Ulfah, Octaviana, and Aqila 2019). In Buddhism, cosmos spirituality is related to the *Paticcasamuppada* law related to the other, including micro-components in the self, consisting of mind and body (Sugianto 2019).

## CONCLUSION

Internet technology has played a significant role in spreading Buddhism during the COVID-19 pandemic by allowing the formation of virtual religious communities that encourage the study of Buddhism, particularly among millennials, who tend to be digital natives. By facilitating the dissemination of *dhamma* lectures that anyone can access without visiting a Buddhist monastery, the Internet has become vital in increasing interfaith dialogue as well. Thus, many in the digital generation tend to reconstruct their spiritual identity based on subjective experience; their source of religious teachings is not their parents but the Internet, which allows them to acquire religious knowledge without religious barriers.

This study is in line with several previous studies on youth and spirituality. Critics of studies on millennials in Indonesia often use moral lenses to judge the religious disaffiliation that the younger generations experience—that is, their resistance to the religious values passed down by their parents. These critics see such youths as problematic and being afflicted with mental instability. However, religious disaffiliation occurs because Indonesian society generally tends to pressure the young into conforming to societal values and norms, especially religious ones. These pressures come at a difficult time for young people who are transitioning into adulthood; this transition is a process of "becoming", which entails intrapersonal conflicts about the social and cultural constructs that try to shape them into others. Added to parental and societal pressures is the turmoil that youths encounter when the state interferes excessively in the private sphere of its citizens, namely the spiritual dimension. Indonesia is one of several countries that encroach into the private space of religion. It requires that every citizen should have an absolute religious identity, as stated in the national ID, and should practise that religion. This requirement causes a sense of exclusion for Indonesian millennials who practise religious teachings other than those of the religion declared on their IDs. Therefore, while experiencing spiritual disruption, some millennials negotiate their identity by converting or reconstructing a hybrid identity as a process of self-discovery.

Through this study, it was found that non-Buddhist millennials who studied Buddhism at Vihara Karangdjati in Yogyakarta interpret spiritual identity as a process of searching for meaning and purpose in their lives during their transition to adulthood. What motivated these millennials to study Buddhism was its rationalism, inclusiveness and focus on mental health, and, in some cases, their nostalgia for Indonesia's ancient Hindu-Buddhist civilization. How they negotiate spirituality can be seen from their intrapersonal dialogues about the clash of values that must be reconstructed before facing interpersonal conflicts with their families and peers. The middle path of Buddhism is to realize the Buddha's teachings in the face of suffering. Moreover, there are no conversion rules in Buddhism, so anyone can learn Buddhism without having to leave the religion of their birth. Some youths become absolute Buddhists through total conversion by changing the status on their national IDs to Buddhism. Others choose a hybrid path—retaining their birth religion on their national IDs but practising Buddhist precepts as a way of life.

## Notes

1. *Visudhi* is the ordaining ceremony to become *upasakas* (masculine) or *upasikas* (feminine), the Pali language titles for followers of Buddhism who are common people and do not live a monastic life. The process of becoming an *upasaka or upasika* is to practise the *visudhi* or the pledge ceremony to pay homage to the

Buddha, the *dhamma* (teachings of Buddhism) and the *sangha* (the monastic community). In Buddhism, especially in Indonesia, people of any faith can become *upasakas or upasikas* without formally changing their religion because there is no explicit command requiring conversion to Buddhism (Vijjananda 2019).

2. *Tipitaka* is the holy book of Buddhism, which in Pali literally means three baskets, consisting of the *Vinaya Pitaka,* which contains rules for monks, the *Sutta Pitaka,* which contains the sermons of Gautama Buddha, and the *Abhidhamma Piṭaka,* a book containing the philosophy, metaphysics and the science of the Buddha's *dhamma* (Buddharakkhita 2013). The *dhamma* was known to be preached orally in northern India as early as 2,565 years ago and then began to be written down in the fourth Great Assembly in Sri Lanka in 29 BCE during the time of King Vattagamini (Vijjananda 2019).
3. Constitutional Court, Republic of Indonesia, https://www.mkri.id/public/content/infoumum/regulation/pdf/uud45%20eng.pdf
4. In the Sultanate of Yogyakarta, the various layers of the royal family still preserve Kejawen, which is a syncretistic belief that contains elements of animism, Hinduism, Buddhism and Islam. One of the essential elements of Kejawen, which is similar to Buddhism, is known as "Kebatinan", which literally translates as "inner teachings" and regulates the believer's psychological dimension. The royal family preserved the majority of Kejawen teachings, while the purification of the Abrahamic religions—Islam, Christianity and Catholicism—influenced the commoners of Yogyakarta. Therefore, there are two layers of society in Yogyakarta, namely those who are syncretic and those who are puritans.

## References

Adhitama, Satria. 2021. "Studi Fenomenologi Konversi Keyakinan Seorang Pemuda Yahudi Ortodoks". *Humanitas* 5, no. 3: 281–304.

Argawati, Utami. 2023. "MK Tolak Permohonan Perkawinan Beda Agama". In Mahkamah Konstitusi Republik Indonesia, 31 January 2023. https://www.mkri.id/index.php?page=web.Berita&id=18870&menu=2

Bagnall, Nigel. 2005. *Youth Transition in a Globalised Marketplace.* New York: Nova Science Publishers, Inc.

Barnard, Robert, Dave Cosgrove, and Jennifer M. Welsh. 1998. *Chips & Pop: Decoding the Nexus Generation.* Toronto: Malcolm Lester Books.

Beck, Ulrich. 1994. "The Reinvention of Politics: Towards a Theory of Reflexive Modernization". In *Reflexive Modernization,* edited by Ulrich Beck, Anthony Giddens, and Scott Lash, pp. 1–55. Stanford, CA: Stanford University Press.

Bell, Catherine. 1992. *Ritual Theory, Ritual Practice.* Oxford: Oxford University Press.

Bellour, Leila. 2016. "The Religious Crisis and the Spiritual Journey in T.S. Eliot's

'The Waste Land'". *Arab World English Journal* (AWEJ) 7, no. 4 (December): 422–38. dx.doi.org/10.24093/awej/vol7no4.26

Bennett, Andy, and Brady Robards. 2014. *Mediated Youth Cultures: The Internet, Belonging and New Cultural Configurations*. Basingstoke: Palgrave.

Benson, Peter L., and Eugene C. Roehlkepartain. 2008. "Spiritual Development: A Missing Priority in Youth Development". *New Directions for Youth Development* 2008, no. 118: 13–28. https://doi.org/10.1002/yd.253

Binh, Ven. Tran Thi. 2017. "Young Life and Social Networking". *Journal of International Association of Buddhist Universities* (JIABU) 10, no. 2 (July–December).

BPS Statistics of D.I.Yogyakarta. 2022. "Provinsi Daerah Istimewa dalam Angka 2022". https://yogyakarta.bps.go.id/publication/2022/02/25/05661ba4fe09161192c3fc42/provinsi-daerah-istimewa-yogyakarta-dalam-angka-2022.html

Buddharakkhita, Acharya. 2013. *Metta dan Mangala: Falsafah dan Latihan Cinta Kasih Universal*. Yogyakarta: Vidyasena Production Vihara Vidyaloka. https://pustaka.dhammacitta.org/ebook/theravada/Metta%20dan%20Mangala.pdf

Christiansen, Catrine, Utas Mats, and Henrik E. Vigh. 2006. *Navigating Youth, Generating Adulthood: Social Becoming in an African Context*. Uppsala: Nordic African Institute. https://www.engagingvulnerability.se/wp-content/uploads/2016/03/Finnstrom2006_NavigatingYouthwhole_book.pdf

Coleman, James William. 1999. "The New Buddhism: Some Empirical Findings". In *American Buddhism: Methods and Findings in Recent Scholarship*, edited by Duncan Ryuken Williams, and Christopher S. Queen, pp. 91–99. London: Routledge. https://doi.org/10.4324/9781315028019

Davis, Timothy L., Barbara A. Keer, and Sharon E. Robinson Kurpius. 2003. "Meaning, Purpose, and Religiosity in At-Risk Youth: The Relationship Between Anxiety and Spirituality". *Journal of Psychology and Theology* 31, no. 4: 356–65. https://doi.org/10.1177/009164710303100406

Durham, Deborah. 2000. "Youth and the Social Imagination in Africa: Introduction to Parts 1 and 2". *Anthropological Quarterly* 73, no. 3: 113–20. https://doi.org/10.1353/anq.2000.0003

Furlong, Andy. 2013. *Youth Studies: An Introduction*. New York: Routledge.

Genia, Vicky. 1990. "Interreligious Encounter Group: A Psychospiritual Experience for Faith Development". *Counseling and Values* 35, no. 1: 39–51. https://doi.org/10.1002/j.2161-007X.1990.tb00357.x

Giddens, Anthony. 1991. *Modernity and Self-Identity: Self and Society in the Late Modern Age*. London: Polity.

Gilbert Peter, and Madeleine Parkes. 2011. "Faith in One City: Exploring Religion, Spirituality and Mental Wellbeing in Urban UK". *Ethnicity and Inequalities in Health and Social Care* 4, no. 1: 16–27. https://doi.org/10.1108/17570981111189551

Gleig, Ann. 2019. *American Dharma: Buddhism Beyond Modernity*. London: Yale University Press.

Gooren, Henri. 2010. *Religious Conversion and Disaffiliation: Tracing Patterns of Change in Faith Practices*. New York: Palgrave Macmillan. https://doi.org/10.1057/9780230113039

Gordon-Finlayson, Alasdair, and Michael Daniels. 2008. "Westerners Converting to Buddhism: An Exploratory Grounded Theory Investigation". *Transpersonal Psychology Review* 12, no. 1: 100–19. https://doi.org/10.53841/bpstran.2008.12.1.100

Hay, David, and Rebecca Nye. 1998. *The Spirit of the Child*. London: HarperCollins.

Hidayat, Rofiq. 2022. "Perlu Memperjelas Aturan Perkawinan Beda Agama di Indonesia". Hukum Online.com, 24 June 2022. https://www.hukumonline.com/berita/a/perlu-memperjelas-aturan-perkawinan-beda-agama-di-indonesia-lt62b5753c22db4?page=all

Hughes, Philip, Parichart Suwanbubbha, and Janran Chaisri. 2008. "The Nature of Spirituality among Young People in Australia and Thailand". *Social Compass* 55, no. 3: 359–72. https://doi.org/10.1177/0037768608093697

Ichwayudi, Budi, Ahmad Marzuki, and Hasan Sayfullah. 2021. "Konversi Agama Pada Masyarakat Perkotaan: Reshaping Pendidikan Muallaf di Lembaga Sosial YDSF Kota Surabaya". *Multicultural* (Journal of Islamic Education) 4, no. 2: 1–16. https://jurnal.yudharta.ac.id/v2/index.php/ims/article/view/2607/1843

Jiang, Ting, Chris Ryan, and Chaozhi Zhang. 2018. "The Spiritual or Secular Tourist? The Experience of Zen Meditation in Chinese Temples". *Tourism M Management* 65: 187–99.

Jubba, Hasse. 2019. *Kontestasi Identitas Agama: Lokalitas Spiritual di Indonesia*. Yogyakarta: Phinisi Press.

Kim, Hyun Mee Kim. 2016. "Becoming a City Buddhist Among the Young Generation in Seoul". *International Sociology* 31: 450–66. https://doi.org/10.1177/0268580916643089

Lazzi, Antonio, Paola Scorrano, Pierfelice Rosato, and Balakrishna Grandhi. 2019. "Millennial Generation Preferences for Rose Wine: An Exploratory Study of the Italian and French Markets". *British Food Journal* 122, No. 8: 2443–61. https://doi.org/10.1108/BFJ-07-2019-0478

Luhrmann, Tanya, and Martin Fortier. 2017. "The Anthropology of Mind: Exploring Unusual Sensations and Spiritual Experiences across Cultures. An Interview with Tanya Luhrmann". *ALIUS Bulletin* 1: 25–36. https://www.aliusresearch.org/uploads/9/1/6/0/91600416/lurhmann_-_the_anthropology_of_mind.pdf

Lynch, Gordon. 2007. *The New Spirituality: An Introduction to Progressive Belief in the Twenty-First Century*. London: I.B. Taurus.

Mariano, J.M., and W. Damon. 2008. "The Role of Religious Faith and Spirituality in the Development of Purpose in Adolescence". In *Positive Youth Development and Spirituality: From Theory to Research*, edited by R.M. Lerner, R.W. Roeser, and E. Phelps, pp. 210–30. West Conshohocken, PA: Templeton Foundation Press.

McGrath, Alister. 2004. *The Twilight of Atheism: The Rise and Fall of Disbelief in the Modern World*. London: Doubleday.

Ng, Eddy S. W., Linda Schweitzer, and Sean T. Lyons. 2010. "New Generation, Great Expectations: A Field Study of the Millennial Generation". *Journal of Business and Psychology* 25, no. 2: 281–92. https://doi.org/10.1007/s10869-010-9159-4

Page, Sarah-Jane, and Andrew Kam-Tuck Yip. 2021. "Navigating Youth Transitions as a Buddhist: Privilege, Reflexivity, and Sexuality". *Journal of Global Buddhism* 22, no. 2: 380–98. https://doi.org/10.5281/zenodo.5764629

Pagis, Michal. 2010. "Producing Intersubjectivity in Silence: An Ethnographic Study of Meditation Practice". *Ethnography* 11, no. 2: 309–328. https://doi.org/10.1177/1466138109339041

Prasi, Ben. 2017. "Practicing Meditation for Youth in Digital Era". *Journal of the International Association of Buddhist Universities* (JIABU) 10, no. 2: 13–26. https://so06.tci-thaijo.org/index.php/Jiabu/issue/view/15570/Vol%2010%20No%202%20%28July-December%2C%202017%29

Rambo, Lewis. 1993. *Understanding Religious Conversion*. Yale University Press. https://yalebooks.yale.edu/book/9780300065152/understanding-religious-conversion

Reich, K. Helmut. 1998. "Psychology of Religion: What One Needs to Know". *Zygon: Journal of Religion and Science* 33, no. 1: 113–20. https://doi.org/10.1111/0591-2385.1301998130

Schedneck, Brooke. 2021. "Educational Philosophies and Celebrity Monks: Strategies for Communicating Buddhist Values to Thai Buddhist Youth". *Journal of Global Buddhism* 22, no. 2: 123–40.

Schulze, Gerhard. 2008. *The Experience Society: The Sociology of Contemporary Civilization*. London: SAGE.

Setiawan, Andri. 2020. "Ashin Jinarakkhita Membangkitkan Agama Buddha di Indonesia". *Historia.id*, 18 December 2020. https://historia.id/agama/articles/ashin-jinarakkhita-membangkitkan-agama-buddha-di-indonesia-P9Brz/page/1

Shek, Daniel T. L. 2012. "Spirituality as a Positive Youth Development Construct: A Conceptual Review". *Scientific World Journal* Vol. 2012: 1–8. https://doi.org/10.1100/2012/458953

Sinaga, Tika. 2015. "Menyiasati Hukum dalam Perkawinan Beda Agama". *Kompasiana*, 24 June 2015. https://www.kompasiana.com/tikasinaga/55287dab6ea834b4638b4582/menyiasati-hukum-dalam-perkawinan-beda-agama

Spencer, Anne C. 2018. "A Response to the Oxford Handbook of Religious Conversion from Two Perspectives". *Pastoral Psychology* 67: 219–226. https://doi.org/10.1007/s11089-016-0712-6

Sugianto, Sugianto. 2019. "Persepsi Umat Buddha Terhadap Kegiatan Pelatihan Meditasi Di Vihara Siripada Tangerang". *Vijjacariya* 6 no. 1: 35–50.

Suprijanto, A.B., and T. Rudyansjah. 2021. "Pivot: Sebuah Tinjauan Weberian Atas

Rasionalitas Tindakan". *Antropologi Indonesia* 42, no. 2: 87–102. https://doi.org/10.7454/ai.v42i2.13328

Taylor, J. 2004. "New Buddhism, Urban Space, and Virtual Civil Society". In *Civil Society in Southeast Asia*, edited by Lee Hock Guan, pp. 78–100. Singapore: Institute of Southeast Asian Studies.

Thomson, Rachel. 2009. *Unfolding Lives: Youth, Gender and Change*. London: Policy Press.

Tirri, Kirsi, and Brandy Quinn. 2010. "Exploring the Role of Religion and Spirituality in Developing Purpose: Case Studies of Purposeful Youth". *British Journal of Religious Education* 32, no. 3: 201–14. https://doi.org/10.1080/01416200.2010.498607

Travisano, Richard V. 1970. "Alternation and Conversion as Qualitatively Different Transformations". In *Social Psychology Through Symbolic Interaction*, edited by Stone, Gregory Prentice, and Harvey A. Faberman, pp. 594–606. Waltham, MA: Ginn-Blaisdell.

Turner, Bryan S. 2011. *Religion and Modern Society: Citizenship, Secularization, and the State*. New York: Cambridge University Press.

Tweed, Thomas. A. 1999. "Night-Stand Buddhists and Other Creatures". In *American Buddhism: Methods and Findings in Recent Scholarship*, edited by D.R. Williams and C.S. Queen, pp. 71–90. Richmond: Curzon Press.

Ulfah, Siti Maria, Dilla Nur Octaviana, and Muhammad Aqila. 2019. "Esensi Meditasi Terhadap Spritualitas Umat Buddha". *Al-Adyan: Jurnal Studi Lintas Agama* 14, no. 2: 269–82. https://doi.org/10.24042/ajsla.v14i2.5787

Umam, Mohammad Khaerul, and Muhammad Syafiq. 2014. "Pengalaman Konversi Agama Pada Muallaf Tionghoa. Character". *Jurnal Penelitian Psikologi* 2, no. 3: 1–9.

Vijjananda, Handaka. 2019. "Sammasambuddha: Guru Dewa dan Manusia". Jakarta: Ehipassiko Foundation, June 2019.

Williams-Oerberg, Elizabeth. 2021. "Youth Buddhism: The Centrality of 'Youth' in Modern Buddhism". *Journal of Global Buddhism* 22, no. 2: 322–40. https://www.globalbuddhism.org/article/view/1984

Worthington, Jr., Everett L., Joshua N. Hook, Don E. Davis, and Michael A. McDaniel. 2010. "Religion and Spirituality". *Journal of Clinical Psychology* 67 no. 2: 204–14. https://doi.org/10.1002/jclp.20760

Zachara, Malgorzata. 2020. "The Millennial Generation in the Context of Political Power: A Leadership Gap?". *Leadership* 16, no. 2: 241–58. https://doi.org/10.1177/1742715019885704

Zemke, Ron, Claire Raines, and Bob Filipczak. 2000. *Generations at Work: Managing the Clash of Veterans, Boomers, Xers and Nexters in Your Workplace*. New York: American Management Association.

Zizek, Slavoj. 2001. *On Belief*. London: Routledge.

# 8

# Antagonism and Afterwards

## Millennials in Indonesian Participatory Art after *Reformasi*

Chabib Duta Hapsoro

### ABSTRACT

*Indonesian participatory art discourse has not caught up with the development of its practices over the last twenty years, especially those by millennial artists. The discourse also tends to be Eurocentric and fails to notice participatory phenomena in Indonesia rooted in the heteronomous spirit of Indonesian art and other factors. The forms of participatory art in Indonesia have begun to emerge concretely in the art practices of a few young artists' work as an output of resistance or antagonism towards restrictive homogenization and paternalistic culture in art schools due to the depoliticization of art during the New Order era. These expressions manifested in the form of practices that violate conventional norms of art medium and invite the participation of marginalized populations affected by the New Order's centralistic pembangunan (development) policies. This chapter specifically examines the art practice of a Yogyakarta-based millennial artist, Anang Saptoto, as an example of post-Reformasi participatory art that differs from participatory art practices during the New Order era. As a millennial artist, Saptoto, whose participatory work responds to local agrarian problems, inherits the distinctive artistic spirit of Reformasi, which departs from the spirit of decentralization and localization of information technology to achieve the desired goals. Saptoto's participatory art practice is marked by a rupture from the antagonistic nature of young artists during the New Order era. The non-antagonistic temperament manifests in Saptoto's flexibility in encountering more complicated challenges: the neoliberal economy and education regime, and a commercialized and depoliticized art sphere, among others.*

## INTRODUCTION

This chapter discusses participatory art by millennials, which differs from that by previous generations. Millennial artists who practise participatory art cannot be subsumed under one rigid ideological category. They focus more on pursuing strategic solutions to achieve concrete results for marginalized communities. These artists who engage in activism unavoidably encounter more complicated challenges: the neoliberal economy and education regime, a commercialized and depoliticized art sphere, and regional feudalism, among others.

Participatory art substantially deconstructs the artist's role in creating art. Artists no longer monopolize the authorship of artwork; instead, they initiate cooperative authorship with the audience. The expanded role of the audience potentially cultivates their emancipation. This chapter aims to scrutinize the contemporary participatory art discourse and practice in Indonesia, especially by millennials. It argues that millennials develop participatory art practices while taking cues from an existing tradition that has emerged organically in Indonesia. Participatory art is an organic consequence of the heteronomous[1] endeavour of Indonesian artists since pre-independence and of sociopolitical factors.

Several Indonesian thinkers and sociologists have discussed the phenomenon of Indonesian participatory art and its epistemology, describing it as a response to the spirit of the existing art practices in Indonesia, especially during the time of independence. This heteronomous spirit that characterizes participatory art is attributed to the epistemological legacies of vernacular and traditional art.

As this chapter will show, participatory art in Indonesia relates to youth resistance, specifically against the older generation or the old and dominant establishment. Examples of participatory art and proto-participatory art will show the activist spirit that violates the regulated art practice in the academy or the dominant established practice taught by teachers and the older generations. This spirit proves the vigorous influence of heteronomy in Indonesian art practice.

Linking the art practices in Indonesia before and after *Reformasi*—the period after the fall of President Soeharto—arguably can provide an enriching dimension to the Indonesian art discourse during two historical periods. The dominant discourse usually places the works of artists in the 1980s and 1990s as those that were critical of the repressive administration of the so-called New Order under Soeharto. The antagonistic temper of several young Indonesian artists in those decades shows that their critical voices through rebellious behaviours and artworks were relevant in their most immediate context of daily life, that is, the art academies. The dominant discourse, though, fails to provide a sufficient perspective on millennial artists, who are only seen as dealing with recent opportunities in virtual and commercialized art distribution under the blockchain system. This chapter unveils millennial artists' activism, which is no longer fused with an antagonistic temper.

In Indonesia, artists' circumstances, and consequently practices, always encounter practical and ideological choices. The public perception that the art ecosystem is imbued with the spirit of freedom is far from reality whereas arbitrary choices are the underlying spirit. In contrast, creativity or freedom, according to the feminist art sociologist Janet Wolff, "cannot consist in its somehow escaping from social and (and other) determinants" (1993, p. 21). At least, there are many conditions and challenges in the manifestation of freedom, where, for example, some actions are "free" because an agent can make a "deliberate choice" and not be under any pressure situation (ibid.). Theories of the sociology of art emphasize that art production always lies in the context of the "art world", where social structures and institutions, directly or indirectly, enable someone to act (ibid., p. 23). It is this deterministic framework that confirms that freedom in art production is a myth.

In this chapter, the works of the artist Anang Saptoto (1982–) will be examined to see how his rebellious artistic innovations can be explained in terms of the structure, institutions and resource logic. In sociological terms, an innovation does not make an artist the most decisive figure in change. It is the situation and social factors that make an artist inevitably innovate. Within the sociological framework, Anang Saptoto's participatory practice reflects the changes in youth values that motivate their work, a shift from the previous generation of artists, who were enabled by the structure, institutions and resources to which they were subject. Despite the changes, the practice of participatory art continues and regenerates outside the mainstream art ecosystem, allowing possibilities for artists to reach new sources and capital.

## PARTICIPATORY ART: A THEORETICAL OUTLOOK

Participatory art in the West is conceptualized as the linear progress of art in the Euro-American modern art discourse after the art of the Renaissance era began to abandon its function of serving the needs of religious devotion. The French curator and art philosopher Nicolas Bourriaud perhaps was the one who coined the term "relational art", a term used interchangeably with participatory art. He defines relational art as:

> a set of artistic practices which take as their theoretical and practical point of departure the whole of human relations and their social context, rather than an independent and private space (Bourriaud 2002, p. 113).

He argues that relational art is not a revival of any movement of the past "nor is it the comeback of any style" (ibid., p. 44); instead, it is a kind of recent development in art progress:

> Its basic claim—the sphere of human relations as artwork venue—has no prior example in art history, even if it appears, after the fact, as the obvious backdrop of all aesthetic praxis, and as a modernist theme to cap all modernist themes (ibid., p. 4).

He continues that relational art expands its theoretical horizon to the realm of human interactions and its social context instead of the claim of an independent and private symbolic space (ibid., p. 14). Thus, relational art points to a radical upheaval of the aesthetic, cultural and political goals introduced by modern art (ibid., p. 14). He locates the emergence of relational form essentially in the birth of worldwide urban culture (ibid., p. 15), in which the opening up of connections and the growing urbanization ironically create crampedness, where art audiences can afford no more contemporary artwork as a space to be walked through; instead, audiences need more artwork as a period to be lived through (ibid., p. 14).

The feminist art historian Claire Bishop (2012, p. 11) takes a more radical stance than Bourriaud regarding the significant objective of participatory art, which accentuates activism:

> why participation is important as a project: it rehumanises a society rendered numb and fragmented by the repressive instrumentality of capitalist production. Given the markets' near total saturation of our image repertoire, so the argument goes, artistic practice can no longer revolve around the construction of objects to be consumed by a passive bystander.

Bishop (2012, p. 12) argues instead that such practice should be active, interacting with reality and taking steps to repair social bonds. She claims that the participatory trend is unavoidable, indicating a critical detachment towards the neoliberal new world order. Through this art form, the aesthetic judgement of beauty is extended. As a result, beauty is no longer seen only in the quality of formal composition but is challenged to be relevant to how social activities are carried out.

However, it is known that relational aesthetics tends to overlook the artistic discussion or value of its artistic practice. Or, in the words of Bishop (2006, pp. 178–83), "there can be no failed, unsuccessful, unresolved, or boring works of collaborative art because all are equally essential to the task of strengthening the social bond." She discusses participatory art's social turn, a tendency to leave aesthetic judgement and to merely value an artwork in sociological criteria. An example is how the curator Charles Esche reviewed a participatory art project *Tenantspin* (1999) by a Danish collective Superflex:

> His central judgement about *Tenantspin* concerns its effectiveness as a "tool" that can "change the image of both the tower block itself and the residents"; in his view, the major achievement of this project is that it has forged a "stronger sense of community in the building". Esche is one of Europe's most articulate defenders of politicized artistic practice, and one of its most radical museum directors, but his essay is symptomatic of the critical tendency I am drawing attention to. His decision not to address what it means for Superflex to be doing this project *as art* ultimately renders these value judgements indistinguishable from government arts policy with its emphasis on verifiable outcomes (Bishop 2012, p. 17).

Through her deep research on many participatory-mode artists, Bishop finds that aesthetics has become a "dangerous word" for them (Bishop 2012, p. 21) and that they dismiss it as "merely visual, superfluous and academic" since it is less significant than concrete results (ibid., p. 22). However, she insists that there is a way to value participatory art projects as art, asserting that "the aesthetic doesn't need to be sacrificed at the altar of social change, because it always already contains … ameliorative promise (ibid., p. 29)." Bishop gets inspiration from Jacques Ranciere's "aesthetic regime of art" in Western art history, which creates confusion and tension between autonomy (desire to remove art from everyday life) and heteronomy (desire to blur art and life). The urge to support the autonomy of art to endorse aesthetics is to deny that art also has a domain to "promise a better world" (ibid., p. 29). She then concludes that to value collaborative projects, we need to depend on basically two things: (1) an assessment in terms of whether they are good or bad models of collaboration, and (2) the art history's comprehensive familiarity with medium progression regarding materialization and dematerialization. Every detail of collaboration could depend on these standards. By this statement, arguably, Bishop is sure that social engagement art is one of the most recent sophisticated aspects of art development.

However, the scholar Elly Kent (2022, p. 231) suggests that little academic or discursive observation has been addressed to participatory art practice outside the United States and Europe. In her book, *Artists and the People: Ideologies of Art in Indonesia*, Kent offers a thorough description of a range of art practices and discourses in Indonesian participatory art which deal with "aesthetic implications for artists' work when it relies on the involvement of other people as a fundamental conceptual element" (ibid., p. 231).

It is reductive then to apply universalism, as the Euro-American concept of modern art, to the other hemisphere, especially as the knowledge production overlooks concrete socio-political situations in diverse historical trajectories. In some contexts, universalism has a class bias since modern art is also the knowledge product of the bourgeois class. A multi-modernism, instead, reveals that every part of the world has its trajectory of modernity, such as the art practices in Indonesia, which initially emerged from a particular discourse on account of heteronomous factors related to the creation of the nation-state (ibid., p. 220), including colonialism and Indonesian art.

## DEVELOPMENT OF PARTICIPATORY ART IN INDONESIA

Colonialism has a significant epistemological role in art development in Indonesia. During the colonial period, Indonesian traditional and primitive social order shifted to serve colonial interests. As a result, the structure of traditional art production, which deals with the essential life system, changed. Traditional art production does not require a specific appreciation of a certain medium, like painting or sculpture; the artists paint or create a sculpture to be an accessory for performatively sacred ceremonies. Indeed, traditional art production is holistic and communal and serves a utilitarian function. Community members are involved in the art production to fulfil their transcendental needs and the artists are not familiar with the notion of authorship, which modern artists strongly believe in. Therefore, traditional, or premodern art, is holistic in realization and demands every aspect of the community's everyday life. It also deals with the people's active participation, not only as audience but also as producers.

The introduction of modern art in colonized Indonesia and the new colonial capitalist order created a new and unpleasant social situation for traditional art. The late prominent art critic Sanento Yuliman (2020a, p. 7) says that traditional art reduces its relevancies to social situations, although it is still practised by communities due to the new logic of capitalist production that values capital accumulation and profit. In contrast with modern and capitalist plantation nowadays, the vernacular plantation logic not only pursues daily needs but is also a part of the religious and spiritual call which require sacred ceremonial art. Today, the ceremonial art tradition has lost its function of serving a holistic art production, and art production has become separated from daily life (Yuliman 2020a, p. 7). Forced modernization results in the *adat* (custom) ethos and *kerakyatan* (socialist) tradition going into oblivion (Isabella, 2018, p. xvii). It can be argued that colonial capitalism and the imposition of modern art in colonial Indonesia are significant factors in uprooting the participatory manner of Indonesian traditional or premodern art practices.

Yuliman is then sure that the history and development of (modern) art in Indonesia depend on endogenous and exogenous factors that always set art as autonomous and heteronomous. As it happens, Kent (2016, p. 44) maintains that some Indonesian artists have been experimenting with deconstructing the boundaries between the endogenous and exogenous in the quest for how art functions in society, which creates a motive for them to pursue a participatory mode:

> I contend that the combination of participatory and individual practice in Indonesia remains strongly influenced by originally a discourse combining autonomy and heteronomy, which were set out at the advent of modernist art discourse in Indonesia. Yet through practice, artists continue to test these values against exogenous art discourse. This continual discursive and practical testing of the endogenous against the exogenous is embedded in Indonesian art discourse. In this way, Indonesian artists are developing new and varied responses to early Indonesian forms and discourses that sought to conjoin autonomy and heteronomy and are claiming a place for distinctive practices that should rightly be recognised at the forefront of contemporary art practice in the aesthetic regime.

Yuliman (2020b, pp. 285–86), observes how in the 1970s young artists—under the banner of GSRBI (Gerakan Seni Rupa Baru Indonesia), or the Indonesian New Art Movement, which will be discussed later in this article—started to deny individualism, deconstruct authorship, and explore concreteness. He explains further and provides useful characteristics to define participatory art:

> Artwork does not have to be different from the ordinary stuff that accompanies our daily life. On the other hand, artworks may even be objects, selected and combined in a way to express thoughts and the environment. It is even possible that the "artwork" is not in the form of goods, but also of processes, events, or deeds (actions). It may not be the result of one's efforts, but of collaboration, perhaps even with the participation of the audience or the public (whose role thus changes, so do artists). "An artwork" does not have to be a transformation and abstraction to filter the "universal" from "the particular" and distance themselves from actual reality. Rather, it can maintain the actuality and uniqueness of events or circumstances. An "artwork" can take the form of an intervention towards a fragment of social life to drive a change.

Yuliman (2020b pp. 285–86) then examines the specific ends of concrete-ended and non-individualistic art to create objectives for the social and environmental sphere. First, by giving some examples of artworks that invite engagement from the audience, Yuliman argues that the artists pursue concreteness. He underlines the artistic objectives of creating communication to avoid any misinformation caused by artworks. Then it is not strange when an artist also presents research data and documents.

Another Indonesian thinker who has been interested in this kind of art practice is the late sociologist Arief Budiman (1987, p. 21), through his questions of universalism in Indonesian cultural production. Universalism can be understood as a belief that ideas have universal applicability. In the modern intellectual sphere, it manifests as the Western objective of consolidating all social systems across geography under Western values. To Budiman, artists who believe in universalism are keen to overcome time and space. Instead of making artworks about social situations, they aim to unite themselves with the transcendent, based on "a kind of creed among them, that it is a taboo to associate their creations with the people around them. The resulting art is impure; art that serves the community; a prostitute art; a commercial art."

He offers, instead, an alternative to universal art, that is, contextual art. On a contextual frame, art loses its transcendent and sacred value. Budiman is convinced that contextual art is not ahistorical:

> In other words, contextual aesthetics links aesthetic experience with historical developments, where space and time factors are important. Aesthetic values are processed by concrete humans. It is not a transcendental value that is located outside history. It is a value that proceeds with the history of mankind itself. If you want to compare, it is like the value of morality, which also changes throughout history, across places, and over time. Aesthetic values, in the contextual aesthetic paradigm, lose their magical and sacred properties (1987, p. 27).

At this point, some conclusions can be drawn. First, participatory art practices deal with aesthetics in terms of expanding the aesthetic conception beyond the Eurocentric and the dominant ideas in the legacy of modern art. Second, Indonesian art critics and scholars have acknowledged premodern art practices and art's heteronomy that appear in a participatory manner. Although they have not specifically defined what participatory art is, they have indicated its traits in young, Indonesian artists in the 1970s and 1980s regarding their tendency towards the concrete involvement of the audience.

Being part of the youth culture, the emerging movements and innovations in Indonesian art have distinctive sociological origins. One of them is the dissatisfaction of the younger generation of artists with the dominant art teachings or practices adhered to by the older generation, whether in an academy or an art ecosystem. S. Sudjojono (1913–85), for example, in the 1930s represented a dissatisfied voice in responding to the dominant practice of colonial painting (of beautiful landscapes) from the nineteenth to early twentieth centuries in colonial Indonesia.

At the age of twenty-six, Sudjojono (2000, p. 1) sarcastically referred to these landscape paintings as Mooi Indie (Beautiful Indies), arguing that these paintings did not make sense to the native colonized Indonesians and even supported the colonial power's exploitation of them.[2] Mooi Indie did it through the artistic practice of disguise, which includes, first, subtle obfuscation of the reality of rural nature in Indonesia allotted as monoculture plantations, hiding forced cultivation and forced labour; and, second, the wrong depiction of farmers as lazy and spoiled by the fertile, tropical climate. This mythical depiction of the Indonesian human character legitimized the colonial power in its exploitative practice of the native population. It also supported the internalization of inferiority among the colonized so that they accepted their destiny as colonial subjects (Alatas 1977, p. 77).

Instead, Sudjojono invited Indonesian artists to have the courage to choose a path that loves the truth more, to dare to be poor[3] and simple but at the same time confident in establishing themselves as "Indonesian artists" (2000, p. 99). His *jiwa ketok* (visible soul) ultimately does not only take into account the liberation of Indonesian people from inferiority but also puts Indonesian painting into a utilitarian nuance; art is a potential tool to show the full dignity of the Indonesian human being, degraded for years by colonialism. Sudjojono did not only perform his activism through ideas but also manifested it through realism in painting, conscientiously depicting Indonesians who suffered from colonial capitalism. Realism mushroomed in the period between independence and the revolution (1945–49) during which many Indonesian artists pursued the style and incorporated propaganda to support the Indonesian sovereign cause against the Dutch military aggression.

Another young artist who used realism to express his empathy towards the people was Hendra Gunawan (1918–83). As one of the founders and main mentors of the Yogyakarta-based Sanggar Pelukis Rakyat—an art studio at the time of the revolution that served as an important cultural space where people acquired artistic skills under the auspices of a mentor—he encouraged his pupils to interact as much as possible with the *rakyat*—the people—and empathize with them. In return, the *rakyat* would understand the artist's work:

> If you want to understand *rakyat*, you have to live with them, feel their suffering, joy, filth, wish. These things are the main resources. With good skill, you can paint the people's lives with a realistic portrayal in order the make them understand (Hapsoro 2017, p. 19).

An underlying participatory awareness or objective can be inferred from Gunawan's statement above. His encouragement for engagement persisted in *Turba* (*Turun ke Bawah*—or down to the grassroots), a movement by Lembaga Kebudayaan Rakyat (LEKRA, the Institute of People's Culture), a leftist art organization where he was an active and prominent member. During the 1950s–1960s, LEKRA artists carried out *Tiga Sama* (three togetherness), in which they had to eat, live and work together with village farmers (Shackford-Bradley 2007). The objective of this method, according to LEKRA's writer Hersri Setiawan, was to introduce urbanized leftist artists to the physical deprivations and psychological hardships of village life. It was hoped that during and after implementing *Tiga Sama*, LEKRA artists would be personally transformed into supporting the bigger communist orientation to convey research and create revolutionary art forms (ibid.).

Indeed, *Turba* was a "revolutionary realist" focused on immediate, concrete issues and the fight for justice under a radical nationalist ideology (Bodden 2012; Jurriëns 2013). However, there have been no significant findings on LEKRA's real participatory practice in which the audience was a co-creator in art production, although it is clear that the artists maintained the people as subject matters and sources of inspiration. These artists' practices often expressed antagonistic and agitative attitudes towards their "enemies" through artistic propaganda, portraying them as imperialists, capitalists, middlemen and loan sharks, among others. Nonetheless, LEKRA's efforts to mainstream art, implemented through massive artist training, production and exhibition costs, and art distribution towards the *rakyat*, were remarkable—although, unlike other organizations, it was later extirpated by the New Order.

Another episode of dissatisfaction with the dominant art practices occurred in the 1970s—as previously mentioned. A group of art students at the Yogyakarta Fine Arts Academy (Akademi Seni Rupa Yogyakarta, or ASRI; today Indonesia Institute of the Arts or ISI, Yogyakarta), such as FX Harsono (1949–), Hardi (1951–), Siti Adiyati (1951–), Nanik Mirna

(1951–2010) and Bonyong Munni Ardhi (1946–), pursued antagonistic deviation in responding to the stagnation and rigidity in the teaching model at ASRI, dominated by the decorative painting style taught and practised by their teachers (Wiyanto 2022, p. 97). The deviation involved, for example, producing orderly geometric paintings—even using a ruler and eraser—as well as the use of found objects (ibid., p. 94).

The antagonism[4] peaked in a protest against the jury of the 1974 edition of the Great Indonesian Painting Exhibition I (Pameran Besar Seni Lukis Indonesia I), a biennial event in which the students participated. They objected to the jury's decision to award senior artists and some of their instructors at ASRI, who stuffily pursued decorative painting. Their protest was expressed in a mourning bouquet with the message, "Our deep condolences to the passing of the Indonesian painting" at the closing of the event.[5] Accordingly, their teachers, who had strong authority in ASRI, set out punishment for them, which came out as obstacles for them in continuing their education.

The friction spurred the protesting students to form a coalition with art students at the Art Department at Bandung Institute of Technology[6] who were experiencing a similar stagnation. They exhibited together at the Cipta Gallery in Jakarta in 1975 under the title "Pameran Seni Rupa Baru Indonesia" (Indonesian New Art Exhibition), and as a group were then known as Gerakan Seni Rupa Baru Indonesia, or GSRB (Indonesian New Art Movement), as noted earlier. Their artworks departed from the dominant and well-established art practices through the use of found objects and popular visual culture, making art objects undistinguished from everyday objects. For them, artistic expression could not only be limited to lyrical expression resulting from the artists' filtered experiences in abstract and decorative paintings; it should be able to pursue a more direct form, allowing the audience to receive an intended message.

A more direct expression using found objects suggests the concreteness of the audience's experience, allowing them to produce meanings. This engaged artistic expression enabled subversion in art production during the New Order. This new art movement offered opportunities for people to aspire, something avoided and repressed by the regime, which demanded a vertical instructional hierarchy.

Another case of artistic practice that must be considered is an artwork by Moelyono, *Kesenian Unit Desa* (KUD or Village Unit Art), which was supposed to be the artist's final project to fulfil ASRI Yogyakarta's requirement in 1985 for a bachelor's degree (see Figure 8.1). However, the examination committee rejected the work since it violated the ASRI painting studio's criteria. KUD came as an installation work consisting of found objects, i.e., banana leaf bowls containing soil planted with seeds and vegetable stems, among others, which were put out on traditional mats. There was also a small hut containing a drawing book of a conglomerate figure and a podium with a microphone and noise from a transistor radio news broadcast (Moelyono 1997, p. 93). In the presentation, Moelyono performed a speech, offering a dialogue with the campus authority. Needless to say, he came up against the campus authority's hostility.

KUD contains the artist's subtle antagonism.[7] As a student, Moelyono no longer believed that he had to dedicate himself to one medium, painting. Instead, he believed more in the wide choice of suitable mediums to express ideas and contextualize social conditions. Arguably, he tested the limit of his teachers' conservatism in painting. Fortunately, he was given a chance to create a conventional painting to fulfil the conditions to graduate.[8]

Despite the rejection, KUD set a foundational pavement for Moelyono's artistic practice. Presenting dialogue as the primary practice, Moelyono (2005, p. 30) believed it could facilitate a critical attitude because dialogue connects everyone as equal subjects and demands each other's respect. KUD gave Moelyono a foundation for participatory research, a combination of social research, education work, and communal political action.

In 1986, Moelyono worked in Brumbun and Nggerangan villages in Tulungagung, East Java, teaching drawing to elementary school students using simple means and through art that encouraged them to build awareness concerning their lives and well-being. It was a meaningful practice and a breakthrough by way of practical methods inspired by social sciences and activism discourses.[9] (See Figure 8.2.) However, in the New Order period, such participatory art projects could become provocative. He encountered repression from the state authorities because he drew a crowd and even developed critical faculties among the villagers, creating an inconvenient situation for the established local authority.

## INDONESIAN YOUTH CULTURE AND ART (ACTIVISM) BEFORE AND DURING *REFORMASI*

The youth spirit with an antagonistic temper has been capable of sparking innovations in art production in Indonesia—and, in art development,

**FIGURE 8.1**
**Kesenian Unit Desa**

*Note:* An installation work by Moelyono, featuring a rice field hut, rattan mats, soil, banana leaves, cassava stems, and sound, 1985.
*Source:* FX Harsonos' documentation.

**FIGURE 8.2**
**Moelyono, *Seni Rupa Refleksi Kehidupan Brumbun dan Nggerangan* (1994)**

*Note:* Mixed media, variable dimension. The installation artwork was an artistic output of his participatory activism in Brumbun and Nggerangan villages, Tulungagung.
*Source:* Moelyono.

novelty is a kind of absoluteness. However, Sanento Yuliman emphasizes that in the half-century since independence Indonesian art had only encountered slight changes or turmoil. Among several reasons for this state, Yuliman identifies the older generation's inability to accept reform.[10]

During the New Order, the growth of higher art education or art academies did not necessarily contribute to increasing the number of young artists who would enter the arena but instead hindered novelty. Among the few, not many had new creative tendencies because only young artists who followed in the footsteps of their teachers were supported, with works that were variants of the old types already made by their predecessors (Yuliman 2000, pp. 102–3). It was a uniformity that avoided dialectics of ideas which then blockaded the emergence of new ideas (ibid.). From another perspective, Chandra Johan finds that the need for growth in a capitalistic modern order requires standardization and specialization to facilitate modern life. These are not only applicable institutionally in the art academies but also internalized as standards by the individuals who teach there. This system is felt to be too restrictive and even absurd for the students (Johan 1987, p. 42).

The development of art academies that operated on the logic of homogenization opened greater opportunities for paternalization towards young people. The young were required to keep following in the footsteps of their elders. This rigidity and orthodoxy in maintaining the status quo were a manifestation of the New Order's penetration of power, which was felt in the microsphere, pivoting not only in political life but also in the educational and domestic spheres. The paternalistic model, later referred to as typical of Javanese feudalism, disparages young people who were perceived as rude to their parents. Criticism of parents should not be conveyed openly because it would demean their dignity (Yudhistira 2010, p. 151). The maturity of critical young people was always doubted. FX Harsono and friends and Moelyono were subjected to such scepticism. The despair in facing this suffocating situation led to youth antagonism.

The New Order also co-opted young people's representations: those who obeyed were role models, and, conversely, those who were critical were rogues. Doreen Lee's argument makes sense that during the New Order era, especially after 1978,[11] there was "a long break in youth's nationalism's lineage, until it was revived again in 1998 with *Reformasi*" (Lee 2016, p. 7). The young people's representation of dissent and criticism rarely appeared during the peak of the New Order.[12] On the contrary, youth identity was almost always associated with criminal acts of the underclass, which then brought youth association to thugs (ibid., pp. 7, 151). This co-optation at the same time suppressed young people's opportunities for activism. In addition, under the anti-communist New Order regime, activism could be alleged to be an offshoot of communism, which could threaten the lives of youth activists. So, FX Harsono's and Moelyono's choices of rebellious expressions put them at risk. In this regime, every power apparatus was vertically centralized in the person of Soeharto, who held military and political powers in his hands. As in Foucauldian biopower, Soeharto's New Order positioned everyone's biological and mental body as a political body, which was essential for governmentality (Miller and Yudice 2002, p. 4). The vision manifested in various procedures to pursue and establish submission. Youth activism was resisted, for example, through the depoliticizing educational policy of "Normalisasi Kehidupan Kampus/Badan Koordinasi Kemahasiswaan" (NKK/BKK) in 1978 that forbade students from engaging in political activities on campus. Students, however, managed to initiate underground platforms for free speech and youth politics, as well as organize study clubs and student presses, creating networks to NGOs, among others (Lee 2016, p. 35; Juliastuti and Lestari 2006, p. 141).

In the *Reformasi* era, as there was no longer a single common enemy, an arena emerged where progressive social forces and conservative powers contested to gain institutionalized changes in the democratic administration (Lee 2016, p. 210). *Reformasi* has been marked by decentralization, rife with social problems both on national and regional levels. Horizontal conflicts escalated as predatory local or national state administrative actors strengthened their positions while the disenfranchisement of the poor and rural areas continued (Klinken and Barker 2009, as cited in Lee 2015, p. 307).

The die-hard youth activism thus faced threats on a level that was tantamount to those in the previous period, even trickier. The shift of the higher education paradigm under neoliberalism has driven students to take a pragmatic approach, finishing their studies soon to get jobs and staying away from sociopolitical issues (Juliastuti and Lestari 2006, p. 141). The art scholar Nuraini Juliastuti finds that it is difficult to determine whether young people hold certain ideologies or merely consume the commodification of art although leftist books or icons are no longer banned by the state apparatus (ibid., p. 142). Nevertheless, youth activism also discovered many options. For example, Juliastuti witnesses that creativity flourishes beyond the previous era's imagination, providing youth with many ways of expression, and there is an intersection of media, allowing them to consume "global issues through various aspects of cultural products in their everyday lives" (ibid., p. 142). Extending Juliastuti's argument, Lee argues that activism has been transformed into a more diverse field of engagement, such as environmentalism, indigenous rights, press freedom, LGBT rights, and religious freedom, among others (Lee 2016, p. 211).

After *Reformasi*, Indonesian youth activist art, which deals with awareness of important issues and encourages people's participation in social transformation (Wright 2000, p. 49), is not merely carried out by artists focusing on criticism of national problems (Lee 2015, p. 302). Instead, it has turned out as a more diffuse counter-establishment and localized approach (Lee 2015, p. 302). Juliastuti explains counter-establishment as an "alternative", indicating that ordinary people, instead of state apparatus, can initiate and develop alternative infrastructure in art production to overcome the lack of state support for art development (Juliastuti 2008; Juliastuti 2012, pp. 119–25). It is unlike during the New Order when the state's formal infrastructure dominated the social-political sphere and civil-private initiatives were limited because the government-imposed restrictions on people gathering and expressing their opinions. Just as youth and students played an important contribution in toppling Soeharto, youth movements now create many initiatives, including alternative art infrastructure. Thus, Juliastuti makes sense in stating that alternative initiatives in art production are incorporated into the youth movements after it was previously denied by the New Order government (Juliastuti 2012, p. 119). As the youth discover the contemporary global culture, alternative movements also embrace the do-it-yourself (DIY) culture. In some regards, the DIY spirit or subculture is suitable for various communities that focus on self-sufficiency, creating things outside of formal-professional knowledge as resistance against consumer culture. Bruhn (2012 p. 110) notices that DIY culture is applicable in discussing Indonesian alternative spaces or artists' collectives, especially in Yogyakarta.

In *Reformasi*, Indonesian youth's encounter with the contemporary global culture would not have happened without the Internet in the mid-1990s. Merlyna Lim (2012 p. 159) notes that the arrival of commercial Internet service providers (ISPs) did not prompt the significant growth of Internet users. Rather, it was the *warnets* (*warung Internet*—small, informal establishments that provide Internet access in booths for hourly rent) that significantly contributed to Internet popularization among Indonesian society at large. Lim continues that *warnet* offers some benefits. *First*, it does not require computer ownership for an ISP subscription; anyone can access the Internet by the hour. *Second*, *warnets* owned by civil-private and micro-scale businesses not only reflect the absence of the state's telecommunication infrastructure (Lim 2012, p. 159) but also the wide access to the Internet for upper- and lower-middle classes. *Third*, a *warnet* inherits the vernacular design of typical Indonesian *warung* (café): the bamboo screening and *lesehan* (seats on the floor) style allow customers to buy meals, eat, drink and just hang out (Lim 2003, p. 278). *Warnet* then "embodies the social function of *warung* in the traditional information network" (Lim 2018, p. 160), providing a place for people to discuss very broad topics, from daily life to hard issues such as politics (Lim 2003,

p. 278). It can be said then that the infrastructure of the Internet, and its early culture, in Indonesia is very much inseparable from the sociological setting of alternative movements. The Internet as a new medium not only provides new means of exchanging information or knowledge but also encourages civilians and the grassroots to adapt, transform and localize technology (Lim 2018, p. 159) beyond the state and capitalist intervention.

The alternative movement in art can be seen mostly in the emergence in the early 2000s of artists' collectives, alternative spaces, communities and study groups, founded by young people in their mid-twenties, especially in three centres of art development: Jakarta, Bandung and Yogyakarta. They promoted new media or new interests in art that previously had not been supported by the state or mainstream art ecosystem, which includes art in an urban context, video and media art, contemporary photography, and art activism. The artists' collective in Jakarta known as *ruangrupa* is a notable example of how such collectives use DIY culture to provide alternative art infrastructure. Born initially to pursue relevant artistic practice and production in Jakarta's urban context in 2000, *ruangrupa* has developed as an important form of art infrastructure in Jakarta and beyond. Comprising visual artists, writers, filmmakers, architects and musicians, among others, it runs to fulfil many functions, such as educating prospective artists, curators and art critics, organizing new media biennales and publishing visual art journals (Juliastuti 2012, p. 119).

Being alternative drives Indonesian artists and cultural producers in *Reformasi* to develop and experiment with many strategies to spread out their impact, or at least to survive. Arguably, it may be unwise for the youth movement in art production to persist with antagonism since the situation becomes more complicated than before. Youth cultural producers tend to see cultural problems in more fragmented ways than before and find solutions practically and pragmatically. Juliastuti suggests that there is a flexible characteristic of alternative space which includes creating activities under changing focuses and contexts, and flexibility in finding funds and resources to run the spaces (Juliastuti 2008). The flexibility also applies to the typical daily organization of the spaces. It is not strange to see an alternative space functioning as a gallery, a library or a showcase room, all under the same roof, sometimes at the founders' house or *rumah kos* (boarding house). It might relate to Ade Darmawan's "contextual response", inseparable works of initiative spaces. Through this response, alternative spaces conduct experiments in their local environment to respond to local needs. The model is thus often irrelevant in other places and sometimes short-lived.[13]

Youth art activism has certainly transformed in more dynamic ways than previously under the influences of alternative settings. In the New Order, youth art activism mostly dealt with the real and constant threats of an authoritarian regime. In *Reformasi*, art activism not only deals with propaganda to express dissenting opinions towards authority but often employs diverse strategies in achieving concrete impact in society, though in a local context. Katherine Bruhn asserts that art activism in *Reformasi* has been driven towards participatory or social engagement practice, thanks to the nature of the alternative spaces enabling their members and audience to hold a discussion—restricted in the New Order era—and confront issues relevant to Indonesia's history and contemporary situations (Bruhn 2013, p. 117). Bruhn suggests that the vast network throughout Indonesia and abroad opens opportunities not only for funding but also for information exchanges that enhance meaningful discussions between the spaces to gain practical knowledge in practising social engagement art (ibid.). The new destiny of youth art activism by this notion is perhaps that it no longer puts artists on the front stage. Instead, artists' collectives find a new role behind the scenes: employing art pedagogy and the intersection of creative fields to supply marginalized communities with relevant skills in coping with the state and capitalist repression or strategies for advocacy that they themselves could use. Bruhn mentions and discusses some artists' collectives in Yogyakarta such as Taring Padi, Teater Garasi and Ketjilbergerak that accompany marginalized communities in Java who suffer from village eviction, youth criminalization, and land exploitation and destruction by mining companies (ibid., pp. 43–65).

Artists' collectives in *Reformasi* are also capable of building mutually beneficial relationships with the state, an impossibility in the New Order. An example is Jatiwangi Art Factory (JAF), one of Lee's case studies and an artist initiative that applies a contextual response towards villagers within social participatory projects in the agricultural, mono-industrial, and post-crisis setting in Majalengka, West Java (Lee 2015, p. 318). This civil-private initiative builds close relationships with the district governments or even local police institutions. Lee finds that JAF's founders were locally well known, allowing them to interfere with local mainstream arts and cultural production. The founders and the Majalengka local governments provide an example of accountability and accessibility in state-society relations which resembles elite convergence (Lee 2015, p. 319). Furthermore, Lee observes that the relationship between JAF and the local governments is not patron-based. Instead, she suggests,

> the JAF community has managed to produce participatory art that leaves space for state involvement without subordinating their artistic vision. *Pak Camat* and *Pak Polisi* have themselves become artists according to JAF's rules, creating a stakeholder portfolio of *karya* (work) as proof of their engagement with the village community (ibid., p. 320).

## ANANG SAPTOTO AND *PANEN APA HARI INI*: INDONESIAN MILLENNIAL PARTICIPATORY ART IN *REFORMASI* ERA

More than twenty years after *Reformasi* began, art practices and infrastructure have encountered and experienced increasingly complex networks of production, distribution and consumption. Global neoliberalism and the increasingly sophisticated development of the Internet have reinforced significant changes in the art ecosystem in Indonesia. An increasing number of multinational corporations and information-based businesses have created a new middle class. These new multinational companies, many of which are extractive, have also penetrated the democratic process and influenced the character of the political elites and the middle class. The art ecosystem in Indonesia, directly or not, is affected by the elites' transactions. The invention of blockchain technology also necessitates changes in art production, placing artists as content creators and increasingly directing them in art production in the virtual world.

The complexity of this decade, despite the freedom of exchange of information and expression during *Reformasi*, has played a role in limiting the number of artists who are critical of state policies, let alone assisting marginalized and indigenous people affected by the excesses of unjust infrastructure development. One reason is self-censorship by artists who want to avoid the trap of dubious articles of the information technology law. Another reason is that Indonesian artists have been keen to become world citizens who participate and contribute to universal humanitarian ideas while at the same time disconnected from their immediate surroundings. Artists and art practitioners are faced with more and more crossroads of ethical choices. During this period, an artist could claim to be a leftist artist.

However, he or she can also be involved in a large exhibition sponsored by a mining company that greedily exploits natural resources in an indigenous (*adat*) land without experiencing a significant ideological dilemma. It can be said that the practice of participatory art in *Reformasi* has been marked by a rupture from the antagonistic nature of young artists during the New Order era. Anang Saptoto will be discussed here as a case study to show an artist's consistency in assisting several farmer groups in Yogyakarta amid this city's art and culture development.

As a graduate of the Faculty of Photography and Television, Indonesian Institute of the Arts (Yogyakarta), Saptoto was familiar with activism during his university days. However, his involvement in the photography collective Ruang MES 56 since 2002 has identified him as an artist who focuses on the medium of contemporary photography. His involvement in this space has led him to participate in many contemporary art exhibitions in Indonesia and abroad, exhibiting both individual and collective works under MES 56. MES 56 was established due to the lack of appreciation for art photography in the Indonesian contemporary art ecosystem in the early 2000s. The space was formed in a typical motif of the development of photographic practices in Indonesia, which always requires a "space" materially, emotionally, structurally and creatively.[14] In the case of MES 56, although not typical of this collective, the members end up disrupting the personal and conventional relationship between the camera and the cameraman as an individual practice. Collective activities in MES 56 are not like that in ordinary photography hobbyist groups whose members photo-hunt together in exotic places. More than that, MES 56 grows in collective works "ranging from social empowerment to one that leans towards creative experimentation" (Tadjib 2015, p. 182). It is this creative experimentation that has brought MES 56 and its members to public eminence in Indonesian art through their distinctive photographic works, displayed at important and commercial art event circuits.

The image of MES 56 being closely related to the art market has obfuscated their involvement in activism, especially in Yogyakarta. One of their collective activist projects is "Bangun dan Gembira" (Wake Up and Be Happy, 2006). This project assisted children affected by the 2006 earthquake in Yogyakarta through the method of storytelling photography, seeking to heal their traumatic experiences.[15] Their last art activism was titled "Alhamdulillah We Made It", a result of their mentoring and empowerment project for Middle Eastern refugees who were stranded on the south coasts of Yogyakarta in 2014. They assisted the refugees through several photography and graphic design workshops (MES 56 2015).

Collective work and creative experimentation in MES 56 more or less inform Saptoto in his individual work or his work with other collectives in the spirit of participatory art and activism. His artistic works are in fact unconventional in accommodating activism practices in Yogyakarta. He has been very vocal in expressing his boredom at the boundaries of art and activism. Activism, for him, is an essential part of an artist's creative process to obtain information (Pea 2018):

> What is the reason that there is always a boundary between artists and activists, and if there are artists who try to get closer to real problems, they are immediately claimed to be activists. This is strange, how come the distribution of information is avoided instead of being understood as something that can be tackled together.

Furthermore, he also believes that the artist's substantial role is needed by the community in terms of amplifying their voices:

> If we are directly involved in being part of the dynamics of society's problems, then we will see that society needs art as a medium to help echo their voices. So that the distribution of information can be packaged in such a way. Because there is a role vacancy, so artistic work is then only carried out by a few people, whether artists or not (Pea 2018).

Therefore, Anang Saptoto's artistic practice is not limited by the choice of a rigid medium for art. Instead, he engages in various mediums and activities and often combines them to achieve the expected impact. One of them is activism in 2018 on behalf of Temon, Kulon Progo, one of the villages affected by eviction due to the construction of Yogyakarta International Airport. Within his capacity, Saptoto did whatever was needed, such as designing fundraising posters and assembling solar panels for the homes of several villagers whose power sources had been cut off by government officials.

The following section will discuss Saptoto's work, *Panen Apa Hari Ini* (What's the Harvest Today). This ongoing work since 2021 aims to distribute harvested and processed products from urban farmer groups and publicize their activities.[16] Through this work, Saptoto not only works as an event organizer but also handles the publication strategy of this activity.

One example of *Panen Apa Hari Ini's* activity is Pasar Tiban Purbayan (Purbayan Pop-up Market) in the Kotagede area which provides an opportunity to gather in one place urban farmer groups and potential customers (Figure 8.3). This event lies in the domain of and under the responsibility of the City Agriculture Service. However, it becomes part of an art exhibition organized by Struggles for Sovereignty, a forum that raises land and food sovereignty issues in Yogyakarta.[17]

*Panen Apa Hari Ini* through Pasar Tiban Purbayan offers a solution to one of the agrarian problems in Indonesia. Unlike conventional farmers, farmer groups are part-timers who use vacant urban spaces in the city. In some cases, although their production quantity is not as much as that of conventional farmers, farmer groups often conduct experiments but have difficulties finding a proper market. *Panen Apa Hari Ini* then connects the supply and demand sides to realize food security in the urban area.

**FIGURE 8.3**
**Pasar Tiban Purbayan (Purbayan Pop-up Market)**

*Note:* The market, which was initiated by *Panen Apa Hari Ini* in collaboration with the Purba Asri Urban Farmer Group, Purbayan, and twenty-six other farmer groups in the Kotagede subdistrict of Yogyakarta. Pasar Tiban Purbayan was organized as part of the Struggles for Sovereignty collaboration programme.
*Source:* Courtesy: Anang Saptoto.

Saptoto's artistic work is manifested in organizing activities, documenting events through photography and website development, and designing event publications through posters and banners.

Reviewing *Panen Apa Hari Ini,* Hsiang-Pin Wu (2021) reveals that one of the strengths of this work is beyond the question of where the art is in this project, although there are some consequences in the form of conventional works produced by this project (Wu 2021). For example, a series of photo works shows surreal imageries that combine the human body and some agricultural products. Saptoto reveals that this serves more as a publication of agricultural products, which later became stand-alone artworks (Figure 8.4).

Hsiang-Pin Wu quotes Saptoto's statement that in *Panen Apa Hari Ini,* art manifests as a common language that seeks to find gaps to develop new knowledge collectively and create new harmonious relationships with the environment. Wu further argues that *Panen Apa Hari Ini* goes beyond the grip of the conventional regime of works and art exhibitions. It can embrace a subversive perspective of emancipation (Wu 2021).

Compared to Moelyono's artistic practices, Saptoto's seem less manifested as a participatory practice. Moelyono uses art pedagogies such as drawing lessons or modules for children. Meanwhile, what Saptoto does in *Panen Apa Hari Ini* revolves around more pragmatic efforts for the distribution of agricultural products and the publication of related events. *Panen Apa Hari Ini*'s participatory nature manifests itself in Saptoto's engagement in his community's real issues.

Moelyono's works are inspired by participatory research methods, which in turn are manifested in works involving the real participation of citizens and are carried out for their benefit. His works show artists as facilitators of the participants' art creation. In contrast, the manifestation of activism in Saptoto's works does not show much artistic participation from his subjects, considering that he does not delegate artistic work to his participants, i.e., urban farmer groups in Yogyakarta. He also does not use the art pedagogy in *Panen Apa Hari Ini* in publishing information on harvests from urban farmer groups. He just utilizes the potential of information technology and design to support his realization of the project.

Compared with Moelyono and his artistic period in the early 1980s to 1990s, Saptoto's art projects do not continue the antagonistic trait of participatory art. He has never designed his artistic practice as a form

**FIGURE 8.4**
**Anang Saptoto, e-Catalogue Cover of *Panen Apa Hari Ini***

*Note:* Title of image: *Cabe Rawit Setan Kredit* (2020).
*Source: Panen Apa Hari Ini/Anang Saptoto.*

of opposition to any dominant artistic practices, let alone issuing an agitative creed. However, Saptoto's artistic practice can still be seen as a continuation of Moelyono's participatory art practice through the development of new methods, such as design, for a tangible end. This non-antagonistic temperament is also manifested in Saptoto's flexibility as an artist. He continues to participate in commercial art exhibitions to support his activism. Like many other artists today, he cannot be identified through one single lens, for example as a leftist artist. The choice to not be antagonistic and ideologically rigid hints at a pragmatic and opportunistic attitude, allowing the artist to realize his practical goals. Such an approach was not adopted during Moelyono's artistic period in the 1980s. Their two approaches are sociologically possible because of the emergence of new local and international sources and the complexity of mainstream and commercial art networks.

Therefore, this era can then be identified as after the antagonism, where artists do not respond antagonistically nor supportively to the hegemonic powers, compared with the generation before *Reformasi*. Without antagonism, a millennial artist like Saptoto remains adamant about creating meaningful impact as well as concrete outcomes for the community through participatory art although it remains an alternative in the Indonesian art world.

Arguably, it is difficult to characterize Indonesian millennial art's uniqueness. Millennial artists still enjoy or very much depend on the structures, systems, institutions and networks established by the previous generation. Anomalous situations within this system's power are nearly impossible to occur. With neoliberal forces increasingly subtle and gripping, artists are faced with real challenges in the art world, which often only offers support for commercial art practices. The millennial generation also encounters more real threats through paternalistic patterns in domestic and professional lives, making them vulnerable to being exploited. Apart from that, Indonesia's current social situation prevents millennial artists from making a breakthrough, especially if they practise participatory art.

In the Special Region of Yogyakarta, where Saptoto carries out his practice, agrarian problems are complex due to an existing feudal social structure. Critical residents confront resistance from fellow residents. Saptoto chooses a different path from most other artists in Yogyakarta by networking and working together with farmer groups, in which he identifies problems. Through joint work and discussion, he and his resident collaborators find a solution by connecting agricultural products to consumers in the province who need them. This is done through a participatory art approach, design and mass organizing which is manifested in various activities. This shows that Saptoto has succeeded in finding his own resources outside of the established system. However, he also continues to utilize well-established resources to amplify the impact of his participatory practices.[18]

In the end, Saptoto's work, as a millennial artist, can be seen as a disruption because it goes against the social structure that has been established by local elites and the capitalist class. Through *Panen Apa Hari Ini*, Saptoto and several farmer groups in Yogyakarta have fostered communal horizontal collaboration to improve their quality of life. The collaboration facilitated by *Panen Apa Hari Ini* provides opportunities for ordinary citizens to collaborate in fulfilling their own basic rights while at the same time proving that the state, to this day, still fails in its responsibility to serve the people.

## Notes

1. Pierre Bourdieu (1996), p. 142. Sociologists have been examining and analysing the art ecosystem as a particular arena that deals with capital exchanges which manifested in ideological contestation and competition in accumulating capital, for example, according to Pierre Bourdieu. Their works prove their ability to demystify the role of the artist and dissect the art ecosystem to show that every agent or stakeholder in an art ecosystem is functional and thus dependent on the other. Furthermore, the demystification demonstrates the dynamic situations within the tension between the autonomous and heteronomous poles in an art ecosystem. The autonomous pole represents the notion of disinterestedness in every art production (ibid., p. 142). Art creation is separated from social life, and in the European context is no longer attached to church patronage. It has won considerable acclaim for its disconnection from functional and economic motives (art for art's sake). In contrast, the heteronomous pole persistently puts art creation as dependent on social and economic influences. By this pole, art creation is a social production that relies on various social situations.
2. According to Sudjojono (2000, p. 1), Mooi Indie paintings only made sense in the eyes of tourists coming to Indonesia, who were used to seeing skyscrapers.
3. To choose a different path from Mooi Indie would not promise an established and prosperous life for artists in colonial Indonesia. The Mooi Indie style dominated the colonial Indonesian market as a commodity (Sudjojono 2000, p. 2). Also, other styles failed to win popularity since artists in the Netherlands East Indies preferred to remain dedicated to their old love (beautiful Indonesia landscape paintings) even though they had explored many other styles. Koos van Brakel, "For evidently, the fine arts do not thrive in the Indies", in *Pictures from the Tropics: Paintings by Western Artists during the Dutch Colonial Period in Indonesia*, edited by Marie-Odette Scalliet and Tropenmuseum, p. 128 (Wijk en Aalburg: Pictures Publishers, Amsterdam: Royal Tropical Institute, 1999).
4. Curator Jim Supangkat coins the term "rebellion" to identify the antagonistic

tendencies of this group and the art students from the Art Department, Bandung Institute of Technology.

5. This was followed by a petition titled "Desember Hitam" (Black December), signed by them and several artists and performers from Jakarta and Bandung. One of the petition's statements, "What has hindered the Indonesian painting development so far are the obsolete concepts, which are still being embraced by the establishment, cultural arts entrepreneurs and established artists. For the sake of the well-being of our painting, now is the time for us to honour this establishment, namely the honour of the retired cultural officer." This protest angered their teachers, some of whom won the awards and felt humiliated by their students, who addressed them openly and cynically disputed them. Wiyanto, *FX Harsono*, pp. 111–16.
6. The Department has been transformed into the Faculty of Art and Design since 1984.
7. It is not strange, considering Moelyono's involvement with an artist group called Kepribadian Apa, which was affiliated with GSRB in the 1970s and shared the same antagonism. Moelyono's involvement in this group influenced his creative process as a young artist.
8. Interview with Moelyono by video call, 11 November 2022.
9. His practice started years before international scholars discussed participatory art practice. By joining the leftist activism circle and learning methodologies from social sciences, Moelyono could organize and carry out his own practice-based learning. Mansour Fakih claims that Moelyono and his cultural action and participatory projects achieved the critical social scientists' goal in communities: a critical analysis of the consequences of capitalism and inequalities. He could even generate critical community conscientization using people's (folk) art. Moelyono's artistic practice arguably put the people as the actors of change. It challenges the dominant and typical social science paradigm that reduces social events and people to formulas. Mansour Fakih, "Aksi Kultural untuk Transformasi Sosial" in Moelyono, *Pak Moel Guru Nggambar*, pp. xxvi, xxxii, xxxiii.
10. The older generation's reluctance to accept reforms by Yuliman caused the emergence of Gerakan Seni Rupa Baru Indonesia in the 1970s–1980s. Sanento Yuliman, "Langkah Kepalang", in *Refleksi Seni Rupa Indonesia Dulu, Kini, Esok*, edited by Biranul Anas et al. (Jakarta: Balai Pustaka, 2000), p. 102.
11. Massive demonstrations by Indonesian students in 1978 in several Indonesian cities against the election of General Soeharto as president for the third time.
12. President Sukarno believed in an open-minded representation of youth. At least, it was put forward by Saya Sasaki Siraishi (2001, pp. 52–53) that the youth representation of mischief towards their parents was exemplified by the kidnapping of Sukarno and Hatta by several young men to Rengasdengklok,

putting Sukarno in the position of a father who decided to hear what the youth wanted. Such representation of youth did not become dominant during the New Order era, a period that Siraishi characterized as being under "Mr President", Soeharto, as the "Supreme Father" (2001, p. 2). Whose words are these? Answer: Siraishi.

13. Ade Darmawan is one of the founders and directors of Ruangrupa, an artists' collective established in Jakarta. The statement is a part of an interview piece in Juliastuti, "Ruangrupa", p. 121.
14. Yudhi Soerjoatmodjo, "The Challenge of Space: Photography in Indonesia, 1841–1999", in *Stories of Space—Living Expectations: Understanding Indonesian Contemporary Photography Through Ruang MES 56 Practices*, edited by Agung Nugroho Widhi, p. 156 (Yogyakarta: Ruang MES 56 and Indo Art Now). MES 56 was not established in an antagonistic temperament. Its founders, Angki Purbandono and Wimo Ambala Bayang, among others, were encouraged by the Photography Department's lecturers in ISI [Indonesia Institute of the Arts] to keep practising art photography in an expressive manner outside the dominant salon photography (Isabella 2015, pp. 117–18).
15. Interview with Akiq A.W., an MES 56 member, 31 October 2022.
16. "Panen Apa Hari Ini", https://parikolektif.com
17. Struggle for Sovereignty, https://strugglesforsovereignty.net/author/panen-apa-hari-ini/
18. One of the essential resources obtained by Saptoto is the Seed Award by the Prince Clause Fund, a funding institution from the Netherlands that has long been known in the Indonesian art scene. Saptoto was awarded the Seed Award in 2022 as an emerging artist "with collaborative practice focused on ecology and social change, using art as a tool to question and open new possibilities". See Prince Claus Fund, https://princeclausfund.org/awardees/anang-saptoto

## References

Alatas, Syed Hussein. 1977. *The Myth of the Lazy Native: A Study of the Image of the Malays, Filipinos and Javanese from the 16th to the 20th Century and Its Function in the Ideology of Colonial Capitalism*. London, New York: Frank Cass.

Bishop, Claire. 2006. "The Social Turn: Collaboration and Its Discontent". *Artforum*, February 2006. https://www.artforum.com/print/200602/the-social-turn-collaboration-and-its-discontents-10274

———. 2012. *Artificial Hells: Participatory Art and the Politics of Spectatorship*. Brooklyn, NY: Verso Books.

Bodden, Michael. 2012. "Dynamics and Tensions of LEKRA's Modern National

Theatre, 1959–1965". In *Heirs to World Culture: Being Indonesian, 1950–1965*, edited by Jennifer Lindsay and Maya Hian Ting Liem, pp. 463–64. Netherlands: Brill. https://doi.org/10.1163/9789004253513_018

Bourdieu, Pierre. 1996. *The Rules of Art: The Genesis and Structure of the Literary Field*. Stanford, CA: Stanford University Press.

Bourriaud, Nicolas. 2002. *Relational Aesthetics*. Dijon, France: Les Presses du réel.

Bruhn, Katherine L. 2013. "Art and Youth Culture of the Post-Reformasi Era: Social Engagement, Alternative Expression, and the Public Sphere in Yogyakarta". Master's thesis, Ohio University.

Budiman, Arief. 1987. "Menduniakan Nilai Estetika yang Sakral". In *Pasar Raya Dunia Fantasi-Gerakan Seni Rupa Baru*, edited by Sanento Yuliman, pp. 20–25. Jakarta: Taman Ismail Marzuki.

Clark, John. 1993. *Modernity in Asian Art*. NSW, Australia: Wild Peony.

Greenberg, Clement. 2003. "Modernist Painting". In *Art in Theory, 1900–2000: An Anthology of Changing Ideas*, 2nd ed., edited by Charles Harrison and Paul Wood. Malden, MA: Blackwell Publishing.

Hapsoro, D. Chabib. 2017. "Pengantin Revolusi-Hendra Gunawan". In *Pusaka Seni Rupa Series*, edited by Hendro Wiyanto. Jakarta: Direktorat Kesenian, Direktorat Jenderal Kebudayaan, Kementerian Pendidkan dan Kebudayaan, Indonesia.

Isabella, Brigitta. 2015. "Stories of Space and Those Who Live in It". In *Stories of Space—Living Expectations: Understanding Indonesian Contemporary Photography Through Ruang MES 56 Practices*, edited by Agung Nugroho Widhi, pp. 240–57. Yogyakarta: Ruang Mes 56 and Indo Art Now.

———, ed. 2018. *Unjuk Rasa: Seni, Performativitas, Aktivisme*. Jakarta: Yayasan Kelola.

Johan, Chandra. 1987. "Penyimpangan: Telaah Pada Karya Perupa Muda Fakultas Seni Rupa dan Desain ITB". Undergraduate thesis, Bandung Institute of Technology.

Juliastuti, Nuraini. 2006. "Moelyono and the Endurance of Arts for Society". *Afterall: A Journal of Art, Context and Enquiry* 13: 3–7. https://doi.org/10.1086/aft.13.20711600

———. 2008. "Alternative Spaces as New Cultural Movement: Landscape of Creativity". Paper presented at the conference "Indonesia 10 Years After". University of Amsterdam, 22–23 May 2008. http://kunci.or.id/articles/alternative-space-as-new-cultural-movement-landscape-of-creativity

———. 2012. "Ruangrupa: A Conversation on Horizontal Organisation". *Afterall: A Journal of Art, Context and Enquiry* 30, no. 1: 118–25. https://doi.org/10.1086/667251

———, and Camelia Lestari. 2006. "Whatever I Want: Media and Youth in Indonesia Before and After 1998". *Inter-Asia Cultural Studies* 7, no. 1: 139–43.

———, translated by Camelia Lestari and Nuraini Juliastuti. 2006. "Whatever I

Want: Media and Youth in Indonesia Before and After 1998". *Inter-Asia Cultural Studies* 7, no. 1): 139–43. https://doi.org/10.1080/14649370500463786

Jurriëns, Edwin. 2013. "Social Participation in Indonesian Media and Art: Echoes from the Past, Visions for the Future". *Bijdragen Tot de Taal-, Land- En Volkenkunde (Journal of the Humanities and Social Sciences of Southeast Asia)* 169, no. 1: 7–36. https://doi.org/10.1163/22134379-12340021

Kartaredjasa, Butet. 1985. "Kesenian Unit Desa Ditolak" [Village Art Unit Was Rejected]. *Sinar Harapan*, 4 March 1985. http://archive.ivaa-online.org/files/uploads/texts/Kesenian%20Unit%20Desa%20Ditolak%20.pdf

Kent, Elly. 2016. "Entanglement: Individual and Participatory Art Practice in Indonesia". PhD dissertation, Australian National University.

———. 2022. *Artists and the People: Ideologies of Art in Indonesia*. Singapore: NUS Press.

Lee, Doreen. 2015. "A Troubled Vernacular: Legibility and Presence in Indonesian Activist Art". *Journal of Asian Studies* 74, no. 2: 303–22. https://doi.org/10.1017/S002191181400223X

———. 2016. *Activist Archives: Youth Culture and the Political Past in Indonesia*. Durham and London: Duke University Press.

Lim, Merlyna. 2003. "The Internet, Social Networks, and Reform in Indonesia". In *Contesting Media Power: Alternative Media in a Networked World*, edited by Nick Couldry and James Curran, pp. 273–88. Lanham, MD: Rowman & Littlefield.

———. 2018. "Dis/Connection: The Co-evolution of Sociocultural and Material Infrastructures of the Internet in Indonesia". *Indonesia* 105 (April): 155–72. https://doi.org/10.1353/ind.2018.0006

MES 56. 2020. "Alhamdulillah, We Made It". Ruang MES 56, 31 December 2019. http://mes56.com/alhamdulillah-we-made-it

Miller, Toby, and George Yudice. 2002. *Cultural Policy*, London: SAGE.

Moelyono. 1997. *Seni Rupa Penyadaran* [Art of Conscientisation]. Yogyakarta: Yayasan Bentang Budaya.

———. 2005. *Pak Moel Guru Nggambar*. Yogyakarta: Insist Press.

*Parikolektif.com*. 2020. "Panen Apa Hari Ini". https://parikolektif.com

Pea, Kiki. 2018. "Anang Saptoto: Seniman Harus Hadir di Tengah Masyarakat". *Visual Jalanan*, 5 April 2018. https://visualjalanan.org/web/anang-saptoto-seniman-harus-hadir-di-tengah-masyarakat

Shackford-Bradley, Julie. 2007. "Mao's Ghost in Golkar". *Inside Indonesia*, 30 July 2007. https://www.insideindonesia.org/maos-ghost-in-golkar-3

Siahaan, Semsar. 2017. "Oleh-oleh dari Desa II" [Souvenirs from the Village II]. In *Seni Manubilis Semsar Siahaan (1952–2005)*, edited by Hendro Wiyanto, pp. 46–65. Jakarta: Yayasan Jakarta Biennale 2017 & Penerbit Nyala.

Soerjoatmodjo, Yudhi. 2015. "The Challenge of Space: Photography in Indonesia, 1841–1999". In *Stories of Space—Living Expectations: Understanding Indonesian*

*Contemporary Photography Through Ruang MES 56 Practices*, edited by Agung Nugroho Widhi, pp. 156–75. Yogyakarta: Ruang Mes 56 and Indo Art Now.

Struggles for Sovereignty. 2021. "Panen Apa Hari Ini". https://strugglesforsovereignty.net/author/panen-apa-hari-ini/

Sudjojono, S. 2000. *Seni Lukis, Kesenian dan Seniman*. Yogyakarta: Yayasan Aksara Indonesia.

Tadjib, Ferdiansyah. 2015. "Living Expectations: Understanding Indonesian Contemporary Photography Through Ruang MES 56 Practices". In *Stories of Space—Living Expectations: Understanding Indonesian Contemporary Photography Through Ruang MES 56 Practices*, edited by Agung Nugroho Widhi, pp. 178–89. Yogyakarta: Ruang MES 56 and Indo Art Now.

Wiyanto, Hendro. 2022. *FX Harsono: Sebuah Monografi*. Jakarta: Penerbit Gang Kabel.

Wolff, Janet. 1993. *The Social Production of Art*, 2nd ed. London: Macmillan Education UK.

Wright, Astri. 2000. "Thoughts from the Crest of a Breaking Wave". In *AWAS! Recent Art from Indonesia*, edited by. Alexandra Kuss et al., pp. 49–69. Yogyakarta: Cemeti Art Foundation.

Wu, Hsiang-Pin. 2021. "Dari Narasi Hibrida ke Bahasa Umum". *Jawa Pos*, 31 October 2021. https://www.jawapos.com/minggu/halte/31/10/2021/dari-narasi-hibrida-ke-bahasa-umum/

Yudhistira. 2010. *Dilarang Gondrong! Praktik Kekuasaan Orde Baru Terhadap Anak Muda Awal 1970-an*. Tangerang: Marjin Kiri.

Yuliman, Sanento. 2020a *Keindonesiaan, Kerakyatan dan Modernisme*. Jakarta: Penerbit Gang Kabel.

———. 2020b. "Perspektif Baru Dalam Seni Rupa Indonesia?". In *Sanento Yuliman—Estetika yang Merabunkan: Bunga Rampai Esai dan Kritik Seni Rupa 1969–1992*, edited by Danuh Tyas Pradipta, Hendro Wiyanto, and Puja Anindita, pp. 254–55. Jakarta: Dewan Kesenian.

———. 2000. "Langkah Kepalang". In *Refleksi Seni Rupa Indonesia Dulu, Kini, Esok*, edited by Biranul Anas et al. Jakarta: Balai Pustaka.

# 9

# The NFT Phenomenon among Indonesia's Millennial Artists

Genardi Atmadiredja, Arief Hartanto, Andrian Wikayanto, Sentiela Ocktaviana, Riri Kusumarani, Ari Cahyo Nugroho, Dida Dirgahayu and Ahmad Budi Setiawan

## ABSTRACT

*The art industry has been influenced in recent times by the emergence of the phenomenon of non-fungible tokens (NFTs), that is, unique objects validated by digital encryption technology. Indonesian millennials have been quick to harness the potential of NFT technology as a means of showcasing and marketing their artistic creations. However, research on the impact of NFTs on the Indonesian art ecosystem is limited. This chapter aims to fill that gap. Applying a qualitative method with a phenomenological approach, the researchers examined how millennial artists engaged with the NFT world. The study showed that access to the NFT digital art market and the NFT community has advantages for artists such as obviating the need to use intermediaries, allowing freedom of expression, fostering networking with their fellow artists and collectors, and even providing an inclusive space for female artists. Conversely, digital artists also face certain shortcomings, such as regulatory uncertainties surrounding NFTs, the volatile nature of cryptocurrency rates, the inherent risk of cybercrime and the potential for digital art theft. Nevertheless, the NFT trend epitomizes the zeitgeist of the digital era, where millennials actively seek validation and recognition from their digital communities.*

## INTRODUCTION

A non-fungible token (NFT) is defined as a one-of-a-kind digital object validated and protected using blockchain[1] technology (Terry and Fortnow 2021). This technology is widely used to claim asset ownership, particularly in the form of creative works known as NFT art. Popkova (2022) adds that blockchain offers authentication of ownership, rarity and immutability of related objects. NFT art includes videos, images, games, audio, books, texts and photography. Even though the NFT market is highly volatile, the artwork becomes valuable when it is a unique collection (Frye 2021).

The NFT phenomenon is growing due to technological advancements and the ability of artists[2] to monetize their artwork. However, new challenges emerge, such as concerns about the legal protection of these assets. Irrespective of this challenge, artists or creative industry players can monetize their digital assets to create new revenue streams (Ante 2021). This phenomenon has altered the buying and selling of digital artwork worldwide, which was initially distinct from the conventional art market. According to Horky, Rachel, and Fidrmuc (2022), when the conventional art market failed to transition to digital platforms, NFTs became a global phenomenon. Initially, the conventional art market made it difficult for digital artists to be a part of its ecosystem. Currently, owing to NFTs, digital artists have the same opportunity to monetize their artwork as established conventional artists do.[3]

The NFT ecosystem is currently expanding and has the potential to serve as a new medium for networking purposes. The trend has attracted young Indonesian artists to participate in this creative world. An example is Sultan Gustaf Al Ghozali, an Indonesian NFT creator who earns a large income from artwork and has attracted many young people to NFTs (Maulida 2022). These artists show their enthusiasm by creating various

NFT art pieces that have flooded several platforms and marketplaces,[4] such as OpenSea, OBJKT and Tokomall. According to the "Modern Indonesian Consumption" report by Populix (2021), only about one-third of the 1,002 respondents in a survey were aware of and had purchased NFTs. Of the types of NFTs purchased, the biggest category was various online NFT items (44 per cent), followed by video games (39 per cent), virtual fashion (31 per cent), artworks (24 per cent) and music (24 per cent). The data showed that in the past two years, NFTs have become a critical component of Indonesia's digital art revolution (Populix 2021).

The current explosion of NFT art in the country is inextricably linked to the long journey of global art development. NFTs are classified as part of new media art, a subset of contemporary ones, with various approaches and responses to the circumstances under which the works were created. As a result, when reading about the phenomenon of NFT art, it is necessary to (1) consider how artists use this technology to communicate their ideas to the audience, and (2) how the art sector responds to NFTs.

This study attempts to determine how the NFT phenomenon impacts millennial artists in Indonesia. However, because it is digitally savvy millennials who are primarily driving this movement, it is paramount to concentrate on their motivations and the barriers to technology adoption more broadly.

The chapter is divided into five sections. The next section discusses the ecosystem of NFTs. It also outlines the history of the art market in Indonesia. The third section explains the methodology of this research. This section contains more detailed information about the backgrounds of the informants and the research approach, which is a phenomenological approach. The fourth section involves a discussion and analysis of the findings. We end the chapter with a short conclusion and recommendations section.

## THE EMERGENCE OF DIGITAL ART AND THE NFT MARKET

The most distinguishing characteristic of the NFT market, which differs from the conventional marketplace, is the ability of artists to sell digital artwork without a third party or an intermediary. An artwork is sold on an online platform, and the token is directly transferred to the buyer (Wang et al. 2021). Meanwhile, because NFT items can be resold or transferred from one collector to another, the distribution process of these works can continue after the initial purchase.

Prices in the digital art market are progressive; they rely on many factors such as collectors' appraisal of an art piece and its popularity. Based on the system implemented by various NFT marketplaces such as OBJKT, OpenSea and Superare, whenever their artwork is sold artists receive royalties, which are usually set at 5–10 per cent of the price. This concept makes the NFT market distinct from the conventional art market, and the royalties allow artists to monitor the current owners of their artworks. Transactions are transparent and can be easily tracked in the blockchain.

In addition, NFT collectors play an essential role in justifying works worthy of collection. For example, in a book titled *Real Life*, Rob Horning (2021) reported that in the current era of people needing validation from the Internet, one can only prove the worth of a work of art by buying an NFT collection. Some of the world's top NFT collectors are well-known public figures in their respective fields (Horning 2021).

Digital art—works involving the use of technology—has become a medium for contemporary artists. The increasing use of technology to create art is identical to Gerhard Richter's (1978) blurred images and the digital manipulation techniques of Jacqueline Humphries (2018) obtained using computer programs and captcha codes (the tools to differentiate between automated programs and real humans). These were transferred onto canvas through a stencil technique and further stacked with oil paints to produce abstract works in response to industrial needs (Lesso 2020). When artists perceive digital technology as a tool to create artwork, they transfer the visuals produced to conventional media.

The NFT art market explosion is reminiscent of the Indonesian fine art market boom phenomenon from the early 1980s to around 2000. The present study refers to Sanento Yuliman's article in *Dua Seni Rupa* (2001), Yuliana Kusumastuti's *Market Forces: A Case Study of Contemporary Art Practice in Indonesia* (2006); and Danuh Tyas Pradipta's *Kajian Boom Seni Rupa Dalam Medan Seni Rupa Kontemporer Indonesia* (2014). The three works are focused on Indonesian art, particularly the involvement of market forces in its development.

Several NFT artists are currently attempting to fill digital market spaces. Their endeavours are in response to the massive shift in society's behaviour today, which entails spending more time in the digital world. Various digital artworks have flooded social media pages in recent years although one often needs more time to appreciate these digital art pieces. There is a mechanism for appreciating digital works that involves clicking on "like", "love", or "+1" response buttons on social media such as Facebook, Instagram and Twitter. There are also types of social media such as Karyakarsa, Trakteer, Patreon and Onlyfans that serve as direct platforms for artists to earn revenue from fans.

NFTs guarantee ownership of digital assets, but they also provide an opportunity for the public to appreciate digital assets that have been purchased by a collector. This feature differs from conventional art market practices, where the general public is unable to enjoy works owned exclusively by collectors. The NFT art market is filled with millennials who are familiar with digital life and fluent in using technological devices, so, automatically, the actors involved (not just artists, but also collectors, developers and flippers) are also mostly from the millennial generation. In practice, NFT transactions are different from the mode of transactions in the conventional art market in that artists or collectors who intend to enter the NFT world must possess a web3[5] digital wallet,[6] cryptocurrency,[7] and an account with a cryptocurrency exchange[8] in order to exchange cryptocurrency for conventional fiat money. This disruption process distinguishes NFTs from the conventional art market.

## METHODOLOGY

This study focuses on the Indonesian millennial generation although there is no consensus on the upper and lower age limits of this generation. Strauss and Howe (2000) consider millennials as those born between 1982 and 2004. Researchers from the Alvara Strategic research firm define millennials as those born between 1980 and 1999 (Ali and Purwandi 2017). Milkman (2017), on the other hand, defines this group, also known as Generation Y, as those born after 1980, who are becoming the new political generation because they are part of the digital age. Based on data obtained from the Indonesian statistics agency in January 2021, 25.87 per cent of the total population were born between 1981 and 1996, and 27.94 per cent were born between 1997 and 2012 (BPS 2021).

According to DeVaney (2015), millennials are optimistic, civic-minded, exercising close parental involvement, practising work-life balance, impatient, multitasking and team-oriented. Milkman (2017) emphasized that millennials in general are more highly educated and tech-savvy and adapt more quickly than the previous generations.

This generation is expected to lead society in adapting to the changing digital art era, including the NFT phenomenon. Adding to these general findings, the Alvara research team discovered that Indonesian urban middle-class millennials are connected, creative and confident (Ali and Purwandi 2017).

Our research involved a study of nine male and female millennials from Jakarta, Bandung, Makassar and Yogyakarta who are NFT artists and collectors. They use NFTs for various reasons, mostly economic. For privacy and security purposes, the data presented here has been anonymized.

This qualitative research, which was aimed at conceptualizing life experiences, adopted a phenomenological approach. This approach serves to highlight and explain the richness and diversity of human experiences in relation to a specific phenomenon (Tracy 2019). Therefore, we conducted in-depth interviews with the informants as the primary method for collecting data, besides observation and literature review.

We observed NFT community forums on OpenSea, Foundation, Discord and Twitter. This initial observation gave us insights into the NFT stakeholders' promotional activities and discussions. This was followed by in-depth interviews and work tracing with selected NFT artists or collectors. Most of the informants were interviewed online for one to two hours through Zoom and Google Meet.

The collected data was evaluated using interpretative phenomenological analysis (IPA). IPA considers the active role of researchers during the interpretive process. Its purpose is to uncover sociocultural experiences and how these shape the participants' subjective understanding of the phenomenon (Siddiqi 2021). In this context, the phenomenon is the involvement of Indonesian millennial artists or collectors in the NFT world and how existing NFT trends have influenced them in creating and distributing art.

## FINDINGS AND DISCUSSION

We analysed the findings in terms of opportunities and challenges.

### 1. Opportunities

The opportunities arising from using NFTs come from both internal and external factors. Those factors drive artists to engage more in the NFT world.

### *Tangible and Intangible Benefits*

In terms of tangible benefits, the informants acknowledged the relatively high financial profits that NFTs can offer, compared with those arising from the conventional art market. In December 2021, one of our informants sold her artwork for 2.98 ETH (or Ethers, the cryptocurrency used by the Ethereum blockchain), which is equivalent to US$4,100. The huge profit factor is the most notable reason for Indonesian artists entering the NFT marketplace. Once an artist converts their cryptocurrencies into conventional currencies, such as the US dollar or the Indonesian rupiah, the exact worth and benefit are determined. Besides the profits arising from their first transactions, secondary market royalties provide these artists with a lifetime of passive income as long as their work is transacted and distributed (Park et al. 2022). Because of the tremendous economic potential of selling or collecting artwork in the NFT marketplace, some artists have been able to focus solely on their digital art careers as a primary source of income.

The intangible benefits of utilizing NFTs that the informants reported included networking opportunities with other digital artists or collectors from various backgrounds and genres. The nature of NFTs promotes decentralization, openness and transparency (Wang et al. 2021) and enables artists to create networking groups with the facility of tracing transactions in real-time. The business process in the NFT marketplace enables artists to know their collectors. Furthermore, by tracing transactions and accessing other people's collections, artists can forecast trends in the NFT market. More importantly, artists can identify the preferences of potential collectors or buyers of their artwork.

Since blockchain technology offers an inclusive environment, artists from diverse genres, ethnicities, nationalities and genders have equal opportunities in the NFT marketplace. These individuals' success is solely determined by their artwork. Therefore, many Indonesian digital artists have become well-known internationally after their artwork gained popularity in the NFT marketplace, due to the consistency and originality of their masterpieces. According to most of the informants, one is less likely to achieve that kind of opportunity in conventional art markets. Before the emergence of NFTs, digital artists in the country had only a few options for selling their works.

### *Social Media as Promotional and Learning Tools*

The strength of social media as a promotional tool lies in its ability to help artists expand their potential market and sell their artwork globally. Most artists use social media platforms such as Instagram and Twitter to promote NFTs by posting a preview of their art pieces on these accounts. These efforts offer visibility to the artists' most recent work, attracting potential collectors to participate in the buying and selling process as well as the bidding wars on NFT platforms (Dwivedi et al. 2022). The artists also engage in social media to expand their networks and then direct their fans to the NFT marketplace to complete the transactions.

Furthermore, the informants use social media to expand the distribution and marketing of their digital works. The ability to consistently mint[9] NFTs promotes their reputation in the art market. The informants further stated that they learnt about NFTs out of curiosity and used NFTs by trial and error. Besides learning from their peers, the respondents obtained information from social media, such as how to engage in minting, open an account on OpenSea, and learn about gas fees.[10]

### *Time Flexibility and Freedom of Expression*

Flexible time management was one of the attractions of NFT technology, as reported by the informants. Users are able to manage their work time without being constrained by deadlines. This flexibility allows artists to put more effort and detail into artwork and mint NFTs. The informants claimed that this attribute boosted their productivity. The number of NFT platforms available allows artists to be on each platform under a different username, so they can adjust the standard and quality of their customized works based on their markets.

The NFT ecosystem enables digital artists to express ideas limitlessly, unlike the restrictions present when carrying out commissioned work. Artists are free to try out new techniques. Consequently, NFT art becomes more personal and unique. NFTs also allow artists to use alter egos to represent themselves, an alter ego being an alternative identity consciously created by a person (Buck-Pavlick 2020). Artists have no obligation to provide real identities but can create alter egos to set up an account in most NFT marketplaces. Based on the interviews, we learnt that artists sometimes create second accounts to appear as a different version of themselves so that they can create works of different intensities and styles. These artists are eager to experiment with new techniques and styles for their work. They push their boundaries and ultimately grow as an artist. By diversifying their artistic expression, they can satisfy their creative impulses while keeping their main accounts focused on their established styles. It is fascinating how these artists use different platforms to showcase their versatility and creativity.

### *Absence of Intermediaries*

Artists and collectors interact with one another in places such as museums and art galleries and at offline events. Digital artists frequently demand an equal place in such mediums as their conventional counterparts, namely painters, sculptors and craftspeople, who have a long history of developing world art (Pérez-Ibañez and López-Aparicio 2018). Curators, art dealers and critics play a highly dominant role as intermediaries in the conventional market because they act as filters to display artwork to appreciators and collectors.

In contrast, in the context of NFTs, the role of the intermediary is irrelevant. Digital artists perceive the NFT market as a medium that allows them to sell their masterpieces directly to collectors (Zeilinger 2016). Network openness causes many artists to finally believe that art is a viable career for them because the NFT market is more accessible than the physical art world and the opportunities to sell, promote and distribute their works are extensive and free from barriers.

### *Community Support*

The hype surrounding NFTs among Indonesian millennial artists is linked to how the community, which is dominated by millennials and those from Generation Z, reacts to the latest technology. As more members become interested in NFTs, information about the technology becomes easily accessible. The majority of informants reported that the role of the community is essential, especially for beginners. Some communities assist these individuals not only with technical but also financial support. This support is necessary for the informants to become professional NFT artists globally. The formation and expansion of networks facilitate the entry of millennial artists into the NFT world, which is more easily identifiable and reduces certain risks, such as artwork theft and concept plagiarism (Trivic et al. 2020).

One of the most notable NFT communities in Indonesia is IDNFT. The artists who are members of the community initiated the IDNFT Academy, an educational programme to help increase NFT literacy in society. The artists involved in IDNFT asserted that there is no competition in the field of NFT art, and NFT communities are not only based on sharing knowledge and information about the art; according to one informant, an NFT community even offers funding schemes for anyone, not just professional artists, who wishes to start selling their digital art on the various NFT platforms.

## Space for Women

Our findings did not allow us to make any definitive conclusions about gender equality in the NFT market. However, in terms of motivation, some intriguing points concerning gender issues were highlighted by the female informants. This platform can be viewed as a safe space for females to work in. The creator and the buyer have no physical contact. Besides, they can also use pseudonyms in their transactions to feel more secure. Unlike the conventional art market, the NFT market seems equal for artists of all backgrounds, including gender, fame and nationality. The NFT environment provides equal opportunities for both female and male artists to have their artwork appreciated.

The female informants confirmed that owing to the NFT industry they have better opportunities to explore and actualize their artistic talents. The time flexibility referred to above gives female artists the ability to navigate their offline lives as mothers or homemakers while earning income through NFTs.

The works of Indonesian female artists in the NFT marketplace are personally and emotionally distinct, with varying themes or concepts. The works of male artists, on the other hand, are mostly series-generative, created manually or with the assistance of artificial intelligence, and their themes and concepts lack variety. The identity of female artists with multiple roles in daily life, such as mothers, wives, lovers, children, sisters, friends, caregivers, and, of course, artists, contributes to the uniqueness of their works. Female artists also quickly adapt to NFT's changing dynamics and connect globally with female artists from other communities, who help them build confidence in the NFT market.

## 2. Challenges

The challenges are the constraints faced by NFT artists and aspiring artists to enter the world of NFTs.

### *Lack of Government Regulation*

As of the time of writing, the Indonesian government does not monitor NFT transactions, including issues related to copyright, technical and legal matters. Likewise, cryptocurrencies, which are closely related to NFT transactions, are unregulated. However, the Ministry of Communication and Informatics (KOMINFO) has initiated collaboration with the Financial Regulator Authority (OJK) to supervise cryptocurrency asset trading.

Despite the lack of a monitoring system for NFT transactions, KOMINFO has advised the public to exercise caution in responding to the trend of increasing NFT transactions. It also reminded NFT platforms to ensure that they do not facilitate the distribution of content that violates existing laws and regulations, whether in the form of personal data protection or intellectual property rights (KOMINFO 2022).

The informants expressed their hopes that more regulations related to NFT governance will be available soon in Indonesia. They considered it critical to have clear regulations in order to lower the risks and eliminate legal problems. The regulations would need to address problems related to the legal status of NFTs from the perspective of intellectual property rights. As the blockchain system allows certain parties to take possession of copyrighted works and then convert them into assets through the tokenization process, every NFT transaction needs to protect the original creators' copyrights to their works. This means that no matter how many times an NFT is transferred from one buyer to another, the copyright of the NFT needs to belong to the creator.

### *Cryptocurrency Volatility*

The NFT market continues to fluctuate depending on collector interest and cryptocurrency rates. Even though NFTs were popular and received much attention in 2020 and 2021, NFT volumes have declined since then due to uncertain market conditions. According to Dune Analytics, NFT trading volumes have dropped by 97 per cent since early 2022 due to reduced collector interest (Shukla 2022). Such volatility makes investors doubt whether NFTs are good investment assets.

To become sustainable assets in the future, all stakeholders in the NFT ecosystem need to work together to create a robust digital art market. NFT prices fluctuate partly because the NFT artworks are seen as a symbol of wealth by some people, who flaunt their possession of such assets on social media. Although it makes no sense, many wealthy people buy NFT masterpieces worth millions of dollars simply because NFTs have become a yardstick for measuring one's social status.

Our informants viewed the value of NFT art from four perspectives: (1) the cost of production arising from the complicated creative process, (2) its originality, (3) the quality of the artwork, and (4) the credibility of the NFT artists themselves. These four attributes serve as references in determining the sale price of NFTs, thereby ensuring that the value remains relatively high and stable due to factors other than the art itself.

## *Gender and Vulnerability*

Although the NFT space is relatively safe, it is a well-known fact that the blockchain platform still introduces numerous risks and weaknesses, especially for women. These include scamming and digital data fraud or theft (Kshetri 2022). Artworks are also susceptible to loss, and it is often not known whether loss is due to application problems or deliberate ploys on the part of platform owners. Besides such vulnerabilities, women lack access to information and technology. Most of our female informants noted that they learnt about NFTs from their male counterparts, particularly their spouses, with the majority becoming aware of and engaged with this phenomenon after 2020. The lack of information affects women's proficiency in mastering technology, thus making them more vulnerable to artwork loss.

## *Impact of NFTs*

The informants stated that NFTs play a role in artwork creation, production, distribution and consumption. Indonesian artists use NFTs to experiment with new techniques, from creation to production. One of the informants experimented with new techniques and media, using augmented reality (AR) in their digital works while maintaining the uniqueness and characteristics of the visual style.

Regarding distribution, several informants reported that the quality of their artwork varied, depending on the marketplaces where they were distributed. This disparity in treatment is due to the value of the cryptocurrency associated with each NFT platform. In other words, artists' decisions on where they sell their artworks of varying quality would depend on the value of the cryptocurrency used in a particular NFT marketplace.

The informants noted that collector preferences tended to shape their artwork process and creation. Some followed market trends, while others avoided them and remained consistent with their branding. However, some others attempted to bring out the characteristics of their styles while also considering market trends. Some of the artists offered additional benefits, such as special bidding privileges and bonus masterpieces specially created for collectors.

## CONCLUSION

This research has shown how millennial artists in Indonesia respond to the growing NFT trend. Indonesian millennial artists generally try to keep abreast of new developments in the digital era and hope the platform creates a sustainable ecosystem that can be used as a guide to the future. Unlike the conventional art market, NFT technology gives optimism not only to millennial artists but also to society at large to enter the art market. NFT art is popular among millennial artists because they see opportunities to collaborate and share their work. NFT artwork reflects the personalities of millennial artists who appreciate collaboration, networking and social connection. These attributes are necessary when joining an NFT community because the value of an NFT work is determined by how the community perceives it. However, NFT art based on blockchain technology is also appealing to millennial artists because the authenticity of a digital asset can be maintained, as well as the authenticity of the creator's work and historical ownership. This reflects the zeitgeist of the digital era, where millennials seek validation and recognition from their digital communities.

The findings show that blockchain technology allows greater and safer access to digital assets such as NFTs. NFTs constitute a unique form of art. The uniqueness can lie in the beauty of the artist's work, the complicated creative process, and the ideas or concepts projected through the artwork, among other things. The NFT business has significant opportunities, but it takes a careful reading of the market to create a potential NFT for sale.

The development of the NFT market creates job opportunities in Indonesia. Indonesian millennials can contribute to the NFT business by taking on roles such as NFT marketplace developers, NFT artists, or managers of NFTs owned by others (in the capacity of consultants or managers). As an NFT creator, foresight in creating unique works is the key to creating a valuable asset. For NFT collectors, care in assessing which NFT assets have the potential to appreciate in value rapidly is one of the key factors to consider. However, the ability to manage measurable risks is critical. Using NFT technology, any physical work, such as paintings, photographs and other collectibles can be listed as digital assets. Blockchain technology increases the value of art pieces by ensuring their originality.

NFTs are still evolving, and there are advantages and disadvantages to engaging with them. However, the appreciation of digital artwork can improve with a more established and sustainable ecosystem for all relevant stakeholders. As mentioned by our informants, NFTs also carry disadvantages, such as inadequate copyright protection for digital works sold on the NFT marketplace and the lack of legal protection from the Indonesian government. While there are several regulations in place relating to intellectual property rights, implementing them is difficult since transactions in the NFT market often take place at the global level.

## Acknowledgement

This research was conducted by the Arts, Design and Intermedia research group from the Research Center of Society and Culture (PMB), National Research and Innovation Agency (BRIN), Indonesia. Apart from the authors, who were the main contributors, Genardi Atmadiredja, Arief Hartanto, Andrian Wikayanto, Sentiela Ocktaviana, Riri Kusumarani, Dida Dirgahayu, Ari Cahyo Nugroho and Ahmad Budi Setyawan contributed to the design and implementation of the research, the analysis of the results, and the writing of the manuscript. Special thanks are due to all informants and IDNFT for their assistance, contributions and recommendations towards this research, Lilis Mulyani as head of BRIN's community and cultural research centre, and Damar Ayu Cahyani as a member of the Arts, Design and Intermedia research group.

## Notes

1. Blockchain is a digital encryption technology in the form of a ledger (archived folder) that guarantees the authenticity of any integrated digital data transaction.

2. Artist is used in this chapter as a term that includes creators, designers, illustrators and other artistic producers.
3. Conventional artists in this chapter refer to artists who produce their work using non-digital media.
4. NFT marketplace is a site for NFT digital asset transactions. In this chapter, OpenSea, OBJKT and Foundation are classified as marketplaces.
5. Web3 is the third generation of the Internet. Web 1.0 (web1) was a one-way, read-only static web for information flows. Web 2.0 (web2) involves interactive, reciprocal, user-friendly social media, where users are allowed to upload text, images and sound to a website platform. Web 3.0 (web3) goes beyond that. It is a blockchain-based decentralized technology that allows direct and secure communication among users, data and applications, and is used to authenticate the transfer and ownership of digital assets.
6. Digital wallet is a "wallet" for storing digital currency. It entails a unique address that becomes a distinguishing account for transactions with other digital wallet users.
7. Cryptocurrency is defined as encrypted digital currency based on blockchain technology. This chapter mentions several cryptocurrencies such as Bitcoin (BTC), Ethereum (ETH) and Tezos (XTZ), each of which is used in a different marketplace.
8. Crypto exchange is a business that allows customers to trade cryptocurrencies for other assets, such as conventional fiat money, or other digital currencies. Such exchanges include Tokokripto, Binance and Indodax.
9. Minting is an activity that users engage in when they upload digital assets to an NFT platform (usually an NFT marketplace) by paying a gas fee (see below) to issue a smart contract of asset ownership.
10. Gas fee is the fee that NFT users need to pay (in cryptocurrency) to successfully conduct a transaction or execute a contract.

## References

Ali, Hasanuddin, and Lilik Purwandi. 2017. "The Urban Middle-Class Indonesia: Financial and Online Behavior". Alvara Research Center, February 2017. https://alvara-strategic.com/wp-content/uploads/whitepaper/The-Urban-Middle-Class-Millenials.pdf

Alqaryouti, Omar, Nur Siyam, Zainab Alkashri, and Khaled Shaalan. 2020. "Users' Knowledge and Motivation on Using Cryptocurrency". In *Information Systems 17th European, Mediterranean, and Middle Eastern Conference, EMCIS 2020, Dubai, United Arab Emirates, 25–26 November 2020, Proceedings*, edited by Marinos Themistocleous, Maria Papadaki, and Muhammad Mustafa Kamal, pp. 113–22. Springer Nature.

Ante, Lennart. 2021. "The Non-Fungible Token (NFT) Market and Its Relationship with Bitcoin and Ethereum". SSRN Scholarly Paper. Rochester, NY. https://doi.org/10.2139/ssrn.3861106

Badan Pusat Statistik (Statistics Indonesia). 2021. "Berita Resmi Statistik No. 07/01/Th. XXIV", 21 Januari 2021. https://bps.go.id/

Buck-Pavlick, Helen. 2020. "The Superhero in Me: Connectivity between the Dual Identities of Inner Superhero and Outer Alter-Ego". *Journal of Dance & Somatic Practices* 12, no. 2: 267–87. https://doi.org/10.1386/jdsp_00028_1

*CoinMarketCap.com*. 2022a. "Ethereum Price Today, ETH to USD Live, Marketcap and Chart". https://coinmarketcap.com/currencies/ethereum

———. 2022b. "Tezos Price Today, XTZ to USD Live, Marketcap and Chart". https://coinmarketcap.com/currencies/tezos

DeVaney, Sharon A. 2015. "Understanding the Millennial Generation". *Journal of Financial Service Professionals* 69, no. 6: 11–14.

Dwivedi, Yogesh K., Laurie Hughes, Abdullah M. Baabdullah, Samuel Ribeiro-Navarrete, Mihalis Giannakis, Mutaz M. Al-Debei, Denis Dennehy, et al, 2022. "Metaverse beyond the Hype: Multidisciplinary Perspectives on Emerging Challenges, Opportunities, and Agenda for Research, Practice and Policy". *International Journal of Information Management* 66, (October): 102542. https://doi.org/10.1016/j.ijinfomgt.2022.102542

Frye, Brian L. 2021. "NFTs & the Death of Art." *SSRN Scholarly Paper*. Rochester, NY. https://doi.org/10.2139/ssrn.3829399

Gillovic, Brielle, Alison McIntosh, Cheryl Cockburn-Wootten, and Simon Darcy. 2021. "Experiences of Tourists with Intellectual Disabilities: A Phenomenological Approach". *Journal of Hospitality and Tourism Management* 48 (September): 155–62.

Horky, Florian, Carolina Rachel, and Jarko Fidrmuc. 2022. "Price Determinants of Non-Fungible Tokens in the Digital Art Market". *Finance Research Letters* 48 (August): 103007. https://doi.org/10.1016/j.frl.2022.103007

Horning, Rob. 2021. "The Presence of the Original". *Real Life,* 26 February 2021. https://reallifemag.com/the-presence-of-the-original

KOMINFO (Ministry of Communication and Informatics). 2022. "Siaran Pers No. 9/HM/KOMINFO/01/2022: Tentang Pengawasan Kementerian Kominfo Terhadap Kegiatan Transaksi Non-Fungible Token (NFT) Di Indonesia". 16 January 2022. https://www.kominfo.go.id/content/detail/39402/siaran-pers-no-9hmkominfo012022-tentang-pengawasan-kementerian-kominfo-terhadap-kegiatan-transaksi-non-fungible-token-nft-di-indonesia/0/siaran_pers.

Kshetri, Nir. 2022. "Scams, Frauds, and Crimes in the Nonfungible Token Market". *Computer* 55, no. 4: 60–64. https://doi.org/10.1109/MC.2022.3144763

Kusumastuti, Yuliana. 2006. "*Market Forces: A Case Study of Contemporary Art Practice in Indonesia"*. Master's thesis, Charles Darwin University, Australia. https://doi.org/10.25913/5eb3453fbadda

Lesso, Rosie. 2020. "The Rise of Digital Painting: A Contemporary Phenomenon". *The Collector*, 27 October 2020. https://www.thecollector.com/digital-painting-contemporary

Maulida, Lely. 2022. "Tren NFT Di Indonesia, Ekosistem, Dan Minat Masyarakat". *Kompas*, 28 February 2022. https://tekno.kompas.com/read/2022/02/28/11110067/tren-nft-di-indonesia-ekosistem-dan-minat-masyarakat-?page=all

Milkman, Ruth. 2017. "A New Political Generation: Millennials and the Post-2008 Wave of Protest". *American Sociological Review* 82, no. 1: 1–31. http://doi.org/10.1177/0003122416681031?

Park, Andrew, Jan Kietzmann, Leyland Pitt, and Amir Dabirian. 2022. "The Evolution of Nonfungible Tokens: Complexity and Novelty of NFT Use-Cases". *IT Professional* 24, (Jan–Feb): 9–14. https://www.computer.org/csdl/magazine/it/2022/01/09717330/1BaW5O7ratW

Pérez-Ibañez, Marta, and Isidro López-Aparicio. "Art and Resilience: The Artist's Survival in the Spanish Art Market—Analysis from a Global Survey". 2018. *Sociology and Anthropology* 6, no. 2: 221–36. https://doi.org/10.13189/sa.2018.060204

Popkova, Elena. 2022. *Imitation Market Modeling in Digital Economy: Game Theoretic Approaches*. Vol. 368. Lecture Notes in Networks and Systems. Switzerland: Springer. https://link.springer.com/book/10.1007/978-3-030-93244-2

Populix. 2021. "Indonesian Modern Consumption". Report. Jakarta, Indonesia: PT Populix Informasi Teknologi. https://info.populix.co/report/indonesian-modern-consumption

Pradipta, Danuh Tyas. 2014. "Kajian Boom Seni Rupa Dalam Medan Seni Rupa Kontemporer Indonesia". Master's thesis, Institut Teknologi Bandung, Indonesia.

Shukla, Sidhartha. 2022. "NFT Trading Volumes Collapse 97% from 2022 Peak". *Bloomberg*, 28 September 2022. https://www.bloomberg.com/news/articles/2022-09-28/nft-volumes-tumble-97-from-2022-highs-as-frenzy-fades-chart

Siddiqi, Nasrina. 2021. "Gender Inequality as a Social Construction in India: A Phenomenological Enquiry". *Women's Studies International Forum* 86 (May–June): 102472. https://doi.org/10.1016/j.wsif.2021.102472

Strauss, William, and Neil Howe. 2000. *Millennials Rising: The Next Great Generation*. New York: Vintage Books.

Terry, QuHarrison, and Matt Fortnow. 2021. *The NFT Handbook: How to Create, Sell and Buy Non-Fungible Tokens*. John Wiley & Sons.

Tracy, Sarah J. 2014. *Qualitative Research Methods: Collecting Evidence, Crafting Analysis, Communicating Impact*. John Wiley & Sons.

Trivic, Zdravko, Beng Kiang Tan, Nina Mascarenhas, and Quyen Duong. 2020. "Capacities and Impacts of Community Arts and Culture Initiatives in Singapore". *Journal of Arts Management, Law, and Society* 50, no. 2: 85–114. https://doi.org/10.1080/10632921.2020.1720877

Wang, Qin, Rujia Li, Qi Wang, and Shiping Chen. 2021. "Non-Fungible Token (NFT): Overview, Evaluation, Opportunities and Challenges". *ArXiv*. https://doi.org/10.48550/arXiv.2105.07447

Yuliman, Sanento. 2001. *Dua Seni Rupa*. Jakarta: Yayasan Kalam.

Zeilinger, Martin. 2018. "Digital Art as 'Monetised Graphics': Enforcing Intellectual Property on the Blockchain". *Philosophy and Technology* 31, no. 1: 15–41. https://doi.org/10.1007/s13347-016-0243-1

# Index

www.ingramcontent.com/pod-product-compliance
Lightning Source LLC
Chambersburg PA
CBHW072100040426
42334CB00041B/1518

* 9 7 8 9 8 1 5 1 0 4 6 0 8 *